Pittsfield
Then & Now

A Good Place to Call Home

Jane Woodruff

and

Community Contributors

Cover design by Barbara Denaro

Cover photo by Mark Schumpert

Formatting Assistance by Yvonne Blake

Published by Amazon: createspace .com

ISBN 13: 978-197440096
ISBN 10: 197440093

For Don ... who lived every word of this book with me

Contents

PREFACE

Pittsfield: Then & Now will look at the town and its people today 225 years after the first family made their way to settle on the shores of the Sebasticook River and 200 years since the town's incorporation. It will look not only at what was - its people, its traditions, and its landmarks - but what they are today.

Readers are referred to Sanger Cook's *Pittsfield on the Sebasticook* detailing the history of the first family settling in the wilderness to the 1960s when the town had grown to near its current population. *Pittsfield: Then & Now* represents a collaborative effort by writers and photographers seeking to showcase the town as they see it now against the backdrop of its past. Portions have been researched, written, and photographed by community members who joined in the compilation of this book to commemorate the occasion of Pittsfield's bicentennial celebration in 2019.

Of special note is the initial section elaborating on Pittsfield's first family and the area in which they lived which was contributed by Warsaw Middle School's 2016 class of 8th graders resultant from an expeditionary learning project. Special thanks go to them and to all who helped make this publication possible.

And finally, special thanks to those who helped in the construction of this book: Barbara Denaro for her cover, design and computer help, to Yvonne Blake for her assistance in the publishing process, to Don Woodruff who heard and read the entire book more times than he could count, and to Brenda Seekins and Norm Clarke for their generous assistance in editing all this material honing it to its final product.

INTRODUCTION

Pittsfield - a good place to call home - and that's what Moses Martin did. In 1794, Martin moved his family from Norridgewock to the area now known as Peltoma Woods after having hunted there with native friends several years before. Others followed coming from places such as Gardiner or Fairfield to settle near Sibley Pond or East Pittsfield in what is now known as downtown.

The town's name would change many times over the years as wealthy out-of-towners wielded their influence and Maine would become independent of Massachusetts. Beginning as Plymouth Gore, it would change to Sebasticook Plantation then become Warsaw, Massachusetts onto Warsaw, Maine and ultimately to Pittsfield, Maine.

What has remained unchanged is that this community has attracted and retained a number of energetic, creative, and caring people who have chosen Pittsfield to call home. Now coming from as near as Waterville and as far away as California and Canada, people have joined long-term residents such as the Humphrey and Higgins families who have been here since near the time of the town's incorporation. They - like earlier families - have come to call Pittsfield home.

Evergreen

Monoprint by Barbara Denaro

Along the banks of the Sebasticook River, the Natives hunted, the first permanent settlers arrived, murder was committed, and a feud fueled. In 2016, 8th grade students from Warsaw Middle School, in an experiential learning project, studied and completed an ecological and historical presentation that is displayed on the kiosk at the trailhead for Peltoma Woods. Fortunately, they shared their work here.

Natives

The Legend of Peltoma

The Town Farm Property, also known as Peltoma Woods, is a piece of land with a story behind its name. As legend has it, a Norridgewock Native named Peltoma and the tribal princess, Laughing Eyes, fell deeply in love. Unfortunately, Laughing Eyes was betrothed to marry Sly Fox, who was a Penobscot Native, to promote peace and friendship between the two tribes. One day, the two tribes met in a forest while hunting, and soon after, a battle broke out.

The Legend of Peltoma

Done by
Hannah Peacock
and Makaila Bailey

In this battle, Peltoma was severely wounded and pronounced dead. Meanwhile, Laughing Eyes was with her father on a branch of the Sebasticook when she heard of Peltoma's death. It was too much for her to undertake, so she took her own life by riding a birch bark canoe over a waterfall. Meanwhile, Peltoma, who was actually still alive, heard that Laughing Eyes had taken her life. The legend of Peltoma suggests he lived the rest of his days at Peltoma Point.

While the story of Peltoma is just a legend, there is evidence of early Native American activity on the Town Farm Property. When the Sebasticook River is extremely low, a fishing weir can be seen peeking through the water. Weirs were created by placing rocks into a river and stacking them to create a "V" shape. The weir directs fish and traps them in spots, making fishing more effective. On the northern portion of the trail, one can see the oldest recorded fishing weir in North America. This method dates back to the first indigenous people of Maine. Many claim to have found arrowheads at this location as well. These, and the stories and legends told, hold evidence of an early Native presence on this property.

Moses Martin

Pioneer of Pittsfield

The first successful homestead in Pittsfield was built by pioneer Moses Martin. Originally from Norridgewock, Moses Martin traveled with the Norridgewock Natives on a hunting expedition and made camp at what later became Peltoma Point. They had ventured down the Kennebec River from Norridgewock, and then traveled upstream on the Sebasticook River until they reached their destination of what became Pittsfield. On this trip, Moses Martin immediately fell in love with the land.

Four years later, he, his wife, and four children moved onto the property and built a log cabin on land near the river bend. In 1818, Martin and his family used his skillful craftsmanship to their advantage by building the first framed house in Pittsfield. "He was a hardy woodsman and a shrewd trapper; a skillful hunter and fisher and was much versed in all the perilous accomplishments which were so necessary to the frontier settler."

After the Martin family settled here, word spread about the potential opportunities this area offered. When it was first developed, the town was called Plymouth Gore. After this, the name became Warsaw, and was later changed to Pittsfield. This simple hunting expedition prompted the development of our town.

Moses and Anna Martin would have twelve children in all. Their fifth born, Jesse, was the first documented birth in Pittsfield. The Martin descendants lived on this property for over one hundred years. Their grandson, William Perry Martin, owned the property until his death. He willed it to family member Sophia Martin, who eventually sold the property to the town of Pittsfield in 1927. At that time, it included the homestead farm of David Martin which became the Town Farm. Pittsfield's annual reports from the 1930s and 1940s show that the Town Farm supported many people during that time. Sources say the farm was there until it burned to the ground in either 1965 or 1967.

Peltoma Woods

The forest habitat of the Town Farm Property is home to a number of different plants, fungi, and animal species. There is a large amount of wildlife in this forest habitat. Everything from salamanders squirming under rocks, or pileated woodpeckers tapping against a tree can be seen and heard in these woods. While white tailed deer and birds like chickadees and pileated woodpeckers are commonly seen amongst the trails, black bears and moose are scarce.

There are at least 12 different types of trees located throughout the property. In fact, the forest itself is home to an impressive number of mature eastern white pine that tower over the trails, some of which are most likely over 90 years old. While exploring the forest, one can hope to find northern red oaks, American elm, American beech, hemlock, and quaking aspen.

One of the most amazing tree stands one will encounter is the silver maple. This stand can be found along the sandy banks of the river and is unique due to its purity and size. Within this 16-acre tree stand, there are very few other plant species. The silver maples develop in a peculiar way. Because they grow in a floodplain, their trunks split in order to keep upright when the plain floods. Their roots protect the area against erosion and preserve the tree against being washed away.

Many of the trees on the property have been here for several decades. The trails on this property allow opportunities to see the different coniferous and deciduous tree types. While on the trails, be sure to respect that this is town property.

Vernal Pools

The Town Farm Property's vernal pools provide the beginning of life for many important species and are incredible places to observe. Vernal pools are temporary wetlands that fill with water during the springtime. This time of year, the pools are swarming with life, while in the autumn and winter some freeze, and others may even seem to disappear. All of the species in the vernal pools benefit the larger ecosystem by providing a food source for a variety of organisms. These temporary habitats are extremely productive hatcheries. Vernal pools are special places to observe the cycle of life.

These pools are delicate habitats to a variety of amphibians, insects, and reptiles. The species include Wood Frogs, Spotted Salamanders, Eastern Red Backed Salamanders, Snapping Turtles, Painted Turtles, Dragonflies, Water Striders, and Mayflies. These species, and many more, thrive in this habitat, and are very important parts of the food chain. Great Blue Herons will pluck small Wood Frogs from a pool of water. Tiny squiggling tadpoles will turn to active adult frogs that provide food for many larger animals all around the Town Farm Property.

Damage from pollution, litter, acid rain, human interaction, and climate change can all ruin the delicate balance of a vernal pool. The consequences are unbalanced ecosystems. These beautiful pools can be conserved by litter prevention and following current regulations. Protecting vernal pools is essential to the health of the entire ecosystem.

Wetlands

The wetlands of the Town Farm Property are significant to the larger ecosystem because they are home to a variety of species. They also provide water, nourishment, and breeding grounds for a multitude of organisms. Wetlands are very important because they act as sponges; they soak up rainwater and help prevent flooding.

Wetlands act like huge filters and improve water quality for the surrounding areas. The Town Farm Property has a number of remarkable wetland habitats, from 16 acres of Silver Maple flood plains to delicate vernal pool hatcheries.

Seasonally, life in wetlands can be experienced in different stages. In the winter months, many of the sedges (marshy areas), vernal pools, and floodplains are covered in glasslike sheets of ice. As spring arrives, and the snow and ice melts, the wetlands soak up the water. New life will flourish in these hatcheries where a number of species will thrive and reproduce; broken pieces of shells scatter along the edges of the wetland as turtles tread to the water.

These wetlands are also prime bird habitat. Some of the birds that can be seen year-round on this property are bald eagles, mallards, and wood ducks. Seasonally, one might see American bitterns, killdeers, great blue herons, and black terns during their migration.

As fall approaches, much of the mature wildlife will have returned to the river. This is a wonderful time of year to catch a peek at deer, foxes, and beavers as they drink and forage in the wetlands.

Sebasticook River

The river habitat on The Town Farm Property is a serene place full of natural beauty. The Sebasticook River is the largest tributary to the Kennebec River. This river has a 606,000-acre watershed that helps support over 50 ponds and other local water ecosystems. The Sebasticook begins in Dexter, Maine and ends in Winslow, Maine, making the river an approximate total of 50 miles long. One of the unique features of this property is that it includes 5,700 feet of riverfront. 13,500 years ago this property was covered by a glacier. The river was carved out by the weight of the glacial ice. When the ice started to melt 11,000 years ago, the weight of the ice had left an imprint of the river.

The Sebasticook River provides food, water, and shelter for both land and aquatic organisms. Some of the plant life in this river includes mosses, algae, and zooplankton. There are also many animals such as snakes, turtles, salamanders and fish. The Sebasticook River is home to nine different species of fish, including brook trout, bass, and brown trout. Many endangered species that also call this river home are the tomah mayfly, the yellow lamp mussel, and the tidewater mucket.

Although they face many threats, numerous organisms live and thrive in the Sebasticook River. For example, this river is home to many types of beavers, including the river beaver. This beaver is an aquatic rodent that lives in rivers, streams, and other wetland areas. These beavers dig burrows and tunnels in the banks along the river to make underground trails that travel to and from their feeding spots. There are many signs of beaver activity along the riverbank.

One of the many problems the Sebasticook River faces is erosion. Take notice of the exposed tree roots and concave dirt bank along the river. These are signs of aggressive erosion. There are many possible reasons for this problem, including people walking off trail down the bank, the fast release of dam water, and the natural flow of the river. Please stay on the trails to prevent any further damage to the river.

Massacre at Peltoma

Douglas Fernald

Just prior to the close of the Civil War, a grisly tragedy unfolded on the banks of the Sebasticook at Peltoma.

Two area men, Charles Knowles of Troy, a member of the Seventh Maine, and Isaac Grant of Palmyra, a member of a Massachusetts regiment, both deserted. Together they embarked on a career of stealing horses and wagons throughout Waldo County.

Warrants for their arrests were issued in Belfast, and law enforcement officers followed in hot pursuit. Grant shot the Belfast Chief of Police before disappearing into the woods. Immediately a posse of armed volunteers formed a search party to locate and capture the fugitives. Joining this search party were three Detroit men, Constable William Jenkins, Myrick and Hurd who searched the lowlands of the Sebasticook.

From the riverbank reeds at Peltoma, Grant and Knowles suddenly rose and fired upon Jenkins, Myrick and Hurd who carried cocked guns and responded instantly. A ball from Jenkins' rifle passed through Grant's head severing both earlobes but touching no vital part. At the same time a ball from Grant's pistol pierced the heart of Constable Jenkins who fell dead. Myrick got a ball in the leg from the pistol of Knowles while the latter got two balls - one from each of his opponents' rifles - in his body. In the melee, Knowles was beaten to the ground and his skull crushed. He died the next day. Grant, attempting to club the wounded Myrick, was clubbed to death at the scene.

The three casualties of this bloody massacre at Peltoma were transported by farm wagons to the Detroit village school where Waldo and Somerset authorities conducted inquests. The guns - all broken at the breech and barrels bent and covered with hair and blood - were brought to Belfast. The three corpses were buried in their respective towns.

Peltoma Bridge Feud – 1889

Douglas Fernald

A colorful episode involving the towns of Pittsfield and Detroit reached a dramatic climax in 1889 following the construction of the Peltoma Bridge spanning the Sebasticook River.

For four decades Detroit citizens had resisted funding a bridge at Peltoma as its location in a remote corner of the township offered little benefit for Detroit residents. Eventually two of the three county commissioners approved the bridge proposal, but they required a bond of indemnity that was signed by business leaders of Pittsfield village.

The original $3,000 estimate for bridge construction costs escalated into expenses exceeding $8,000. Detroit, only half a township and one eighth the valuation of Pittsfield, balked at paying half the expenses. While awaiting for the case to be resolved in court, Detroit's attorney proposed that attachment be made on Detroit's municipally owned properties until a court verdict could be reached. Pittsfield's government officials were satisfied.

However, the Pittsfield business men who had signed the bond of indemnity for the Peltoma Bridge took matters in their own hands. On March 14, 1889 they descended on Detroit and seized horses, carriages, cattle and inventory from a local store. Farms whose livestock were stolen encompassed homesteads on North Road (Route 100), Village (Route 220) and River Road (Route 69). The plunder was taken to Pittsfield.

Irate Detroit citizens conducted a special town meeting - "Indignation Meeting" - and "resolved to declare a general non-intercourse until reparation is made." Consequently, Detroit subscribers to *The Pittsfield Advertiser* transferred subscriptions to a Newport newspaper. A Pittsfield physician attending a Detroit pauper was notified to discontinue his visit; a Newport doctor was his replacement. Half a century later Detroit joined a school union with Newport and Corinna. But time eventually heals all wounds. Today Detroit combines forces with Pittsfield and Burnham in operating Maine School District #53 in peaceful coexistence.

Peltoma Bridge of the 1889 dispute

PITTSFIELD THEN

PITTSFIELD NOW

Pittsfield Then

Post Card of Perkin's and Vickery Blocks:

Published for H.H. Nutter, Prop. Reg. Pharm.

Pittsfield Now

Photograph by Mark Schumpert

Part of what ties a community together with its past are the landmarks left behind reminiscent of bygone days and with its continuing traditions, its townspeople are linked together in the present.

Pittsfield Landmarks - Traces Left Behind

Looking carefully around town, one sees the traces left behind by some earlier generations. The stone weir in the Sebasticook River in the Hunnewell Avenue region is a clear indicator of the early presence of native people.

Follow the river along to Peltoma Woods and the remnants of Pittsfield's first permanent family are seen in the stone foundation of their home indicated by a commemorative plaque.

A ring on a rock in the river near C.M. Almy provided a tie-up for boats in earlier days.

Brickwork atop the Pinnacle prompts stories of Pittsfield's oldest water tower that would splash water when overfilled causing an icy slope at the top for skiers. Folks would wonder whether pigeons perched on the tank's edge would face in or out knowing that the tank did not have a top. This old tower became a news item when it snapped cables and oscillated between its round shape to oval and back again as attempts were unsuccessful in pulling it down in 1987. In the end, it had to be cut in vertical strips and slid down the hill.

Some homes in town still sport hitching posts while former watering troughs have been re-purposed as planters. These items reflect the days when horses were the frequent form of transportation just as it is for the Amish which have recently been moving into this area and now are seen on the streets of Pittsfield.

Reborn as a recreational trail, the rail trail by its very name reminds one of its earlier function. It provides a peaceful trail from downtown Pittsfield with parts adjacent to the river all the way through to Hartland.

Some streets and parks bear the names of men and women who left their marks on this town: Dobson, Manson, Lancey, Hunnewell, Stinson, Hathorn and more recently Stein, Connors and Fendler.

Hathorn stable recently moved to near its point of origin after 120 years. With the break-up of the Hathorn estate and removal of its buildings to elsewhere in town, the stable was moved to Hunnewell Avenue where it served as the headquarters for *The Pittsfield Advertiser* and *The Valley Times* building's demise in 1981 with the demolition of the east side of Main Street. The cupola was saved by Ken Cianchette with thoughts toward preservation. It was given to the town and was stored in the vicinity of the Town Garage where it was restored and subsequently returned to Hathorn Park in 2017.

Left with some visible reminders of the past - along with the luscious recipe from the famous Lancey House, one wonders what the next generation will leave behind that will endure as traces of their past.

Lancey House Hotel, Pittsfield, Maine

Lancey House Cheese Ball

Chop

1/2 green pepper

1 small onion

Mix with

1 oz. pimento

Crumble

8 oz. blue cheese

2 lbs. cottage cheese

Season with

Tabasco sauce

Salt & pepper

Garlic salt

Worchester sauce

Mix all & form ball.

Pittsfield Traditions

Seasons come. Seasons go. Yet what remains are some traditions that have endured over the years with the same regularity as the seasons.

Seemingly gone is the tradition of hanging May baskets, a favorite of children in the 1950's. Hang the basket with candy on a friend's door, ring the bell, run. Maybe caught and kissed. Maybe not. Gone too is the Girl Scouts' May Breakfast held either at Manson Park or the Pinnacle where Scouts cooked over a campfire and Brownies "flew up" by crossing a bridge to become Girl Scouts.

While the tradition of the Girl Scouts' Winter Carnival with its races in winter sports of skiing, snowshoeing and skating did not survive, Maine Central Institute's did though the sports look vastly different as classes compete in activities such as tug-of-war and snow softball as well as building snow sculptures. This annual Winter Carnival culminates in the crowning of the Sno-ball King and Queen at the formal dance.

Some scout traditions remain as the Cub Scouts make and race those familiar pinewood cars in the annual Pinewood Derby as the troop has done for decades but they can also be seen racing their homemade cardboard sleds at MCI. While not an annual event, the attainment of Eagle Scout is not infrequent as many young men from Troop #428 reach this highest award.

At the Pinnacle Ski Slope the annual Bud Dow Races of the past have morphed into races held at the newly developed Pinnacle Fest which celebrates the ski season's end with an outdoor barbecue, music and games.

As winter is nearing its end, the juniors at MCI are finishing their Manson Essays. This tradition began in 1871 when Dr. John C. Manson originated this annual event to promote writing and speaking skills continues today as part of the requirements leading to graduation.

Come spring the Pinnacle becomes decorated with colorful plastic eggs filled with treats as children scamper up the slopes gathering them at the annual Kiwanis Easter Egg Hunt.

As the school year nears its end, the traditional Memorial Day Parade is held where generations of children and veterans have participated in this time-honored parade that has followed the same route decade after decade. From the North Main Street bridge where a wreath is thrown into the Sebasticook River in honor of lost seamen to the Veterans Park Monument and the Soldiers' Monument on the library grounds where wreaths are placed the parade continues until it reaches the Village Cemetery where students play music, concluding with "Taps" near the flag pole at the mausoleum.

 Summer brings the Kiwanis Karnival and Egg Festival drawing folks back home and those from away to this July festival. For over a half-century, generations of children have dressed up to march in the Kiddie Parade where these little ones march down Main Street to Manson Park to open the Kiwanis Karnival with its ever-present Fish Pond guaranteeing each child a prize. While once known for the world's largest frying pan, it is the store fronts painted with the festival's theme and the Egglympics held in Hathorn Park that draw folks' attention year after year. Civic organizations join the Kiwanis in promoting and working for this town-wide event.

Several new traditions have emerged in recent years. Once again folks can enjoy concerts in Hathorn Park as music pours forth from the Griffin Gazebo each week reminiscent of bygone days when Pittsfield had a town band playing from this same bandstand. From June to October monthly lightings of braziers floating on the Mill Pond draw people to its perimeter to see its beauty on full moon evenings.

 Fall descends with its cooler and shortening days as sports teams take to playing fields and ring out their victories from the old bell atop Founders' Hall hopeful that this will especially happen during MCI's annual Homecoming. And for over 100 years the Ladies Aid Society of the Universalist Church has held its annual Harvest Dinner open to the public to partake of local foods and enjoy one another's company.

The former tree lighting in Stein Park has been replaced by one in the gazebo at Hathorn Park complete with the arrival of Santa. Youthful voices of school children from Vickery and Warsaw join in song in a lively presentation of Christmas carols. Downtown, as well as many residences, are lit with elaborate displays that light up the night and MCI's Bossov Ballet performs the Nutcracker Suite in nearby Waterville's Opera House.

The year draws to a close and the new one is set to begin with this cycle of traditions repeating and drawing our community together once again.

Pittsfield's Traveling Water Trough
Donna Laux

A cast iron watering trough, used to provide water for horses, first appeared in Pittsfield in 1894 when the town's water pressure system was created. In 1926, the trough was moved to the west shore of the Mill Pond, on Hartland Avenue, where the guardrail is located.

In 1960, the Pittsfield Community Garden Club, interested in historic preservation and beautification, decided the trough needed flowers; geraniums and petunias, to be exact.

 After caring for the garden for several years, members were interested in expanding the site. With this in mind, they approached two of the town's selectmen and invited them for coffee and a chat. After the meeting, officials agreed to expand the site and improve the soil. The water trough remained at this location until Hartland Avenue was widened. The trough was safely put  into storage, or so we thought.

Fast forward to the early 1970s when, on a lovely summer day, Bev Newton, Garden Club member and two friends, drove to Fairfield to preview a country auction. Turning into the driveway, Bev noticed a cast iron water trough, full of flowers, that looked suspiciously like the one being safely stored in Pittsfield. When Bev approached the auctioneer, she learned he had purchased it from a local picker. Once he understood the origins of the trough he willingly returned it to Pittsfield, where it now proudly sits, just to the right of the recently installed arbor, in beautiful Stein Park.

Pittsfield: A Walking Tour

Holly Zadra

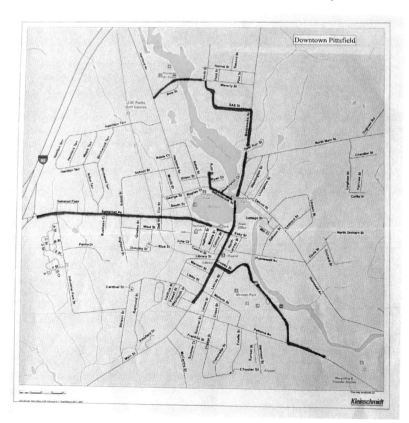

If you want to understand the heart of Maine, you must head inland, beyond the splendor of the oceanside and its boutiques to the rural towns that populate the labyrinthian highways of Central Maine. It's here you'll discover both unique local attractions and salt-of-earth people.

About halfway up or down 1-95 at Exit 150, where the interstate begins to turn east/west instead of north/south, lies Pittsfield, a town of roughly 4200 Maine people who live, work, and have fun in their own backyards. Hard-workers with a dry sense of humor, a do-it-yourself sensibility, and that famous taciturn nature that John Steinbeck describes in *Travels with*

Charley, the people who live in Pittsfield are proud of their town. Be careful if you ask for directions, you might get a walking tour of the whole town. Entering town from the interstate leads you first and foremost to the locally owned grocery store, Bud's Shop 'N Save, truly the social hub of Pittsfield. Park there, pick up any essentials at Bud's, and take a walk. You'll wander through a tree-lined residential district to Hathorn Park. During the summer months, you might find live music in the gazebo, a farmers' market, or public barbecue, and games in Legge's Field. Kids shoot hoops almost year-round clearing snow off the court to play mid-winter. Young ones enjoy the playground. One block closer to the center of town and just east of Hathorn, you'll find Stein Park on the banks of the Mill Pond so named for the woolen mills that Pittsfield depended on for a century. Fendler Park and Remembrance Park on the Sebasticook — both on the other side of the Mill Pond — are sites for loon, heron, and eagle watching as well as fishing and canoeing/kayaking (access at Fendler Park).

At the intersection of Somerset and Main streets, you can travel either north or south to explore Pittsfield. If you go south down Main Street, you'll find Vittles, an outstanding restaurant in the heart of the village that features locally grown produce, meat, and cheese from area farms and not-to-be-missed house-made gourmet ice cream, creations of the gregarious and humbug chef (so-called with love). Or, if you're in the mood for quicker fare or scrumptious freshly baked goods with coffee, try Pop on Overs. Want burgers, fries, and Gifford's ice cream? Head out back to Big Bill's, perhaps Pittsfield's most popular warm-weather hang-out.

Next door, you'll find Renys, a Maine institution without which any rural town is left wanting. Renys carries pretty much anything you need: from non-perishables to Carhartt gear to fleece jackets to shoes to sheets to office supplies to rolls of 50/50 tickets.

You can touch up your nails and get your hair done at Eden Day Spa. Or, for a simple buzz or cut with no bells or whistles, see Stan the Barber easily found by the barber's pole outside.

Catch a movie at the community-owned and operated Pittsfield Theatre, and visit an historic 1888 railroad depot that now houses the Pittsfield Historical Society. Veteran's Park across from the train depot honors Pittsfield's veterans.

At the recently renovated Carnegie library — the Pittsfield Public Library — you can stop in to read a book, gaze at the artwork in the dome painted by Maine's famous humorist Tim Sample, and view the wood reliefs by famous Maine sculptor Bernard Langlais.

Walk a little further south, past Pittsfield's oldest church, First Baptist, and you'll find Maine Central Institute, once a rearing ground for young, religious scholars on their way to Bates College, now a vibrant academy school for area high school students and students from abroad. MCI is also home to the Bossov Ballet.

If you head east from the library, you'll run into Manson Park with 40 acres of playgrounds, ball fields, riverfront on the Sebasticook River, tennis courts, and an expanse of cool grass and trees all carefully designed by the heirs of Frederick Law Olmsted, well-known for designing Central Park in New York City. There's a community swimming pool in the southeast corner of the park near Manson Park School. Home of the Central Maine Egg Festival, Manson Park hosts the ever-popular celebration each July.

If you walk all the way through Manson Park to the east, you'll find yourself at the Village Cemetery where Civil War Colonel and Congressional Medal of Honor Winner Walter Morrill is buried among local loved ones. Once there, across Peltoma Avenue, you'll find Pittsfield's Municipal Airport where you can skydive with Vacationland Skydiving for those of you who wish to mark off bucket list items while on an otherwise leisurely stroll through town.

If, instead, you head north up Main Street from the Somerset Avenue crossing, you'll first see the Unitarian Universalist Meeting House of Pittsfield. Inside this 1890's beauty are exquisite stained-glass, hand-painted, triptych windows portraying the life of Jesus, crafted by-then contemporary competitor to Tiffany - Redding, Baird & Co. of Boston. Also, inside the church are 16 paintings by Harry. H. Cochrane, a famous Maine ecclesiastical muralist and a working organ with more than 600 speaking pipes.

Cross the bridge and follow the pond toward Copper Salon and the Maine Federation of Farmers Markets. Down Ruth Road, you'll find C.M. Almy founded in 1892 in New York City and moved to Pittsfield by Thomas and Ryan Fendler who were descendent family members of the founders, English master tailor Clarence Mortimer Almy and his son James.

If you follow Main Street north over the bridge and along the water, you'll arrive on the grounds of the former San Antonio Shoe manufacturer on the shores of the Sebasticook. The historic multi-story brick building overlooks the River, an evocative and strong, but abandoned building that could be…

Nearby one can paddle through Douglas Pond, watch birds, and hike the slope of Pinnacle Park where folks ski and ice-skate by winter and gather for bonfires by summer. If you're in the park at the right time, you can find wild blueberries growing on the slopes otherwise packed with snow during ski season.

Past the Pinnacle on Hartland Avenue, you'll find the beautiful JW Parks Golf Course, a 9-hole course lined with glorious white pines. The course offers a full-service golf shop and driving range and features lesson by PGA Professional Mike Dugas.

For those who seek solitude, the rail trail — easily accessed from mid-Somerset Avenue — runs through town and can be walked or biked all the way to Hartland.

Pittsfield's Social Capital

While not clearly visible as you walk the streets, a description of Pittsfield wouldn't be complete without mentioning its spirit of volunteerism and social support. Pittsfield's social capital — service and neighbor-to-neighbor support — are part and parcel of Pittsfield's integrity as a "good place to call home." This tree-lined, family-centered, park-filled community is made livable, steadfast, inspiring, and beautiful by its volunteer townspeople that give their energy back to the place that supports them. The real mark of an "insider" in this town isn't how long you've lived in Maine or whether or not you are a biscuit (One would do well with the old-timers in getting familiar with Tim Sample's joke "…if your cat happened to have kittens in the oven, would you call 'em biscuits?" …). In this town that welcomes all, the real mark of an insider is how willing you are to jump in, roll your sleeves up, and get to work doing something that benefits everyone.

Bessie & Lou

By Penny Oliphant

Bessie Percival & Lou Bryant – Sisters

Grandmother & Great Aunt to Richard Parkhurst

Families and Their Recollections

Bill Cunningham

Several of the families who have lived in Pittsfield for two or more generations have contributed these stories and recollections about certain of their family members and ancestors that tell about some of the ways they may have contributed to the Town's well-being and progress and about what life and things were like in Town in years past. Family stories are of special importance because they help us not only to learn about Town history but also about the personalities and heritage of our past and present towns people so that they become more than just names and dates. Many thanks to each of you for sharing your wonderful family stories!

A Native Son Returns Home

Floyd Humphrey - The last Humphrey in my Family Living in Pittsfield

On September 9, 1637 my great (9x) grandfather, Jonas Humphrey stepped ashore from a sailing vessel in Dorchester, Massachusetts. The pilgrims had landed in Plymouth just 17 years earlier. He was accompanied by 2 sons, James and Jonas II, all of whom were born in Wendover, England. Jonas II was my great (8x) grandfather and was 17 years old at the time. He had a son Jonas III who fought in the Indian war of 1675 against the native King Phillip who led the uprising. Jonas III begat Jonas IV who had a son John in 1710. One of John's sons accompanied Benedict Arnold to Quebec and was later killed in the Battle of White Plains, N.Y. during the Revolutionary War. This John had a son by the same name born just before Christmas of 1744, and he was the first of my family to come to Maine, specifically Gray, Maine. It was there that my great, great, great grandfather Oliver was born, and produced a son named Elias, the first in the family to come to Pittsfield. Elias purchased a tract of land on the Higgins Road in July 1830 and proceeded to carve a homestead out of that wild land.

Moses Martin had erected the house in town just 40 years earlier on the banks of the Sebasticook River near present day Peltoma Avenue. This eventually became known as the town farm. I remember going there occasionally on Friday nights to play cards with the residents. This was during the 1950s.

Grandfather Elias had 6 children with his wife, Dolly, and two of his sons, Elias Jr. and Timothy, were both called to service when the Civil War broke out in 1861. While searching young Elias's military records, I found that he had died of disease on August 10, 1863 while in a military hospital in Louisiana. His brother, Timothy, on the other hand, is to this day referred to as Uncle Tim by family members. Tim enlisted for service on the 13th of October in 1862 at age 18. He was mustered out in August of 1863 but reenlisted again to serve in the 1st Cavalry with another Pittsfield son named Colonel Walter Morrill, a medal of honor recipient. Tim was captured by the Confederates on the 26 of June in 1864 at Staunton River, Virginia. He managed to escape briefly by wounding a guard with a derringer that he had hidden in his boot, but a mounted Confederate officer brought him in none too gently with a rope around his neck. Tim was incarcerated at Libby Prison until the Union Army was getting dangerously close and the prison was closed. He was then transferred to Andersonville in Georgia. Thirteen thousand union POW's died of disease, malnutrition, and exposure to the elements.

Tim was released in June of 1865 and made his journey home. After getting off the train in Pittsfield, he walked to the old homestead in West Pittsfield and nobody was home. Upon returning later that day, they found Tim in the kitchen with his feet in the oven. They said that he had lost so much weight that he couldn't keep warm.

Uncle Tim didn't leave home a particularly religious man but came back determined to serve the Lord whom he claimed had protected him through so much. Tim bought a small farm on the Crawford Road in Pittsfield, married, and prepared for ministry. He served as pastor of the Methodist Church in Bangor for many years and died there on January 19, 1931. He, his wife, and four of his children who died young are buried here in the Pittsfield cemetery and I visit his grave every year.

Mercier Family

Sandra Mercier Friend

George Mercier left Princeton, Maine and moved to Pittsfield in the mid-1930s following his brother James who had established a barber shop on Park Street. George worked as a cement finisher for Susi's Construction, but decided to pursue his love of cooking. He was working as a cook at Dan's Lunch in Pittsfield when Hazel Boyle came in with the Hardy family from Sebago, who were visiting in the area. George took a shine to her and drove to Portland many weekends until he won her over. George and Hazel were married on New Year's Day 1939 and their first child, L. David was born on December 4th, 1939. George and Hazel had 7 other children after David and they were Sandra, Nancy, Judie, Connie, Jackie, Gary and Danny.

George built a bakery on Somerset Avenue on land he leased form Dusty Wentworth who owned the general store next door. George, Hazel and George's sister, Edith kept the town supplied with their delicious creations of pies, cakes, cookies, bread, brown bread, baked beans, etc. George moved on and built George's Diner on South Main Street in 1954 and it was a very popular eating spot for Pittsfield and surrounding towns. All the Mercier children worked at the restaurant over the years in one capacity or another. George sold the restaurant due to ill health and passed away within 4 months of selling it. David came home from the Air Force and re-established the restaurant as the very successful Embers Restaurant. David sold the Embers to move his family to Virginia and died shortly after the move.

Hazel lived in Pittsfield until she passed away at the age of 84. She was a well-known and respected part of the community and voted Mother of the Year one year along with many other awards. Most of the Mercier children moved away and became successful in their own businesses and careers. Nancy stayed in the area and owned the popular eating spot, Nancy's, with her husband Bob McGinnis. Judith spent many years in very successful areas of the food business in owning a brokerage firm and a pasta plant. In the year 2000 (the year of Hazel's death) Judie created a company called Amazatto Foods & Marketing and they manufactured all the private label line for US Foods for 17 years. Judie wanted the business based out of Pittsfield, Maine and rented two office spaces in the North Lancey building (Pittsfield's old Grammar School). Judie brought her sisters on board one at a time. Sandra was first with her knowledge of accounting, worker's compensation, human resources, etc. Nancy came on board second with her knowledge of food and her great ability to talk with people, arrange and do food shows. Jackie came on board third after 27 years with Cianbro and became a real asset to the company as well with her expertise for detailed planning, the expertise to set-up and do the food shows all over the United States. The sisters worked well together for 17 years in harmony through many difficult times, loss of families and illnesses. They traveled to Europe many times together and never had an issue. One of the favorite sayings is "I smile because you are my sister. I laugh because there is nothing you can do about it." We can never say enough about the great parents we were blessed with.

Mathews Family

Robert Mathews

My great, great, grandfather Cyrus Mathews (1821-1886) was 44 when he joined the Union army. He left behind in St. Albans his wife Loantha Steward Mathews (1827-1895) and three sons, Elwyn (1851-1943), Walter (1855-1873), and Benjamin (1858-1932). Benjamin married and moved to Pittsfield taking up the cobbler trade like his father. He and his wife Josie (1861-1935) had a son Harris Mathews Sr. (1885-1962).

Harris Sr. took over the shoe store in downtown Pittsfield. He served the town as selectman from 1928-34 and 1957-1960. On town meeting day, 3/12/28, he defeated Charles Steward 407 to 20. He also served the town as constable, fireman, cemetery sexton, and overseer of the town farm. He ran the Shoddy mill boilers in his final years. His wife Selina Mathews (1890-1975), served in the Nurse's Corp during WW1. She was Pittsfield's first Girl Scout leader. They had two sons, Harris Jr. (1921-2003) and Benjamin.

Harris Jr. was the town's first Eagle Scout. He was a Master Tech Sergeant for the Marines during WW2. He once managed the Pittsfield airport and was awarded the Department of Transportation (FAA) Aviation Mechanic Award from Governor Longley. He built several airplanes, including a Fokker DR1 German tri-plane for Ken Cianchette. He worked 30 years for the Cianchettes. He was a past master of the Masons and 50-year life member. Harris was a 50 year life member of the Order of the Eastern Star. He was a proud member of The Sons of Union Veterans and the Allagash Alliance Group. His wife Shelia Mathews (1926-2005) worked for Judge Jude in Newport, clerked in stores, and worked 25 years for S.A.D. 53 in food service. She was an Eastern Star life-member. She taught Sunday School and was a Den Mother for the Boy Scouts. Harris and Shelia had three children, Barry, Robert and Ann.

My uncle Ben was an Army veteran during WW2. Ben had a walking postal route in town for 20 years. He also had a television repair shop. He had machine shops and was a well- respected machinist. Ben's wife Barbara (1928-1994) was a gifted seamstress that worked at Church Goods/CM Almy for many years. Ben and Barbara had two sons Laforest and Ben Jr. Ben Jr. and his wife Betsy had two children,

Erin and Anne. Laforest and his wife Julie had two children Joshua and Jen.

My sister Ann is a florist and health care professional. She had a flower shop on Main Street at one time but is currently working in health care. She had three children, Mathew, Heidi, and Peter (Trey) (2000-2009) Duncombe. My brother Barry (1946-2008) married and moved to Alabama where he passed. He had worked years for Buds Shop 'N Save and Edwards Company. He was a past president of the Jaycees. He and his wife Slyvia had a son Kevan. Kevan had a son Lauton. As for myself, I am an Eagle Scout, U Maine grad, and Army veteran. I worked for the Town from 1970 -1980 as a lifeguard, coach and recreation director. Finally, nearly all descendants from Harris Sr. on have graduated from Maine Central Institute.

E.N. Shaw: Harness Maker

Donald Hallenbeck with William Cunningham

Edwin N. Shaw, my great-grandfather on my mother's side, was a long-time harness maker in Pittsfield. This important and very necessary trade flourished up to the early 1900s. Everyone, residents and businesses alike, relied on horses for transportation in town and between towns and as work animals on the farms.

Born in Charleston in 1856, Edwin learned his trade as a teen working as an apprentice doing upholstery work on the seats of carriages and sleighs.

After working a year for another harness maker in town, he opened his own shop on Park Street (now Somerset Avenue) in 1882 across the street from the town hall in a large two-story building he and Orin S. Haskell of town built that year to house their businesses. Orin and his son Charles used half the downstairs to house their newsprint shop for several years from which the local weekly newspaper, the long-running *The Pittsfield Advertiser*, that they first published that year. Edwin used the other half of the building for his harness shop until 1924 when he sold the building to a laundry business and moved his shop just down the street to the former medical office of Dr. T.N. Drake. He considered Pittsfield a good "horse" town during most of the years he practiced his trades.

When he was interviewed by a newspaper reporter in 1936 when he was 80 years old and still working in his shop on Park Street each day he said, "I've seen this street lined with horses. Blacksmiths were busy and so was I. I've bought as much as a ton of leather at once and that's quite an order coming from a small business-like mine." Many of the older houses around town today still have remnants of the horse stables in their attached barns now garages that existed in this time when horse ownership was common and widespread.

While the automobile put the horse out of business as a means of transportation, it was the bicycle that first hit the harness-making business hard according to Edwin. His sales fell off as bicycle use around town became more and more popular. He admitted that he might have helped this new mode of transportation get a start in Pittsfield by being the first person in town to own one. He also stated he was the first person in town to own a car.

As the use in the cold and winter weather of cars with heaters became more widespread, his sales of carriage and sleigh fur coats, robes, lap blankets and trunks took a nosedive too. He had sold 40 plus fur coats and robes, 400 blankets and 300 trunks a year besides a high number of horse harnesses during the heyday of horse transportation era.

Edwin told a story about how it was not only the horses on the roads and fields that would panic at the sight of one of these early 'horseless carriages.' "Just after I got my car, my wife and I were out riding in the country when we came upon two women walking along the road. They stopped still for a moment and then dived over a fence and ran for all they were worth across the fields. The car was as new to them as to their animals!"

Edwin although selling fewer and fewer harnesses as the last work horses on area farms were slowly replaced by tractors, kept his shop open daily almost to 1941, the year he died.

Edwin and his trade contributed greatly to the success of the town during its early years when horses played a big role in the personal and business life of the community and its surrounding farms.

Dysart Family

Susan Quint Cassidy

In the fall of 1934, and in the middle of The Great Depression, my grandparents took a risk and opened a Five and Dime Store in Pittsfield. The store, LA Dysart, would become a household name here and in the surrounding towns.

Lawrence and Mabel Dysart became entrenched in their dedication to this community. They were devout Roman Catholics who worked tirelessly to run what became a very successful business, raise a family and earn the reputation of helping those in need.

The store began on the first floor of the Perkins Building on Main Street. Eventually, my grandparents purchased the building and after a bit of trial and error, they ran a store with two floors of merchandise.

My grandmother was extremely proud of the women's apparel department that she ran on the second floor. She sold everything from undergarments to wedding gowns. If your apparel needed an alteration my grandmother would do the work on a single stitch sewing machine. That machine has been handed down to my daughter and she cherishes it. Nothing made my grandmother prouder than seeing a satisfied customer exit her department excited about their purchase.

When I was a young girl I would often work for my grandmother. Before I would commence to my duties Grammy would always say, "Now remember, the customer is always right."

My grandfather ran the first floor with inventory such as cookware, children's clothing, make-up and toiletries, sewing notions and fabric, comic books, and too many other things to list. But, to many of the people who remember Dysart's the most appealing products were the candy counter and the peanut warmer. There was nothing more sensational than walking into the store and smelling fresh cooked nuts!

Though involved in many interests my grandparents were known for two very important reasons. The love of their family has been a model for my family for generations and has had a huge impact on those of us who have had the honor of knowing them.

Their care and generosity for people in need made them beloved members of our community. Their lives were an act of kindness.

Gould-Dean-Reilly Family

Lynn Gould Cianchette

At this point the fifth generation for the Gould/Dean/Reilly family is thriving in Pittsfield. Four of those generations are MCI grads or on the way. The manufacturing growth pre-World War II drew the Gould's to Pittsfield for its employment opportunities and the school system. After the three boys graduated from MCI, all enlisted and served overseas for the war. My dad, Ralph, (the Romeo of 38) returned and married his sweetheart, Muriel Dean. The opportunity to buy a local business from Jesse and Earl Banks, Banks Boot Shop, became reality. Ralph, Muriel, sister Eloise and brother-in-law Pat Reilly made the leap to local business. I remember growing up on Main Street with Hugh Hersey (hardware) and Earl Fletcher (A&P) across the street. Mrs. Lagorio's candy store and Richuette Frederick's hot dog stand were the bookends for Gould and Reilly. Life was pretty good! As the post war economy grew so did the business. Televisions, radios and vinyl records were added to meet the public demands. There is a hilarious family story about the dad's running up Franklin Street with a ladder to install one of the first tv antenna in town. They didn't own a truck, so shoe leather express was the mode of transportation. I also realize, in retrospect, that giving to the community was important to them. There was never a time when they were not involved in multiple local service organizations. Town planning, SVH foundation and Auxiliary, Kiwanis, Arts Club, Alumni, church, and coaching, come to mind without effort. In time their vocation changed but the sense of community, respect and kindness did not.

Pratt - Burton Family

Wesley Burton

Massachusetts natives, Francis and Janis Pratt, came to live in Pittsfield after an eight year period of living in the neighboring town of Dixmont. They were both drawn to the town's closeness to amenities such as the hospital and grocery store that they had lived so far away from for those initial years of retirement in Maine. Francis had purchased a modest 1920s cape-style house on Bates Street just across the shoreline of Mill Pond. It was a project house, destined to be remodeled and severed into two apartments. Fran enlisted the help of his son, David Pratt, a master electrician and carpenter to help with the remodels. After a period of some months and a new paint job, the house was ready to become a permanent home.

While settling in, Janice quickly found a home in the town's First Universalist Church and quickly became a member of the congregation. Retired Harvard-educated history teacher, Fran, became active in the political agenda of the church and could be regularly seen protesting near Hathorn Park. Fran and Jan's grandchildren, Wesley and Christine Burton, were also regular visitors of the new estate and were involved in the church's Sunday School program. After eight years of living in Pittsfield, Francis Pratt passed away in 2010, leaving Janice Pratt as the only remaining resident of the home. In 2011, Jan's grandson Wesley moved in and began attending school at MCI. He was an active part of the school's music and academic community. He graduated after four years on the National Honors Society, and shortly after, left for college. Deciding only after two months, that campus life wasn't for him, he returned to Pittsfield to live with his girlfriend and grandmother.

During this time, he found a job at Reny's, the local department store. During his part-time job there, and when his grandmother had put the house up for sale, Wesley began the process of buying the house. He wanted to keep the house in the family and felt that buying the house was an option that would benefit everyone. He now resides in the same house his grandparents had owned for fourteen years prior, and where he had spent a significant part of his childhood and adolescence. While living here, Wesley wrote and published a book of poetry with the help of Matrika Press, a Pittsfield-native publishing company. His grandmother Janice retired to a local elderly housing facility just down the street. Wesley plans to make his roots here and write more books, just as his grandfather would have wanted him to.

Frederick Family

Kellie Brooks

The Forest Frederick Construction Company was owned and operated for 46 years by Forest R. Frederick, one of the many Italian contractors in Pittsfield, until his retirement in the early 1980's. The shop was located on Somerset Avenue, now known as Sebasticook Valley Family Care.

Special projects for the Forest Frederick Construction Company include the Waverly Avenue bridge in Pittsfield, the JFK Mall in Waterville, and others from Millinocket to Downeast Maine. Forest, nephew to JR Cianchette, was known as a road builder as well as a house builder. He built several houses in both Pittsfield and St. Petersburg, Florida. Forest plowed Pittsfield roads in winter. He was a member of the Masonic Lodge and Odd Fellows Lodge. He was a communicant of the St. Agnes Catholic Church. Forest Frederick was a MCI graduate, class of 1934 and passed away on February 10, 1995.

Forest was the son of Shans and Annie (Cianchette) Frederick. Shans was born in Patterano, Italy in 1889 before moving to Pittsfield. Forest first began working for Ralph Giovannucci in the 1950's at his Pittsfield shop, now known as CM Almy. Ralph was a contractor from the 1930's through the 1950's. Wife, Rosie Sue (Giovannucci) Frederick, daughter of Ralph and Josephine Giovannucci, was office manager and a stay at home mother of Marsha and Dennis Frederick. Sue was an MCI graduate, class of 1937. She passed away on April 1, 2000.

Five generations of the Frederick family have lived in the Pittsfield area. Many current residents of Pittsfield are from the Frederick, Giovannucci, Susi, or Cianchette families.

Story of Two Higgins Farms

Daniel Higgins

Farm 1: In 1808, give or take, Ephraim Higgins Sr. and his wife Phoebe (Atwood) moved inland from Mount Desert Island to Pittsfield (known then as Plymouth Gore in Massachusetts). It's speculated they did so to escape the dangers of working at sea. Ephriam built a farm in 1815, give or take, on what is now known as Higgins Road in the west part of Pittsfield. November of 1820, he received a deed for this

property. In 1828, he acquired the lot across the road which would complete the first Higgins farmstead. The farm was continually farmed up into the early 1990s. The original buildings have been replaced 2 times due to fires. This farm is now occupied by Donald Higgins and his family which would be generations 6 and 7 to reside there (646 Higgins Road).

Farm 2: Between the years of 1839 and 1848 Heman Higgins, one of Ephraim's sons, purchased 2 abutting farm properties. In 1843, give or take, on one of the properties which had an existing barn on it, Heman built the house with used lumber probably from the house they took apart on the second property. Today some of this farm's original buildings still exist and are now occupied by Daniel Higgins and his family. They would be generations 5 and 6 to own this property (731 Higgins Road).

Pomeroy & Elkins Family

Barbara J. Pomeroy

My parents, David and Mavis Pomeroy, moved our family from Mechanic Falls back to the Pittsfield area so that my brother Jeff and I could attend MCI. After looking at houses in both Pittsfield and Detroit, we moved to Detroit in 1979. Jeff started eighth grade at Warsaw that fall, and I started fifth grade at Vickery. Jeff was on MCI's 1980 State Champion soccer team as a freshman, graduating in '84; and I was Valedictorian in '87.

There are members of my dad's family on the U.S. census records living in Pittsfield, from at least 1920 to 2010, although not always the same individuals. The earliest instance of a family member living in Pittsfield was my dad's great-grandfather, Andrew J. Pomeroy (1843-1916), a Civil War veteran (Union) who was a Pittsfield resident when he died in 1916. He and his wife Martha (Reynolds) (1854-1907) had seven children.

My dad's father's parents, Albert and Ellen (Reynolds) Pomeroy, lived on High Street (now Leonard Street) for a time and had four children, one of whom, Carrie, lived nearly all her life in town until the age of 100 years old. As a young girl, Ellen and her parents and others in the Reynolds family went West on a wagon train on the Oregon Trail about 1898/99, wintered over in Montana where her father mined some gold nuggets, and returned to Maine the following year when they bought a farm in Unity. Dad's father would talk about his grandfather showing him the gold nuggets when he was a young boy.

My dad was born in Pittsfield, in a house on the Crawford Road that burned down years ago. His parents, Myron and Carolyn Pomeroy, moved many times during their married lives, but Pittsfield was considered "hometown" for the first four of their six children. Their oldest son, Roy MCI '58 (1940-2009), was always proud that he still held an MCI school record in the pole vault. My grandparents moved to Auburn for work after Roy's graduation, and my father David stayed on in Pittsfield while he finished his junior year at MCI, working at Carl McCrillis' farm on Route 2 and then living with his uncle, Phillip Elkins, on the Spring Road that summer, looking after his cousins. He then joined his parents and younger sisters in Auburn for his senior year. Dad graduated from Edward Little High School in 1960; Mom graduated in 1961.

For a time during my dad's childhood, his parents and both sets of grandparents all lived near one another, and in addition to his siblings, he had many cousins to play with. Aunt Carrie would talk about a 7- or 8-year-old David knocking on her door asking if Allen could come out to play. When she told him, no because it was raining, he, standing on the porch drenched with rain gusting and pouring down behind him from the hurricane, told her, "It's not raining out here!" Ayuh, he's a Maine boy.

My dad's mother's parents were Alma (Overlock) and Joseph Lee Elkins who had 11 children in 13 years. My grandmother, Carolyn Alma Elkins Pomeroy Preble, outlived them all when she died in 2018. Walking through the Pittsfield Village Cemetery on Peltoma Avenue is an adventure in finding the graves of family for generations, direct ancestors, collateral lines, in-laws and "outlaws". Among more than a hundred others, Dad's great-grandmother is buried there next to the third of her five husbands. Hannah Mabel (Gerrish) Overlock Gerald Morse Dore Tarr lived a lot of her life in Pittsfield and worked for many years at the Lancey House. She divorced most of her husbands except (according to family story) the one who was a harness-race-driver who was murdered for gambling debts. Dad remembers Nana Tarr showing him a photo of her and one of her husbands - the race-car driving one - with Henry Ford, and she told him they were business partners in the early days of the automobile.

Dad also remembers his father or grandfather telling a story of a cousin who was a bootlegger killed during prohibition in the early 1930s, whose car was shot up on the Dogtown Road, but whose body was never found.

Woodcock - Woodruff Family

Jane W. Woodruff

The Pittsfield Grange led by Leigh Shorey recruited John Woodcock, DVM to relocate his family to town where he along with his wife Laura opened a veterinary practice in 1949 on Somerset Avenue. Doc Woodcock served the area treating both large and small animals with Laura assisting in surgeries and running the office. Their daughters Lois and Jane grew up and were schooled in Pittsfield leaving to pursue careers in social work and occupational therapy, respectively. Jane returned many years later in 1976 bringing with her a new name (Woodruff) and family to live just a 1/4 mile down the road from her parents. The cycle of returning to roots repeated itself when son Vaughan returned to Pittsfield to live in the Woodcock family home with Holly and sons River and Ari. Initially, he housed his solar business in his grandfather's former vet office. Vaughan's sons Eamon and Goran were both born in the parlor of the Woodcock home. While Don and Jane's daughter Dana has yet to return to live in town, she has followed a similar path as her kin in working in a health field as she has become an herbalist. Brothers Dan and Scott while not returning to Pittsfield did return to Maine bringing their families with them to Camden.

Younger - Daily - Vigue

Carole Daily Vigue with Jane Woodruff

In the late 1920s, James Daily (the 2nd) and his wife Marion moved from Bangor to Pittsfield where he initially worked as a teller at the local bank. He later took a job at the Post Office in the Karam Building and would eventually become a postmaster there. His son James Daily (the 3rd), graduating from MCI in 1938, would follow his father's career path and work for the post office after his four and one-half years in the service. He later would take a job at Pittsfield Chair along with his high school classmate Fred Stafford who seemed to be following the same career path.

James (Jim) Daily would marry his high school sweetheart following her graduation from Bates. Elaine, daughter of Agnes and Andrew Younger, grew up in several prominent homes in Pittsfield. They lived in the house on Main and Easy Streets that had initially been known as the Lancey homestead, a home where Agnes Younger would need to hang a black wreath indicating quarantine when Elaine suffered mumps, measles and another childhood disease. Her father being the boss at the Pioneer Woolen Mill meant that they later lived in the "company house" across from the library known for many years later as the Stein house. Unfortunately, Mr. Younger would die prematurely, and they would need to move yet again. This time to the apartment on the second floor of Sanger Cook's house on Main Street at which time Mrs. Younger would become the seamstress for the Lancey House.

Elaine taught French at Maine Central Institute before becoming known as the beloved 7th and 8th grade English teacher at Manson Park and Vickery Schools. Jim and Elaine would have two girls: Arline and Carole. Arline would move away but Carole would return to her hometown after college to start her career as a first-grade teacher and a year later marry Peter Vigue. Their wedding day on June 21st in 1969 coincided with the town's sesquicentennial and folks will remember the bride and groom still in their wedding clothes being pulled through town in a "jail" as part of the parade. Carole would "retire" from paid employment with the arrival of her children - Peter Andre and Michelle - giving all her time to them and a multitude of volunteer duties to better the town from school board to ski slope to Scouts just to name a few. Her husband Peter moved here in his grammar school years and followed his brother to Maine Maritime Academy after graduating from MCI. The birth of his son Andi was impetus for Peter to come home from shipping at sea to find land side employment. And that he did - working from the ground up to become CEO and President of Cianbro Corporation. Like his wife Carole, he too jumped into many volunteer activities including becoming Mayor.

Their children have followed a similar path as their parents returning home to pursue careers, raise families and give back to the community. Like her mother, Michelle has given countless hours chairing the school board and volunteering for various youth activities. Like his father, Andi became CEO of Cianbro and Mayor. The four grandchildren - Gregory, Caroline, Maggie and Natalie - seem to be following that path of gifting their time to the community with their involvement in school civic organizations like the Key Club and the Kindness Krew. It seems that getting involved is the motto for this community-minded family.

Haskell-Stevens-Cunningham

William A. Cunningham, DMD

So far, I have lived and worked in Pittsfield all my life in the now 102-year-old house that was built by Charles Albert (Bert) Stevens, my maternal great-grandfather. I have several of my Haskell - Stevens -

Cunningham relatives who have had direct ties to this community that reach back many years.

My maternal grandfather, Van Mitchell Stevens was born in Pittsfield in 1896 but soon after, he and his parents moved to Syracuse, NY. Van returned to Pittsfield as a three-year boarding student at MCI where he met his future wife Amelia Haskell. Her grandfather, uncle and father were the Haskells who started *The Pittsfield Advertiser* in 1882 and made it into the highly successful weekly local paper that was published for over a century.

1916 was both a very happy and very sad year for Van and Amelia. In June, they had happily graduated from MCI where Amelia was their class salutatorian. However, for the rest of that year, Amelia was unable to speak due to being so upset from the sudden deaths of both her parents. Van's parents, Bert and Emma, moved back to Pittsfield from NY that year and into their newly built dream house, a large elegant craftsman styled bungalow situated prominently on the corner of Main Street and Peltoma Avenue. Amelia enjoyed the frequent sleigh rides Van took her on that winter and his visits and recovered from the loss of her parents.

In the summer of 1917 when Van turned 21, he enlisted in an artillery division and shipped out to France to fight in WWI. Shortly before the war's end in 1918, Van returned home with his lungs damaged by the enemy's deadly mustard gas. The following year just after Amelia graduation from Nasson College, they were married and lived in the house on Summer Street that Van's father had moved there to clear the lot on Main Street for his new house. Their first child was my mother Patricia born in 1921 in the upstairs front bedroom of her grandparents' house. To help my grandfather to further regain better lung function, the family lived for a while at a camp on Great Moose Pond where the air was thought to be fresher and healthier. In 1924 the family moved to a newly built house in Portland given to them by Van's father since Van was not interested in staying in Pittsfield and working at his father's local grocery business.

My mother remembers as a youngster visiting her grandparents at their large house in Pittsfield and playing with her Haskell cousins. In his later years, Bert Stevens turned his many bedroomed house into a popular tourist home (B&B) named Sunset Lodge. Later, my grandfather, Van moved his parents to Portland to care for them in their last years. The house did not sit vacant for long. Starting in 1943 and for the duration of WWII, the house was rented by MCI to accommodate their female boarding students displaced from Weymouth Hall by the Navy
pilots housed there who were being trained at the local airport. Van then rented the house for a few years to the Carl Cianchette family.

My parents, Patricia H. Stevens and Wallace H. Cunningham, graduated from Farmington Normal School, married in 1944, and taught school in Skowhegan. They moved to my great grandfather's house in Pittsfield in 1950 and I was born in 1951. My mother taught nursery school, sub-primary and first grade while my father taught science courses at MCI the years I was growing up. In those early years, my father ran Wally's Sport Shop out of a back room in the house and to help pay for oil to heat the house, the upstairs was converted into a small rental apartment. For eleven years, they owned and operated a set of sporting camps in the summer on Ebeemee Lake just south of Millinocket. I loved those long summers at the lake spent swimming, fishing, sailing and reading. My paternal grandfather, William A. Cunningham, moved to town, owned and operated the local Taste Freeze for several years with plenty of free samples to my great delight. My parents retired from teaching and moved to their retirement home in Kingfield and spent their winters in Florida. Where ever they went, their former students from years past, would stop them and tell them they were the best teachers they had ever had! My father died in 2004 and my mother at 97 is doing very well and lives at Dirigo Pines in Orono.

I graduated from MCI in 1970 and Bates College in 1974. I went on to graduate with honors from Tufts School of Dental Medicine in 1977. That same year I married Karen Lord of Marblehead MA and started my dental practice in the house which served as my home/office for 35 years. Our only child Alexander was born in 1986. He loved to swim when he was little in the indoor heated pool I added to the house. Alex graduated from MCI in 2004 and Worcester Polytechnic Institute in 2008. In 2014, he was awarded a PhD in robotics from the Georgia Institute of Technology. He is currently working for Toyota in Michigan developing the code to run their line of experimental driverless cars. Karen and I, now retired, keep busy with our many hobbies and new activities. At some time soon, we plan to sell our home and move to a warmer clime since my son and or other relatives are not interested living in it. This is sad since this will mark the end any continuation of my family's strong connections to this house and this community – both places that have meant so much to us for several generations.

The Percival/Parkhurst Pittsfield Connection

Richard Parkhurst

My story starts in 1896 when my great-grandfather, William Percival, moved from Waterville to Pittsfield. The lure to Pittsfield was originally a job as a farm hand, but a friend, Dan Dyer, talked him into opening a barber shop in town. He worked his Main Street shop for over 48 years until his death at age 74. Better known as Bill, he married Angie White in 1898. In 1900, they had a son Wallace, my grandfather and in 1902 had the deed to 5 George Street, the house I currently live in.

Wallace Percival grew up an only child around aunts, Angie's sisters, and went through grade school managing to graduate from MCI. His interest was construction, and he bought a Sterling dump truck. Projects like the Sibley Pond bridge and the Pittsfield dam kept him and his truck busy. When jobs dried up, he would work beside his dad barbering. It was during this period a Mr. McCrillis in conversation while getting a haircut said how he wanted to get out of the coal business. Wallace jumped at this opportunity taking over the coal business around 1942. The business grew to become Pittsfield Coal & Oil with my grandmother Bessie as office manager/bookkeeper. His crew was George Moody and Ted Thompson. Together they kept the town heated.

Bessie and Wallace had two children - Roger and Ruth. Both grew up in town and graduated from MCI. Roger joined the Navy at the end of World War II. Upon coming back to Pittsfield, he signed up in the Army National Guard because of the $60 per month pay. Then the Korean Conflict starts and he finds himself enlisted as quartermaster in charge of transporting troop supplies to a fast-moving troop. Having survived that, he took advantage of the GI Bill and graduated from UMO in finance. His first job was at the First National Bank of Pittsfield. Then in 1958, he moved to South Portland and was hired by Portland Saving Bank as their auditor. He moved up to senior vice president and treasurer. The bank's name kept changing until he retired at which time he was 1 of 3 officials who built the bank up to become what we know as TD Bank North. He is 92 and lives in Portland.

Ruth Percival, born August 9, 1929, married Lester Parkhurst, Jr. in 1947. By 1955, there were five of us - Carol, Rick, Jeanne, John, and Douglas. Money was tight with 5 youngsters. She took a job house cleaning for Joyce Dailey and her 5 kids. It was a challenge preparing meals for 10 twice a day.

Then in 1964, she discovered a talent working with kids with special needs and Pittsfield's school system had a need for such a person. As a trial, the Baptist Church basement was the beginning of what would become the Sebasticook Association of Retarded Children (SARC). The need for more space was met with the town re-opening the Hartland Avenue School which was renamed the Marie Bradford School. The state soon recognized these programs should be incorporated into the school system. This allowed Ruth to be recognized as a teacher by the Maine Teachers Association; thus, as this new attitude toward working with children with special needs and Ruth with a lot of support from local clubs (like the Jaycees and Kiwanis) led the way to aiding children with disabilities in this state.

Lester E. Parkhurst, Sr. and wife Marion moved to Pittsfield from Old Town in 1946. He had taken over the Pioneer Woolen Mill as mill manager. His sole purpose was to close the mill since the war was over and labor was cheaper in the South. They had three children - Mary, David, and Lester Jr. Mary was in college at UMO. David finished up his military service and Lester Jr. started as a freshman at UMO.

Being the new kid in town, Lester struck up a relationship with Ruth Percival. He left college and married Ruth on June 15, 1947. In 1950, the Pioneer Mill closed and Lester Sr. moved back to Massachusetts while his son Lester J. stayed in Pittsfield to raise a family. The 1950s and 1960s were hard times in Pittsfield with the woolen mills closed, but the town proved resilient, always providing a good place to raise a family with great support for education and recreation. As I end this, my head is filled with the desire to list the names of all families that grew up in this great town. There are so many of us and we have been lucky to have lived it.

The Start

By Penny Oliphant

Club Members Going to the Boston Garden Show

Wait at Pittsfield's Train Depot for the Train

1961

From earliest times, Pittsfielders have gathered. They assembled to establish the town and congregated to form spiritual, social, and civic organizations. Many of today's churches began as services in congregants' homes. Today, there are ten churches in Pittsfield serving the spiritual needs of the community.

First Baptist Church

Mark Schumpert

First Baptist Church is the oldest church in the area, having been organized in 1823 as the Free First Baptist Church. It was incorporated according to Baptist polity in 1855. Following a fire that destroyed the original building, the current structure was built in 1892. First Baptist and the Baptist Foreign Missionary Society collaborated in the founding of Maine Central Institute in the 1860s. The current congregation is comprised of people of all ages. There are roughly 200-250 people in attendance for Sunday morning services. Numerous in-home studies and fellowship groups meet at different times during the week. The Church is evangelical in demeanor and Reformed in its emphasis. There is a regular Sunday School program during the school year. Services are of varying styles, incorporating both ancient and contemporary music. Although the Church's identity is historically Baptist, members come from all different faith backgrounds.

Saint Agnes Catholic Church

Rena Hodgins

The first recorded Mass in the Town of Pittsfield was celebrated at the home of the Monahans on May 21, 1893. In 1894 the Catholic community was assigned as a Mission of the Belfast parish. The pastor from Belfast traveled to Pittsfield on the Belfast and Moosehead Lake railroad. Mass continued to be offered in private homes and, as the congregation grew, services were conducted in the Grand Old Army Hall and the Perkins Hall which was on the third floor of the building next to the Pittsfield Community Theater.

In 1903, Father Keely, the pastor of the Belfast Church, recommended that a church be built in

Pittsfield. He promised to obtain funds to match whatever the Pittsfield community could raise up to $1,000.00. In a matter of hours, $1,100.00 was pledged. The first Mass was celebrated on November 17, 1904. The Church was dedicated on July 17, 1910 but remained a mission parish and continued to be served by priests from Belfast and North Vassalboro.

In 1927, St. Agnes was designated a full-fledged parish and Rev. M. L. Ballou was assigned as pastor. He would be the first of 18 priests to serve the parish. The parish territory served ten towns with three more added over the years. In 1929 the Dr. Blanchard house (now the home of Dr. Flint Reid) was acquired for use as a rectory. In 1947 land adjacent to the Church was purchased to provide for a parking area and eventually a rectory.

In 1948, St. Agnes Ladies Guild was founded. On October 11, 1959 Council #1861 of the Knights of Columbus was organized with 29 men installed. Both groups continue to provide spiritual leadership and assistance to the pastor as needed. In 1980 the Knights purchased a building on

Dobson Street to use as a meeting place. They subsequently sold the building in 2010 and resumed the use of the Parish Hall where they hold a monthly breakfast which has been on-going for 21 years.

During the late 1950s the parish hall was erected. It was acquired from the Bangor Barracks at Dow Air Force Base. The barracks remains as the front section of the present parish hall which was enlarged in 1980 and again in 1992 to provide space for educational rooms and social functions.

On October 28, 1963 the new rectory, located beside the church, was dedicated. In 1970 land was purchased for an additional parking lot, together with land behind the Church which contained a small building which was used a meeting place for the Catholic Youth Organization. The lot was later used for a convent to house the Sisters teaching at the school.

In the fall of 1993, a parochial school was opened under the guidance of Sisters of the Presentation of Mary. The first year 26 children enrolled in grades K-2. Grade 3 was added in the fall of 1994. The Sisters of Mercy replaced the Sisters of the Presentation, and the school continued to grow adding grades 4 through 8 and an after-school program. By 2006/2007 the school experienced decreasing enrollment and eventually closed on June 12, 2008.

On October 3, 2006 the Bishop accepted the findings of a study group which recommended that St. Agnes parish join with the Dexter, Dover-Foxcroft, and Milo parishes to form a Cluster which would be served by one Pastor and a Parochial Vicar. Several Deacons have also assisted the priests in their spiritual duties.

On September 12, 2010 the parish celebrated the 100th year anniversary of the dedication of St. Agnes church. Programs and activities were held during the summer of 2010 and culminated with a Mass celebrated by the Bishop, several retired priests and a former Pastor. The Catholic community has continued to thrive over the past 125 years. Religious education programs, both for children and adults, have continued throughout the period with the guidance of several religious orders and the many volunteers who have unselfishly given of their time.

Pittsfield Church of the Nazarene

Pastor Tim Hoyt with Jane Woodruff

Like many churches in the area, the Pittsfield Church of the Nazarene began by holding its services in private homes. The church was organized in 1946 and three years later, they were able to purchase the Leon Moody home on the corner of Somerset and Forest Streets. For ten years, they congregated there for services. With members of the congregation assisting in its construction, in 1959 they erected the structure that stands there today; however, with 9-1-1 the street became re-named as Central Street. A parsonage was built adjacent to the church in the late 1980s.

In 2009, they made statewide news with the gifting of labor by Top Notch Roofing of Clinton. Co-owner of the company Roger Reynolds noticed the stacks of shingles and plywood beside the church that had been there for quite some time. Meanwhile, during that late summer, the roof had started leaking in multiple places. Reynolds conferred with his co-owner Richard Park Jr. and they donated their company's labor to roof the church. The congregation responded with immense gratitude, meals, and a funding drive for donations for Top Notch.

Easter Service

The Church of the Nazarene has been quite visible to townspeople in recent years with its serving some basic needs of the community: distributing over 300 coats as well as non-perishable food. At Halloween, they served over 500 people with bags of candy, hot chocolate, and coffee. When Channel 2 in Portland had a mound of toys, they filled their truck to bring them back to children in town. These are just a few of their outreach activities.

Their newest project they plan to launch in 2019 is Christ 4 Life, a "pop-up" church directed to engage tweens to young adults. A call would be put out on social media to inform them of a gathering place in town where they would meet up with a short devotional using the oral tradition of telling a story from the Bible. This would be followed by fun activities for the different age groups. The thought is that church is not necessarily a building, but the gathering of people. With this new project Pastor Hoyt explains, "We need to come together to serve our community, especially our youth."

The Pittsfield Church of Christ

Clermont Spencer

In the spring of 1957, Ralph Smart of Dexter started a Bible class in William and Mary Spencer's living room on North Main Street in Pittsfield that quickly grew to quite a crowd. Then they moved to the American Legion Hall on Manson Street. Classes were held for preachers and song leaders. The men took turns preaching one Sunday a month. Bible classes were taught twice a week. The Bible is the basis for their doctrine and practice. They moved to Galen Spencer's house in the early 1960s, and from there to the one-room schoolhouse which was on the corner of Hartland Avenue and Spring Road. In 1980, Rea Pennock was the preacher.

The little schoolhouse, which had become bigger, burned in 1982 and the church met in various places around town including the American Legion Hall, the Drift Busters Club House, and Terry Kennedy's on the Phillips Corner Road, until a new building was put up on land donated by Clifford Wright on Phillips Corner Road. The last full-time preacher was Don Chason. The elders and several others teach the classes at the building. Home classes and studies by mail are offered. Visiting preachers hold Gospel meetings at least twice a year.

Deeper Life Assembly

Matthew Bagley

Deeper Life Assembly is a Christ-centered Church made up of a body of believers that are interested in showing and sharing the love of God with our community and beyond. We have been in Pittsfield for 70 plus years. We are a small church with a BIG heart! Throughout the year D.L.A. offers a number of different activities to be involved in: Kids Kampout, T-ball/Farm league barbeque, the Annual Pittsfield Car Show, Winter Carnival, Shooters Breakfast, Ladies Luncheon, and many other activities. We have Sunday School, Children's Church, Weekly Worship Services, Youth group, Bible Study and more. For a smaller church, we do a lot and are very active. The Church property is located at 97 Higgins Road about 2.2 miles from the center of town. We own 53 acres of land and there is a pond on the property that gets used in a variety of ways (fishing, skating, swimming, kayaking).

If you're looking for a church, look no further! DEEPER LIFE ASSEMBLY IS AN UPBEAT CHURCH FOR A BEAT UP WORLD. WE HAVE A VISION FOR THE WORLD THAT DOESN'T OVERLOOK YOU.

God is very good to us and we are glad to be a part of a great community such as Pittsfield. Over the years D.L.A. has had several different pastors, the longest one being the former, Pastor Millard Dickinson who was here for 34 years. Our current Pastor Matthew Bagley and his wife Danielle have been in the ministry for over 20 years and have 4 children ages 16, 15, 13, and 12. They have served as our pastors for 12 plus years. They have a great love for D.L.A. and the people of our community and beyond. Deeper Life Assembly thinks Pittsfield is the best and wishes it a happy 200th. God's Richest blessings to you all!

Calvary Baptist Church

Ted Bragg with Jane Woodruff

According to Sanger Cook's *Pittsfield on the Sebasticook,* several years after organizing in 1952 Pittsfield's Calvary Baptist Church purchased a building on Park Street and converted it for their use. By 1976, the congregation and its pastor, Charles Watson, had literally built the current church that is on Grove Hill.

That spirit of building and doing is apparent today in what Pastor Ted Bragg described as their wood ministry. While they literally burn wood to heat their sanctuary, the church members also harvest wood for others in need. Bragg laughingly tells of his congregants calling him the "red neck pastor." He describes some of their ministries with their "chain saw and mud-out" teams where they have been as far away as South Carolina to help with disaster relief in cleaning up debris. Another ministry is the Sewl Sisters Ministry where church members under the leadership of Jan Frost sew clothes for children in Haiti. As he says, "Everything we do is a ministry. Virtually everybody in this church serves. We can't do things without people. So loving a congregation .... it is a privilege to serve them and the Lord."

The church also has a home-school group serving children from five to 14 years old where the ratio is four children per teacher. The two full-time and one part-time teachers are volunteers who serve the children with programs adjusted to their learning levels. They also meet alternate Fridays with other home-schoolers to afford the children more socialization.

Congregational Church of Pittsfield

Kerma Cordice

In September of 1960, a group of approximately thirty-five people considered forming a new church. Financial support was pledged, a new minister was hired and fifty-one charter members joined. In October 1960, after corporation papers were completed, the First Congregational Church of Pittsfield was underway. Soon after the congregation elected to join with the Maine Conference, United Church of Christ.

Early services were held in living rooms and in the VFW Hall. In 1961, the membership voted to purchase then former Donald H. Shorey Funeral Home property which included three buildings on Park Street. The funeral parlor, which became our current sanctuary, the fellowship hall, and the parsonage.

Membership began to grow as did our Sunday School. In 1968, it was voted by the congregation to purchase the Severance home on the corner of Park and Middle Streets. Its many rooms were converted for Sunday School use. During the 1970's the Severance home was renamed Bennett Hall after Blanche Bennett, our first Sunday School Director. In 1979, fund-raising efforts were underway to purchase and install a spire for the front of our sanctuary building and it stands to this day.

In 1985 it was decided to tear down Bennett Hall and to replace it with a new building. In honor of our 25th Anniversary, it was named Memorial Hall. Over the years Memorial Hall has been utilized for many church functions as well as a meeting location for groups such as the Boy Scouts and Cub Scouts, TOPS, and AA. Because we offer a fully furnished kitchen, Memorial Hall is an ideal place to hold many private functions such as showers, birthday parties, and funeral receptions.

Over the years the church has been led in worship by many part-time pastors as well as students from Bangor Theological Seminary. In 1992, the congregation voted to call Rev. Andrew Gibson, a National Guard Chaplain, as our first full-time Pastor. "Andy" served as our Pastor from 1992 to 2003 at which time he was called to full-time duty in the Guard. Since then, we have again relied on part-time pastors. Rev. Alice Lester is our current Pastor.

The pride and joy of our church has always been the Pennywise Thrift Shop which eventually opened up in Lane Hall after being housed in various town locations. Over the years the Women's Fellowship group volunteered to sort and display clothes and other household items. In 2008, the deteriorating parsonage house was torn down and a new sales floor building was erected on its site. The shop is still maintained by volunteers who spend countless hours sorting clothing and household goods donated generously by the public.  Pennywise is a great source for reasonably priced clothing and household goods for residents of Pittsfield and the surrounding communities. We are a small church but due to the income from Pennywise, we are able, in part, to donate to many charitable organizations such as The Mid Maine Homeless Shelter, The Waterville Animal Shelter, the Family Violence Project, the town oil fund, and the Pittsfield Food Pantry, to name just a few.

Our forefathers wanted our church to be known as "The Church that Love Built", noting that a church is not the building it houses but the spirit and devotion of its congregation. We are hopeful that, with God's grace and presence in our midst, to be able to continue to serve the needs of our congregation and the community for many years to come.

The Unitarian Universalist Meeting House of Pittsfield: Then & Now

Holly Zadra

The Unitarian Universalist Meeting House sits prominently atop a hill in the middle of the Pittsfield village, reminiscent of Pittsfield's former leaders who made the church as it exists now possible: the Lanceys, Vickerys, Dobsons, Parks, and Mansons. Though the interior spaces remain unknown to many townspeople today who've never witnessed its craftsmanship and artistry, the art adorning its walls and cove ceiling and its turn-of-the-century woodwork make it truly a hidden gem unparalleled in Central Maine. Work to renovate and restore as well as revitalize its use as a community center at the hub of town commenced in its sesquicentennial year of 2017. Community members look to the past as a guide for that vision of the future.

One of the first churches in the community, the "East Pittsfield Union Meeting House" was built in 1857 as a simple, rectangular, and non-sectarian meeting house where circuit-riding preachers shared the pulpit. Within ten years as Universalism grew in the region, 42 townspeople established "The First Universalist Society in Pittsfield, Maine." Twelve years later in 1879, the Universalists had nearly doubled their numbers, so a Universalist minister was called to preach on Sundays. Though the church grew slowly, the Ladies Aid Society burgeoned in 1889 and raised enough funds to purchase a parsonage for the minister.

In the years leading up to 1899, Central Maine settlers of European descent thrived in Pittsfield, amidst

the zenith of agricultural production and small family farms and the burgeoning of industrial mills on the Sebasticook. As the town and the state entered their heyday, the church did comparably impressive work, in one year alone raising five times its annual budget in order to build the church you see today.

In 1899, the building was turned 90 degrees and the impressive sanctuary was constructed including the installation of its ornate organ with 600 speaking pipes, the hand-crafted pews and woodwork throughout the first floor, three triptych

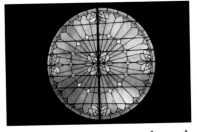

stained glass representations of Christianity on the north, west, and south walls, and sixteen Harry H. Cochrane murals on its domed ceiling. The bell was hoisted and still rings today, and all the art and majesty of 1899 is still apparent despite theological and cultural shifts over the course of the century.

First "Union," then "Universalist" in 1867, the church navigated a brief affiliation with the Congregationalists in the 1950s, and finally settled in 1966 as a member congregation of the newly merged Unitarian Universalist Association. The name "First Universalist Church" was changed unanimously in 2017 to "Unitarian Universalist Meeting House" as part of a larger effort to broaden its welcome and the use of the space. Currently, the Meeting House holds weekly Sunday services; concerts; workshops; reading groups; celebrations of life and rites of passage; local cultural, political, and artistic events; fundraisers; and as always, local suppers where people come together in gratitude to serve, to eat, and spend time together in community. UUMH remains committed to community service, to assisting the needy, and remaining ever-vigilant to the work of social justice in the world at large. The Meeting House also hosts the Welcome Table each Friday all year long serving a homemade meal and socializing open to all.

In many ways, today's Unitarian Universalist Meeting House is in the midst of a kind of rebirth. Strategic planning as well as a renovation and restoration campaigns have begun. Members grapple with how to "do church" in ways that are both relevant and grounded in tradition. Though what came before offers guidance in the journey, it is what comes next that gives these UUs the hope and audacity to imagine a more perfect future.

Her Clubs

People organized and formed social and civic groups to better the community. They have raised and donated money to different causes. They have given their time to coach children in sports and lead them in scouting. Some of these civic groups helped promote economic development. They initiated projects that resulted in the acquisition of a pool, a park, a library, a ski slope, and a hospital. Unfortunately, several clubs that provided the impetus to key projects folded, but they should be remembered.

Pittsfield Tuesday Club

Rae Hersey

The birth of the Tuesday Club occurred on February 23, 1893 after twenty ladies organized a literary society. They met every Tuesday at the home of one of the members. They delved deeply into "the wisdom of the ages," and thus the Pittsfield Tuesday Club was born.

Although the Pittsfield Tuesday Club was organized primarily as a literary club, it had always participated in fund-raising for worthy projects. In the early days of the club, a need was often felt for a larger public library. In 1898, a committee was appointed to see what could be done. This action materialized into a permanent Public Library Association on March 13, 1899 and see what this did - Pittsfield Public Library.

On January 7, 1936, it was voted that the Pittsfield Tuesday Club sponsor a junior club. This was the birth of the Always Ready To Serve Club (A.R.T.S. Club) which is still active today.

The Pittsfield Tuesday Club was a very active club in Pittsfield right up until the late 1990s. Then as inflation took over, American families found it harder to make ends meet with one income, forcing more women into the work force, leaving little time for club work. Membership kept declining. Sadly, the Pittsfield Tuesday Club disbanded in 2008-2009. The history records of the Pittsfield Tuesday Club are kept at the Pittsfield Historical Society.

Athenaeum Club

Jane Woodruff

While it is unclear why the Arts Club initiated the formation of yet another women's club as they themselves had similarly been formed by the Tuesday Club, in March of 1956 they created the Athenaeum Club. Its purpose, as stated in their history, was to "promote the broadening of self, enrichment of life, adjustment of human relations, and service to home, community, state and the world." Beginning with three charter members and twelve others, the club quickly grew to twenty-five members. Its first president was Mrs. Barbara Fendler.

In a nearly 30-year period, this club had a significant impact on Pittsfield. Raising more than ten thousand dollars in just its first 20 years, it contributed to many, many groups such as the library, hospital, schools, and various charities. Perhaps the largest impact this group had was their drive to have a local hospital where their children might be born; thus, they instigated the community-wide project that led to the formation of Sebasticook Valley Hospital.

In its later years, the Athenaeum Club took on another project - what they termed as a Community Improvement Project. This time it was to restore the train station with the thoughts of preserving it to serve as a community center. They initiated the organization of the Depot House, Inc., a corporation organized to support and maintain the station with Byron "Bud" Dow being its first president. The club continued to lead and fund-raise a community-wide effort over a period of eight years until the depot's dedication in 1983.

Sebasticook Club

Brenda Seekins

Elizabeth Sobey was one of seven women who organized a social and service club for their rural community in 1937. The original members all lived on Route 100, or the Burnham Road, and parallel to the Sebasticook River, hence its name.

As a young wife and mother, Sobey joined her neighbors at Annie Ames' home for the first meeting on February 13, 1937. Sobey and Ames were joined by Kate McLeod, Mildred Kenniston, Frances Burch, Florence Mudgett and Alice Dunlop. The small club grew almost instantly as other neighbors learned of the new social group. The function of the group was always to raise money to donate to community projects. They met for many years in the abandoned schoolhouse at the end of the Snakeroot Road, until that practice became too expensive. The club was to survive more than 75 years. From the beginning, the club followed its motto: "Friendships are discovered, rather than made." The saying was borrowed from the work of Harriet Beecher Stowe.

Similar to these now defunct clubs, a number of organizations in town function as did they: to socialize and to promote community projects. Many of these groups help with the major annual celebration to promote the town.

Egg Festival
Norman Clarke

The Egg Festival began in 1973. Local business people teamed with "Toby"' Strong, editor of *The Valley Times,* whose idea it was to promote Pittsfield with a celebration centering around the egg. The egg industry was a thriving enterprise then, especially in Pittsfield, so it was decided to celebrate the egg and the egg producers. It was to be called the Central Maine Egg Festival. The first festival was an elaborate affair featuring Dick Curless, the first Egg Festival Queen, and many other features still in place today, 46 years later.

One of the Many Tee Shirt Designs by Norman Clarke

Dupont and Teflon got together and produced a 12' diameter fry pan, which at that time was the world's largest. The Pittsfield Arts Club served its famous early bird breakfast on that pan, a tradition carried on but the frying pan has been retired. Things such as carnival rides, chicken flying contest, T-shirts, queen pageants, Egglypics, world's largest egg contest, street dance, craft tent, window painting contest, evening chicken barbeque and many more events thrilled and entertained people from all over. Teaming up with the Pittsfield Kiwanis, it became the place to go in July. The Kiwanis served delicious food and provided games to all. Local organizations set up booths and served food of many kinds to festival goers. These organization earned most of their money during the festival and this enabled them to fund their charities throughout the year.

The early policy of nothing but homemade crafts, non-profit organizations only on the grounds, no religious or political groups would be allowed and some of the vendor's money raised was to go back to the festival to help it put on the event year after year.

Kicking off the festival week, the street dance, Egglympics, window painting contest and Kiwanis Kiddie Parade led up to the day of the affair. A big mile-long parade started things off in the morning and ended with the grand fireworks show at night. During the day, the Kiwanis Karnival, Egg Festival and all sorts of fun things to do went on all during the day. Musical entertainment was free and went on continuously while people enjoyed the Bingo Tent, various food options and visited with friends and family, some not seen since the last Egg Festival. It has been said that, at times, you could almost walk on the heads of the thousands of people there and never set foot on the ground.

All these years later, the festival goes on. Some things have changed, the crowds may not be as big and the Kiwanis now plays a smaller part in the festivities, but the festival goes on and on inviting people to come on down and see what's happening. It takes many hands, hard work and much planning to make this continue each year. Your help is much appreciated.

The Greater Pittsfield Area Kiwanis Club

Helping Children in Our Community

Emma Gallimore

The History of the Greater Pittsfield Area Kiwanis Club is the history of Pittsfield. From the club's formation in 1940, it has played a central role in the business and recreation of Pittsfield.

In the 1940s, the club worked with J.R. Cianchette to revitalize Pittsfield's economy. They helped raise more than $6,000 to fund the building of the municipal airport. Soon after the runways were completed, U.S. Navy pilots began training there. They continued using the runway until the end of World War II.

A group of Kiwanians, businessmen all, banded together to buy and rejuvenate the Waverly Mill, bringing more than 300 workers to Pittsfield.

The Development of the Kiwanis Ski Slope on the Pinnacle in the 1950s has had a major impact on the town. Shown here in the 1960s, gone are the ski jump and water tower today, but the facilities and skiers remain.

Not only did Kiwanis play a key role in the business development of the town but they also supported fun and recreation in the community. In 1952, a swimming pool was proposed. The Kiwanis Club jumped in head-first, raising funds and gathering public support. The pool was dedicated and opened to the public in July 1953. The club presented it to the trustees of Manson Park for the joy and entertainment of the whole community.

When President Dwight D. Eisenhower visited Pittsfield in 1955, Willard Lehr, President of the Kiwanis Club, co-led the committee that made preparations for Eisenhower's arrival.

In his historical work *Pittsfield on Sebasticook*, Sanger Mills Cook said, "Never in the history of Pittsfield has a service organization been more active or accomplished more good than this group of men." Since Cook's time, the Kiwanis Club has added many women to its ranks, and the spirit of doing good is alive and well.

Every year, since the 1950s, they've hosted the Kiwanis Karnival, a multi-day event that offers food, games, rides and entertainment for all. Since 1973, the Pittsfield Egg Festival has partnered with the Kiwanis Karnival to make the event even bigger.

Matt Hamrick, Jim & Asa Cianchette Working at the Annual Bike Rodeo

Beyond the Kiwanis Karnival, the club also hosts a yearly Easter Egg Hunt that brings children from miles around to the Pinnacle Ski Club, where the Kiwanis Club developed the ski slope and installed a ski tow in 1955. Each May, local children learn bike safety and get free helmets at the Bike Rodeo. November is time for the Holiday Warm-Up, a fundraising dinner and dance.

In all of these events, the club is helped by the MCI and Nokomis Key Clubs – high school service organizations sponsored by the Greater Pittsfield Area Kiwanis.

Everything the Greater Pittsfield Area Kiwanis does is for the good of area children. If you'd like to learn more about their mission and their work, visit greaterpittsfieldareakiwanis .com

Cub Scouts, Pack 428

Megan L. Hart

Cub Scout Tanner Godfrey placing flag in holder on veteran's grave

Boy Scouts of America was incorporated in 1910 ("History of Cub Scouting"). It was all based on the vision of Robert Stephenson Smyth Baden-Powell. Baden –Powel began his idea of teaching boys about surviving in the outdoors while stationed in India as a British Army officer. He discovered that his men did not know basic first aid or have the knowledge of survival in the outdoors. Baden-Powell wrote a handbook titled *Aids to Scouting* that emphasized how to be resourceful, adapting, and the qualities of leadership that the frontier demanded of the men. Upon his return from war, he gathered around 20 boys and took them to Brownsea Island in England where they set up camp for the next 12 days. The boys had a great time, and little did they know, started the platform of Scouting.

Pittsfield has been a charted Cub Scout pack since 1972. The Cub Scout program is for grades K-5. Cub scouts do fun things, go places, see things, play sports, and build things like racecars and birdhouses. The Cub Scout program builds character and instills values of being good citizens. As a cub scout, you do your best and you help others. The Scout Oath law states that a Scout is trustworthy, loyal, helpful, friendly, courteous, kind, obedient, cheerful, thrifty, brave, clean, and reverent. These character-developing areas are extended into the child's life and throughout all aspects of Cub Scouting.

In just the past few years, the Cub Scout pack in Pittsfield, Pack 428, has participated in a number of community enriching events. We have participated in food drives and hat and mitten drives for those in our community in need. We have decorated Christmas trees at the Pittsfield Library with ornaments the

Scouts made from recycled items. We have gone Christmas caroling around town and visited the hospital and local nursing homes to spend time with patients. We have gone on hikes and collected trash and debris we have found on the trail or at the parks. We have gone camping and participated in Scout summer camps. The comradery and community presence the Scouts bring to the town of Pittsfield is something the Scouts are proud of and cherish.

Boy Scouts

Scott Varney, Scoutmaster

In 2014, Pittsfield scouts marked their 100th anniversary. The Boy Scouts of America began in 1910; thus, Pittsfield was one of the very earliest troops. It later became incorporated with the Pine Tree Council in 1929. Seven years later, Harris (Hap) Mathews attained the rank of Eagle Scout, the highest achievement attainable in scouting. Hap began a long line of young men achieving this rank - forty-seven to date.

Part of this path to Eagle requires that the scout demonstrate community involvement and leadership. The list of Eagle projects is long and varied, but below is a sample of just some of them:

Jim Higgs with Scoutmaster Hap Mathews who was Pittsfield's 1st Eagle Scout

- clean-up of sites such as the length of the Spring Road, where trash collected filled forty-eight pick-up trucks, and the Peltoma boat landing where it was also redesigned and enlarged
- construction projects such as the exercise stations in Manson Park, boxes for nesting ducks, a storage shed for MCI soccer, bookcases for the library, and the small shed over a spring which was later relocated to the Pinnacle to house the motor for the ski tow
- installation of recycle bins at MCI to fund-raise for local athletic programs
- painting and remodeling of all the buildings and concession hut at Hathorn Park
- designing and working with the Town to transform a vacant lot to what is now Remembrance Park

Additionally, the Scouts, as a troop, do many community service activities: serve at the Welcome Table, spring clean-up with the Garden Club, clean-up of streets after the Egg Festival, volunteer to man concessions during athletic events, collect needed items for the Bush Children's Hospital and the Waterville Humane Society to name a few.

When asked the meaning of the Boy Scout motto of *Be Prepared*, founder Robert Baden-Powell answered,"Why, for any old thing," It is apparent that the Scouts in Troop #428 are following that motto.

Eagle Scout Awards
Scott Varney

Harris Mathews	11-25-1936	Jonathon E. Humphrey	5-24-1984
Wayne K. Shorey	9-2-1955	Peter A. Vigue	5-24-1984
Dennis W. Haggerty, Jr.	12-2-1955	Cabot J. Forsythe	5-20-1987
Michael Parker	5-13-1958	Brian C. Philbrick	5-20-1987
Gregory J. Patterson	7-1-1965	Vaughan J Woodruff	8-7-1989
Robert Mathews	10-28-1970	Matthew T. Weaver	3-30-1993
Kirk A. Dahlgren	11-7-1972	Jeff Stevens	3-18-1994
Frank W. Sanborn	1-23-1974	Ryan P. Perry	10-13-1994
Randy L. Raye	8-8-1974	Eric E. Lane	11-26-1996
Gary L. Limatainen	3-27-1978	Daniel J. Cournoyer	8-27-1998
Bruce E. Higgs	9-4-1981	Christopher W. Cochrane	8-20-2000
Troy H. Moon	9-4-1981	Alexander Cunningham	3-24-2002
John E. Plusquelic	9-4-1981	Forrest C. Peterson	3-24-2002
Eric L. Thompson	9-4-1981	Aaron H. Greene	10-18-2005
Daniel P. Williams	9-4-1981	Eliot D. Cochrane	1-24-2007
Aaron C. Bartlett	5-1-1982	Nathaniel J. Olsen	12-22-2008
Timothy J. Cropley	5-1-1982	Patrick K. F. Hapworth	4-28-2010
Charles E. Dickinson	5-1-1982	Christopher A. Spaulding	8-25-2010
Scott Hallett	3-1-1983	Gregory J. Vigue	10-30-2013
Dale D. Rowley	3-1-1983	Ethan P. Duplisea	12-18-2013
Robert B. Speed	3-1-1983	Logan L. Rollins	8-12-2015
Barry G. Brooks	5-24-1984	Brandon C. Stevens	3-2-2016
Brent C. Brooks	5-24-1984	Devon S. Varney	5-25-2016
Harold A. Goodridge	5-24-1984	Carter A. Richmond	9-15-2017

Girl Scouts Then

Jane Woodruff

Apparently from the dated photos at the Historical Society, Brownies and Girl Scouts started in Pittsfield in the 1940s. The troops grew and became extremely active in the 1950s and 1960s when they had some annual events that were unique to Pittsfield. In the winter, a carnival was held with numerous races in skating, skiing, and snowshoeing at the Pinnacle. The day would end with the girls who had accumulated the most points being crowned: the Girl Scout as queen and the Brownie as princess. In May, breakfasts were cooked over campfires in Manson Park and those Brownies who were "flying up" into Girl Scouts would cross a bridge as the symbol of their transition. Badges were earned and ranks achieved with the highest award at that time being the curved bar. Cookies and calendars were sold as fund-raisers to support the activities of the troops and like today's Girl Scouts, values reinforced like "Always leave a place better than you found it."

Crowning of Queen of Winter Carnival Nancy Files by Senator Sinclair in Park Gymnasium

Girl Scouts Now

Kelli Brooks

Girl Scout troop 1328 is one of the multiple Girl Scout troops in Pittsfield, Maine. Currently at the Cadette level, most girls started in their Girl Scout journey as Daisies when in Kindergarten. The troop

was established in 2012 by Kristianna Marcello and Amanda Gillis with meetings held at Manson Park School. Other leaders include Kellie Brooks, Sara Good, and Shannon Peppard with meetings being held at Vickery School. Tuesday has become known as Scout night with several Girl Scout and Boy Scout troops meeting at Vickery School.

Celebrating Girl Scouting's 100th Birthday

During Girl Scouts cookie sales, the girls earn financial literacy and cookie business badges. Each has the opportunity to take part in the cookie share program to benefit Meals on Wheels and earn a week at summer camp. Troop 1328 joined 640 other Girl Scouts in Maine at Acadia National Park in 2016 for Expedition Acadia to help the park service celebrate the 100th Anniversary. In the same year, the girls collected donations for the Barbara Bush Children's Hospital. Troop 1328 earned the Bronze award in 2016, the highest honor a Girl Scout Junior can achieve, with planning, designing, and building a bench for the entry way at Vickery School. The girls spent many teamwork hours and hands on work with tools to benefit their community.

Meeting with Senator Susan Collins in Washinton, D.C.

In 2017, EMT's from Sebasticook Valley Health came to teach troop 1328 about first aid and pet CPR. The first aid badge is one of multiple ways the girls have paired earning badges while reaching out to the community. Donations from troop 1328 include to the food cupboard, animal shelter and Pittsfield's own Children's Benefit Fund. Girls participate yearly in Pittsfield's Memorial Day parade and Central Maine Egg Festival.

The troop joined 300 Girl Scouts of Maine in traveling to Washington DC, June 2017. In celebrating the 105th year of Girls Scouting, they toured the Holocaust Museum, Capital and Air and Space Museum. This is just one experience Girl Scouts offers, giving some girls the opportunity that they would not normally be able to have.

Michelle Carr is Pittsfield's leader facilitator, recruiter, troop leader, and event coordinator for the Chickadee Service unit. She recalls since 1995, Pittsfield has had a Girl Scout at every grade level. Girl Scouts have been in Pittsfield since before Girl Scout Colleen Irish welcomed President Eisenhower to town.

Juliette Gordon Low founded Girl Scouts in Savannah, Georgia on March 12, 2012. The mission of the Girl Scouts is to build courage, confidence, and character in all girls and to make the world a better place. Girl Scouts of America has grown to 1.8 million girls and 800,000 adults. Visit girilscoutsofmaine .org for more information.

The Pittsfield Historical Society and Museum
Norman Clarke

The historical society was formed in 1983 by Trudy Humphrey and Eve Drew, because of concern for items often locked up in the historical room at the library. When remodeling and renovations began at the library, they needed a new home quickly.

It happened that the old railroad depot was vacant and looking for someone to step in to save and occupy the building. The station was a golden opportunity and because it is listed on the National Register Of Historic Places, it seemed like a good fit.

The historical society and museum share the same space which houses over 2000 artifacts from the Egg Festival largest eggs and other items, old railroad and town memorabilia, displays from the town floods of 1924, 1936 and 1987, an X-ray machine from Dr. Stein, farmers' tools and much more.

Local people have donated their time and energy to preserve and add to the collection as well as fix and maintain the building. From outside to inside, many local hands keep the building in shape. An old Maine Central Railroad caboose was added in 1987 and sits just behind the museum on its own tracks. As with the depot, local children and adults have helped paint and maintain the caboose.

A website has been established to provide updated news about the museum and society. It also contains an index to Sanger Cook's book on Pittsfield, which the original book didn't have. Information can be found at pittsfieldhistoricalsociety .org.

Thanks to Tom Brown Sanger Cook's Book has an index on the Historical Society's Website

As with any town volunteer organization, the society needs help and people of all ages to keep things going into the future. Please help in any way you can so we all can enjoy the town's past for many years to come

Sebasticook Valley Hospital Auxiliary

Beverly Rollins

The Sebasticook Valley Hospital (SVH) Auxiliary was chartered May 11, 1960 to raise funds for construction of the new hospital planned for Pittsfield. Alice Baxter served as its first president.

Over the years many dedicated members have served on committees and volunteered at events and fundraisers to support SVH, its patients, and the communities it serves.

In 1988, the Auxiliary took over the holiday Greeting Page from the RN Club, who had started this annual fundraiser around 1970. This gives individuals and businesses the opportunity to wish everyone Merry Christmas in a local newspaper. These funds support two scholarships awarded by the Auxiliary each year - $500 to a Maine Central Institute senior and $500 to a Nokomis senior who are continuing their education in the healthcare field. The holiday Greeting Page continues to support these scholarships.

Auxiliary activities have included participation in the annual SVH Health Fair, blood drives, the Smiley Program, and Daffodil Days, to name a few. Proceeds from Daffodil Days enabled the Auxiliary to donate up to $2,500 annually to the American Cancer Society.

Since the 1990s the Auxiliary supported the Brothers Table and the Welcome Table at local churches.

Connie Thies, Bev Rollins, Marilyn Lloyd, Barbara Jones and Nancy Fiske at SVH Luncheon during Hospital Volunteer Awareness Week

In 1990 the Auxiliary pledged $35,000 to the SVH Capital Campaign. To help meet this financial commitment, they had a Pepsi vending machine installed in the hospital waiting room. Sales from the vending machine, gift nook, and greeting cards helped raise the $35,000.

They host food sales and tables at craft fairs and in 2012, Auxiliary members, family, and friends contributed their favorite recipes to publish a cookbook. The Auxiliary now hosts an annual spring concert and Christmas Home Tours every other year, which is enjoyed by many. These fundraising initiatives enable them to continue their support of the hospital.

Over the years, they made many contributions to SVH including, but not limited to: $3,000 Lifeline, $17,500 Women's Health Center, $10,000 Digital Mammography Machine, $17,500 ED Renovations and Waiting Room, $5,000 Patient Information Brochures and most recently, $25,000 for the SVH Building Campaign.

The Auxiliary appreciates the support of Terri Vieira, President of Sebasticook Valley Health, and her staff for their services and all they do for the Auxiliary. Auxiliary meetings are currently held September through June at the SVH conference room located 130 Leighton Street. New members are always welcome.

Meridian Lodge, #125 Pittsfield, Maine

Lewis (Ross) Fitts III, Lodge Secretary and Historian

The masonic fraternity has enjoyed a long and storied history in Pittsfield. In preparing some insights into the lodge's beginnings, I am indebted to a well written account spanning the first 14 years of lodge activities written by Brother Albion Whitten in 1878. I would borrow the beginning paragraph of his preface "Chosen by the lodge to write its history, I enter upon the task with fear and trembling. Fear of my own ability to accomplish what is desired of me, and lest with the somewhat uncertain sight I have of some of the earlier history, I may not do the founders of the lodge that equal and exact justice which is their due, and that I may disappoint my friends in their estimate of what I ought to do in the premises." This was his sentiment, having the luxury of writing an excellent account of the lodge's beginnings while most of the original members were still alive and active, and available to offer their own accounts. I will need to rely on my personal experience and knowledge of the town, and the masonic fraternity here, based on my 37 years as an active member, and in my role as current lodge secretary. I will not offer insights into the origins, ideology, or methods of Free Masonry in general. It is sufficient to say Meridian Lodge prescribes to the purposes of the organization and its principles which are well documented.

There were originally 14 Master Masons who petitioned the Grand Master of Masons in Maine, William A Preble, for a dispensation to form Meridian lodge, which he granted in June of 1864. The lodge's

official charter was awarded on May 3, 1865. Of the 14 petitioners only 12 became charter members, having all taken dispensations from their home lodges in surrounding towns in order to organize a Pittsfield lodge. The Grand Master appointed Mr. Augustus C. Whitney as the first Master of Meridian Lodge and they held their first meeting in "Lancey Hall" On June 15, 1864. After the official charter was granted the first election of officers took place during the lodge stated meeting of September of 1865 and Brother F.D. Jenkins became the first elected Master. Since this beginning Meridian Lodge has been an active part of the community for 153 years. Respected citizens have been proud members and active supporters. Names on the lodge rolls would be recognized on many prominent buildings, institutions, businesses, and parks around town. This suggests that community leaders were active in the fraternity. The original history provides some interesting insights into the makeup of members who joined in the early years and is evidence that, far from being and elitist society, the masonic lodge was a melting pot of a wide variety of farmers, laborers, teachers, merchants, entrepreneurs, and professionals, much as it remains today.

In perusing the lodge history, it is evident that masons from these early years took their responsibility to live exemplary lives which would reflect well on the fraternity and society of that time seriously. I found examples of 2 lodge hearings to chastise, and eventually suspend a member due to drunkenness, another expulsion due to a member making public statements about masons condoning, and aiding him, following fraudulent financial dealings, which were considered as unmasonic behavior. A resolution approved by the lodge in 1868 read as follows.

"Resolved, that the use of profane language is ungentlemanly, and extremely demoralizing, and in direct conflict with our obligations as masons, and perfectly inexcusable."

The Lodge continued to meet in the Lancey House and records show they made a contract with Mr. H.B Connor "for the Hall in his building to be built". Evidently this hall was somewhat unsatisfactory and in 1873, Going Hathorn, a man whose name features prominently in Pittsfield's history, erected a building which would become the new Masonic temple and was dedicated in 1874. Eventually the Masons

Granite Name Marker from Union Hall

moved into a lodge on the top floor of the Union Hall next door to another prominent fraternal organization, the International Order of Odd Fellows. When the town decided to renovate the old Union Hall in 1973 these 2 fraternities combined resources, along with a generous gift from Earl Vickery (another citizen of some note), and together constructed the Pittsfield Fraternal Hall on Hamilton Drive. The Masons continue to meet in this building today. Sadly, the Odd Fellows membership dwindled to the point where they gave up their charter many years ago.

Meridian Masonic Lodge #125 still remains an active and vital organization which continues to attract a number of promising gentlemen and offers financial support to many community projects. In recent years this includes contributions to local school initiatives as well as capital improvements to MCI. Other projects supported by the masons include renovations at Sebasticook Valley Hospital, Pittsfield Public Library and reconstruction of the municipal swimming pool. The masons of Pittsfield are especially enthusiastic in their support of local youth. More information on masonry in Maine can be found on line at mainemason .org and on the lodge web page, Meridian Lodge #125 A.F. & A.M. The Mailing address is Meridian Lodge #125, PO Box 365, Pittsfield ME. 04967. Membership inquiries are always welcomed.

Order of The Eastern Star

Chapter: Bethlehem #36

Beverly Breau

Nokomis Chapter of Newport Merged with Bethlehem Chapter

The Order of The Eastern Star is one of the largest fraternal organizations in the world for both men and women. Our local Chapter, Bethlehem #36, received its Charter in 1897. The Chapter held its meetings for many years on the third floor of the old Town Hall before moving to the Fraternal Hall built by the Masons and Odd Fellows in 1974 on Hamilton Terrace.

The main focus of the membership is charity and they support local organizations such as the Food Bank, Christmas Community Project, schools and library. Some of the other charities supported are the Shriner Hospitals and ESTARL (Eastern Star Training For Religious Leadership). We also utilize our hall for catering many community events.

Chapter meetings are held on the third Thursday of every month except July and August at 7:00 P.M. There is usually an interesting program and always refreshments.

Bethlehem Chapter has been honored to have had four members serve the Grand Jurisdiction of Maine as Worthy Grand Matrons. They are Josie Mathews, Dorothy Stanley, Cynthia Lewis and Rebecca Johnson.

For 67 years, the Chapter sponsored Pittsfield Rainbow Assembly #15. This was for young girls ages 12-18 and many girls locally and from surrounding towns made lasting friendships while learning lessons for young womanhood.

To become a member, one must have a Masonic affiliation such as father brother, uncle, etc. Petitions may be obtained from any member. We would be happy to share our fellowship with any new brother or sister.

American Legion

Burns W. Knowlton, Jr. Post 32

Gary Jordan, Sr. with Jane Woodruff

Chartered on August 5th, 1919, Pittsfield's American Legion celebrates its 100th birthday in the year of Pittsfield's bicentennial. Pittsfield's post is headed by Commander Gary Jordan, Sr. Originally known as the Otis M. Vining Post, it was later renamed for Pfc. Burns W. Knowlton, Jr., who was killed in Vietnam in 1967.

This post meets monthly at the Elks Lodge, a building that they originally had built in the late 1970s/early 1980s. Currently, they are working toward acquiring a new facility on Middle Street on a site where they demolished a burnt-out apartment building after carefully removing saleable parts. The hope is to make a gathering place for veterans where they can meet and socialize.

They support an oratorical program, where high school students prepare a 10-minute speech on the Constitution as well as a speech picked randomly on an article. Adjutant Michael Wyley coaches students who compete at Husson College the second week in February with students representing other Legion posts. They also support the Veterans Park in maintaining the memorial stones.

Marching in the Memorial Day parade, they remind us of their dedication and commitment to our country.

Sebasticook Valley Lodge 2713

Michael Lange

Sebasticook Valley Lodge was chartered in 1986 and their first Exalted Ruler or Lodge President was Spencer R. Havey, a retired Pittsfield Chief of Police and former sheriff of Somerset County. He eventually served four terms as Exalted Ruler and was elected as the lodge's first Honorary Life Member.

The lodge's first organizational meetings were held at the former Wright's Emporium on Hartland Avenue in Pittsfield and later moved to the Cianbro Training Center. The Elks eventually purchased the former American Legion Post at 26

Middle Street in Pittsfield where they are now located.

The Burns W. Knowlton American Legion Post #32 still meets at the lodge once a month at no charge. Pittsfield does not have many large meeting venues, so the Sebasticook Valley Lodge often serves as the town's unofficial "community center." The Pittsfield Senior Citizens' Club meets every Wednesday morning, the lodge hosts four or five Red Cross blood drives each year, and it is the headquarters for the annual quiche and cheesecake contest at the Central Maine Egg Festival. Basically, if a nonprofit, school or civic organization needs space to hold an event, chances are the Sebasticook Valley Lodge will donate the use of the hall.

Social and charitable events hosted by the lodge include karaoke, potluck suppers, holiday celebrations such as the members' Christmas Party, New Year's Eve, Super Bowl Sunday and St. Patrick's Day, the Central Maine Egg Festival parade, an annual scholarship golf tournament, a "Super Supper" and much more. One of the biggest single-night fundraisers is the Night-Before-Thanksgiving Pie and Cake Auction which raises $500 to $700 each year for a designated charity. The lodge partners with the Meridian Masonic Lodge each year for the Christmas Giving Tree. The Elks set up a tree with name tags in their club room for needy children in the community. Once the gifts are collected, the Masons wrap and deliver them to the families.

The Benevolent and Protective Order of Elks (BPOE) has more than 1,900 lodges nationwide – 22 in Maine – with over 800,000 members. Although the Sebasticook Valley Lodge is one of Maine's smallest Elks Lodges, they have a positive impact and excellent reputation in the community.

ARTS Club

Beverly Rollins

In 1936, the Pittsfield Tuesday Club sponsored what was called the Junior Arts club. The charter members of the Junior Arts club were: Ruth Louder, President, Erma Humphrey, Nedra Walker, Doris Healey, Virginia Wright, Elizabeth Lindholm, Geraldine Cargill, Helen Bailey and Georgia Fuller. In 1941-42, the club changed its name to the Arts Club. Meetings were usually held in members' homes and their annual meetings at local restaurants. During the club year 1955-56, the Arts Club organized a Junior Federated Club known as the Athenaeum Club. The Arts Club was very active during these times. Their membership numbers were limited to 25 and if a lady wanted to join, she had to have her name submitted by a club member and put on a waiting list. Openings to the club were when members resigned or left the area. They were then voted in and welcomed as a member.

The club had some worthwhile fundraisers such as its successful annual rummage sale, box socials, fashion shows, food sales and starting in 1975, serving breakfast at the Central Maine Egg Festival. These funds enabled them to support many local and federation causes such as a MCI scholarship, a Community Improvement Project, HOBY, Homes for Little Wanderers, Girl and Boys State, Red Cross, Cancer Drive, School Lunch Program, March of Dimes, and Crippled Children's Fund to name a few. They also sponsored a Girls Scout groups in Pittsfield. One of their CIP projects was financing trees and shrubs to be planted at the MCI campus.

Operation Lifesaver 1958: A Community Improvement Project: The ARTS Club compiled a list of 165 individuals and the list grew to 193, who would donate blood at any time. The club maintained a list with names, phone numbers and blood types and this list was given to area physicians and Community Nurses, as there was no hospital in Pittsfield at this time. The Arts Club women worked very hard to keep this list updated and support the local community over the years.

Barb Jones, Marilyn Lloyd and Connie Thies Receive Certificate of Recognition for Club's 70th Anniversary at the General Federation of Women's Clubs

Pittsfield Community Theatre CIP Project 1980-82: The theatre was the CIP Project of the Pittsfield Arts Club which raised $500 for the curtains and $200 for the stage balcony.

The 25th anniversary of the Arts Club was held at MCI Hall of Science and the 50th anniversary at the First Universalist Church. Many members from the Tuesday Club and the Athenaeum Club along with state GFWC members were in attendance.

The ARTS Club that is in existence now tries to keep some of the traditions that were part of the early years of the Arts Club. The name of the club now is The Pittsfield ARTS (Always Ready to Serve) Club and is a community service group. We have over the years held many fundraisers to keep us in a position to give to many worthwhile causes. Some of these were continuing with the breakfast at the Central Maine Egg Festival, however, now we hold the Cheesecake and Quiche Contest (since 2014). We also have held a Christmas Craft Auction, Lunch to Go at the polls (2014 & 2016), and cookie sales, to name a few.

Some of the donations given by the ARTS club have been to the Keep ME Warm program (thru the town of Pittsfield), MCI scholarships, Maine Youth Leadership, Born to Read Program, HOBY, the Pittsfield Food Pantry, Pinnacle, SVH, the Pittsfield Public Library, the Historical Society, the Pittsfield Theatre, Valentine bags for an area boarding-home residents, gifts for an area Domestic Violence shelter for women are a few that benefit from the ARTS Club. A yard sale and concert was held in 2006 and netted a profit of $1741 which was given to the Library Restoration & Expansion project.

In the past nine years, the club has provided meals three times a year at the Welcome Table here in Pittsfield, which provides meals every Friday. The clubs also host a Meet the Candidates night during election years.

The club has decorated a tree at the Pittsfield Library in December as part of the Friends of the Library for the past few years. The club supported the library in 2017 with their first Wooden Egg Painting where children came in and painted eggs that were then on display during Egg Festival Week.

Over the years the numbers of members have declined from what it was in the past. However, that does not change the spirit of its members and honorary members. Even though once a member has been in the club for 25 years, they become an honorary member that does not mean they slow down. They are asked to bake for fundraisers and events and attend district and state meetings. They contribute to the many charities along with the other ARTS club members for events the club is involved in and do it with a smile. We hope the club can continue for many more years and maybe in 2036, we can celebrate our 100th Anniversary.

Scarlet Dames

Rebecca Johnson with Jane Woodruff

Scarlet Dames, the Pittsfield area chapter of the Red Hat Society, promotes socialization for women over 50. Meeting monthly since 2005 this organization's members are easily identified by their wearing of red hats at various venues when they are meeting. Representing a variety of towns in proximity to Pittsfield, it serves women from Hartland, St. Albans, Ripley, Corinna, Stetson, Brooks and of course, Pittsfield.

Each month a member is responsible for planning outings which may range from trips Down East to eating locally. Their calendar year runs from November on as members meet for a Thanksgiving-style dinner at the local fraternal hall of the Masons.

Moving beyond the pure socialization aspect usually associated with this organization, Pittsfield's chapter has a charitable one as well. Whatever proceeds are made from the fall turkey dinner are divided amongst area food banks. They also buy toys at Christmas for the Home for Little Wanderers in Waterville and make hats and mittens to be distributed.

Any women in the Pittsfield area interested in joining this organization should contact Cynthia Lewis or Rebecca Johnson.

Pittsfield Seniors

Cyndra Knowles

Betty Delong, Jeanne Boisvert & Fran Kirk
Discussing Club Business

The Pittsfield Seniors have been meeting over the last 50 years. Every Wednesday at 9 A.M. this group of 25 to 30 members meets at the Elks Club for a morning of good friendship, great food, and playing games and cards, especially a competitive game of cribbage and 63.

We welcome anyone in the surrounding towns to join us. Over the years, the town of Pittsfield has been generous in helping fund our group. This has enabled us to enjoy an occasional meal out and entertainment. Each month, we celebrate members' birthdays. We have pizza, potluck, or something special that week. In July and August, we visit with the Newport seniors for a cook-out and entertainment and we invite them to our club for lunch and games. This is always a special time to get to meet them.

Our members range in ages from 50 to 95, so please join us if you would like. We would love having you. Stop by the Elks Club any Wednesday morning and check us out.

Friends of the Library

Sue Leibowitz

I moved to Maine in 2007 and being an avid library lover, my daughter took me to see the Pittsfield Library. I fell in love! It is such an elegant and beautiful library building (even before the renovation). I immediately got my library card and the following week (to my great luck), they were having a book sale. I went and there I met Lancy Bradshaw and my life changed. We became friends and we talked about starting a Friends of the Pittsfield Library to help with the things that were needed and were not in the town's library budget. We investigated what other groups had done to begin an actual Friends organization and we followed their recipe. We wrote a constitution and the by-laws for a Friends group and that was the very beginning of the formal "Friends" group. We then went ahead (mostly Lancy, as she knows everyone) and started asking people to join for a $10.00 membership fee and we got quite a few memberships. That gave us enough to file with the IRS to become a 501 (c) (3) organization and we became legal and tax-exempt.

Each year we write a letter to all members for a renewal of their dues and everyone has been extraordinarily generous. We have been able to do things that could not have been accomplished under the town budget. The things that we do for the library are somewhat invisible like keeping up the landscaping, paying to have the walkways into the library shoveled more often than the town would do, painting rooms when needed, decorating the library at Christmas, having the carpets cleaned when needed and putting in a remote monitoring system so the librarians upstairs can see what is happening downstairs. We also pay for many programs for adults and children and a membership to Bangor's Children's Museum.

We and all of our donors/members are so grateful to be able to do this for our most beautiful and timeless Pittsfield Library.

Knifty Knitters

More than 10 years ago, Lyn Smith and Kathy Kehoe began a program at the library to encourage handcrafts such as knitting, crocheting and needlepoint. Since that time this group has provided lessons, shared patterns and donated items to a number of charitable organizations. In December, the Giving Tree is set up in the library's rotunda where more than 100 handmade items are placed. These hats, mittens and scarves are distributed to doctors' offices, schools and the food pantry.

Crafters challenge each other to complete projects that have lain dormant for years, sometimes decades. Over the years the group has ranged in age from 5 to 99. All are welcome to come learn, share and join in on Monday afternoons from 2 to 4 PM in the library's conference room.

Universalist Ladies Aid Society - ULAS

Bev Rollins

The ULAS has been in existence for many years. In the early years, they would hold their annual rummage sale and luncheon, which proved to be quite profitable. They held food sales and would make nice donations to support the church for many years.

Holly Zadra Basting Turkeys for the Annual Supper

The Aid would also hold their annual church bazaar with a lunch that was held the first part of November every year. As AID members aged, this bazaar was discontinued. In the evening, they would host the annual turkey supper where folks would attend from miles around for a wonderful home cooked meal. In later years this was taken over by the younger ladies of the church, the Women's Club. Now this is a joint effort with the church as a yearly celebration of this wonderful event with locally grown foods.

For many years, the ULAS held their wreath project. In the beginning they made the wreaths, decorated them, and delivered to area businesses. In later years, the bare wreaths were purchased and cones were wired, bows were made and wreaths decorated by the Aid members and friends. Deliveries were done by many members and friends of the church. About five years ago, this project was discontinued as it was too much on the aging members.

The ULAS continue to support the church with the Easter Memorial fund, fundraisers of the church, support of Aid members and friends of the church. They also prepare food and serve for special gatherings at the church and whatever is needed at the UU Meeting House of Pittsfield.

Now the ULAS members do not meet on a regular basis but a few times year and have a luncheon/meeting to make any necessary plans. Members keep in touch and support is given whenever needed.

The Welcome Table

Trudy Ferland

The Welcome Table was originally conceived of by a group from Pittsfield's Unitarian Universalist Meeting House (UUMH, formerly the First Universalist Church) as a place for people to come to get out of the cold. In late 2008, when oil was near $4 per gallon, simply staying warm through the winter was a daunting task for many. They decided that their heated, handicapped-accessible downstairs dining area with its large kitchen could help.

Back then, Trudy Ferland, a member of the UUMH, had volunteered to organize Keep ME Warm, a project to weatherize houses as one means of increasing home heating efficiency. On the designated volunteer day, not only did 89 people show up, but they were grateful to have been given the opportunity to help. The enthusiastic response made the UUMH organizers realize that if they were to offer a weekly free lunch, they wouldn't be doing it alone. People in the community from many denominations, businesses, and civic organizations were willing and eager to work.

 The Welcome Table opened its doors on January 9, 2009, to a meal of beef stew prepared and served by employees of General Electric. Since then it has been open every Friday, including holidays like Christmas and New Year's Day, closing only for inclement weather. In the 9 years of operation, approximately 18,000 meals have been served.

The Welcome Table isn't a soup kitchen in the traditional sense. While it is a place for people to eat, they also come to socialize – as important, especially in a rural area, as the need for food. Elaine Turner likes "to get together with seniors to play cards" and she helps out in the kitchen. A group from Living Innovations has adopted the program as their own, wiping the tables each week, donating coffee and tea, and even sponsoring meals.

Although it is based at the UU Meeting House, the Welcome Table has always been bigger than that one church. The administrative team includes UUMH members like Beverly Rollins along with volunteers such as Carolyn Collins who are not affiliated with the Meeting House. At first, a different church, business, or civic group sponsored the Welcome Table each week. Now, the sponsorships have grown to include the Quints and other families, local book clubs and a buying club. Guests have become volunteers helping to prepare and clean up after each week's lunch.

Janet Reid, Melanie Wakefield, Zachary Sposato , Royce Sposato, and Holly Zadra

The First Congregational Church, First Baptist Church, St. Agnes, and Saint Martin's Episcopal Church of Palmyra are regular sponsors. Businesses including ARGO, Cianbro, Kleinschmidt Associates, Somatex Inc., and C.M. Almy can be counted on to provide meals. Bud's Shop 'n Save traditionally provides a corned beef dinner on the Friday of St. Patrick's Day week and also hosts a meal during the summer to allow its group of young seasonal workers a chance to volunteer. Local teachers have regularly contributed while also creating opportunities for the students of MSAD 53 to participate thereby teaching young people the joy of serving the community. The ARTS Club, Kiwanis, the Blue Women, and other local civic organizations have come together in recognition of the importance of the Welcome Table.

The generosity of The Welcome Table supporters has allowed the program to be mostly self-sufficient but there have been several successful fundraisers. Among the most popular friend of the Welcome Table actress Marie Cormier has over the years presented three benefit shows in Pittsfield. You will find Welcome Table supporters serving strawberry shortcake at the Egg Festival Carnival in partnership with the Kiwanis.

To stay current and facilitate the ease of volunteering, the Welcome Table staff set up an on-line sign-up system through the Meal Train website. Any group can choose a date and easily get on the calendar by going to mealtrain .com/r39ddw

After nine years, volunteers are still grateful to have that opportunity to give back to the community as are the guests who come to socialize or to supplement their weekly meals. Everyone is welcome, something that is apparent in the diversity of both guests who come and organizations that sponsor each week's lunch. If you're free on Fridays, drop by. Play cards, chat, enjoy a lunch and maybe you'll find yourself returning each week as part of the Welcome Table community.

MSAD #53 Children's Benefit Fund

Sue Nile

In the mid 1990's, MSAD #53 school nurse, Millie Bachrach, noticed that some students had basic unmet needs, such as food and clothing. She established the Nurse's Special Fund to meet these needs. Over time, the name of the fund changed to the Deserving Students Fund, which in 2003 was incorporated as the MSAD #53 Children's Benefit Fund. While the name of the fund has changed, the focus has always remained on the needs of students.

The mission of the Children's Benefit Fund is to support MSAD #53 students in grades Pre K – 8, identified as being in need, by providing resources and opportunities, as well as soliciting donations to support this endeavor. The goals are to offer and/or provide new and quality used clothing, to enable students to take advantage of an enriching summer camp experience, and to offer support to students facing an emergency situation.

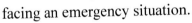

Children's Benefit Fund

This MSAD #53 Children's Benefit Fund is run by a small volunteer faculty and staff committee. The committee receives input from all MSAD #53 faculty and staff regarding the particular needs of students within the school district. The committee members maintain a clothing closet filled with new and quality gently used clothing (coats, pants, shirts, sweatshirts) and a supply of new warm hats, gloves, mittens, and socks that are available to all Pre K – 8 students. For over twenty years, the committee has also financed a summer overnight camp experience for deserving students at Camp Bishopswood in Hope, Maine. All of these opportunities for MSAD #53 students are made possible by the generous donations of clothing items, school supplies, and financial donations from local businesses, individuals, and community groups. This community generosity makes all of the committee's projects so successful.

Heart of Pittsfield

Jane Woodruff

After attending the visioning session for the Town's Comprehensive Plan in the fall of 2012, Ray Berthelette and Vaughan Woodruff initiated an organization that became known as the Heart of

Pittsfield (HOP). The mission of this group is to promote economic development and community connections while aligning its goals with the comprehensive plan. Over the past few years, HOP has been involved co-hosting a number of community activities such as several suppers highlighting local foods along with Pittsfield's Food Policy Council. Along with the library, it also co-sponsored several Maine Humanities Council presentations: *Maine @ Work* and *Local & Legendary*, a Civil War program.

With area youth joining in, members painted the gazebo at Hathorn Park and facilitated the making of planters that are on Main Street. In early December HOP supports the Holiday Lights at Hathorn program and in the summer on full moon nights five braziers are lit for an event known as Pond Fire.

Vaughan Woodruff leads session on Google Map Up

In 2017, partnering with the library, HOP sponsored a program called *The Year of Kindness* with a number activities promoting planned and random acts of kindness. HOP's strong Facebook presence has promoted new businesses starting in Pittsfield as well as a sense of community. It has been involved in supporting citizen input on projects affecting the Rail Trail and Somerset Avenue and continues to work to inform townspeople of issues relevant to the community.

Pittsfield Community Garden Club
Donna Laux

Pittsfield is a town blessed with parks large and small. Well-groomed by town crews, they are also home to lovely gardens. Gardens cared for by an enthusiastic group of dedicated gardeners, members of the Pittsfield Community Garden Club.

The club was organized on May 11, 1932, during a meeting of the Farm Bureau, as the Flower and Garden Club. The purpose of the club was to advance gardening and to improve the beauty of the community. That has been the club's focus in its 87 years of existence and will continue to be as we move forward toward our 100th year anniversary in 2032. Add to that an interest in continued learning and sharing what we know and you have a group that plays a vital role in our community.

Over the years, the club has sponsored many activities and undertaken large projects. In the midst of the depression, with club dues just twenty-five cents a year, the club organized flower shows, which continued until the war years. "Victory Gardens for Girls and Boys" were a way the club found it could support the war effort. Later, members made wreaths and donated gifts to Togus Hospital. Flower arrangements were delivered to the hospital at Dow Air Force Base in Bangor on a regular basis. The Burnham and Pittsfield Nursing Homes also benefited from member gardens.

The 1950s found the club sponsoring "Junior Gardeners". Seed packets were distributed to school children whose gardens were judged in the fall. Meetings, held in various locations continued, as did civic beautification projects. In 1962, The Sebasticook Valley Hospital was built. For several years, the hospital stood in the middle of a rocky, undeveloped, weed-choked field. With help from several other civic and fraternal organizations, the club undertook a two-year project to landscape the building. Once completed, the club-maintained flower beds around the entrance well into the 1990s. This effort did not go unnoticed. For three years the club received the Sears Foundation Beautification Award made to just 10 clubs each year in the state.

By far, one of the most ambitious club projects was the development of the Mill Pond Park garden during the country's Bicentennial year, 1976. Aided by the town, volunteers, and consultants, the club transformed a blank space into one of the most inviting spots in town. It is now complete with benches, pathways, and architectural pieces.

The club continues to meet and works to beautify the town as it has done for so many years in the past. Currently, we maintain gardens at the Mill Pond, Food Cupboard, planters on Main Street and Hathorn Park, the Memorial Garden at Manson Park and beds at the library.

The Community Garden at Outland Farm

Heather Holland

A community garden is "many people using shared land to produce vegetables and fruit for their own use". A garden allows individuals and families who have little or no available space for a garden at their own home to grow food in a shared space. This also allows those who have little experience to learn from others involved.

In 2015, with the benefit of a Kohl's grant administered by Healthy SV, the Community Garden was born. Located at Outland Farm on the Phillips Corner Road, experienced and new gardeners partner together with shared efforts producing a plentiful harvest.

Not Too Young to Help – Goran Zadra-Woodruff

With group work days and once a week work-assignment days, the daily burden of a garden is gone as

78

all share in the workload together. The group plans a planting list and plants the garden as well as hosting weekly group work days to encourage working and learning together. On the weekly assigned days, members are expected to visit the garden, water if needed, weed, check for pests, or find what is ripe. The garden is offered at no cost to its members and hopes to continue this in the future by grants, fundraising, and donations.

In late winter/early spring an informational meeting is held where any questions can be answered and signups begin. Those wanting to get on the community garden email list, contact Heather@OutlandFarm.com.

Pinnacle Ski Club

Jim Cianchette and Jane Woodruff

Vaughan Woodruff and Son Eamon Heading Out to the Slope

The winter season of 1954-55 saw the beginnings of what was to become the Pinnacle Ski Club. In their mission to promote activities for youth, the Pittsfield Kiwanis Club under the leadership of its president Jack Baxter took on the project of developing a ski slope out of the east side of the Pinnacle. Raising $600 in cash and obtaining donated materials, labor, and equipment, they, along with Bud Dow who oversaw this project, transformed this hill of gravel into the Kiwanis Community Ski Slope complete with a rope tow to the summit in just sixty days. By mid-January the Pinnacle Ski Club of Pittsfield, Maine was formed to oversee the functioning of the slope. Club dues were set at $1.00 for adults, 50c for juniors. As noted in Jack Baxter's weekly *Ski Chatter* column, "the purpose of the club is to manage the existing facilities, expand and improve the facilities, and encourage the development and enjoyment of skiing by children and adults in the Pittsfield area." And this they have done and done so very well for over 60 years.

Over the years, trails and a bunny slope with another rope tow were developed as well as a ski lodge and a skating rink built by this ambitious club. The lodge has been rented out throughout the year to various civic groups and families for celebrations. Folks have come to snowboard and a half-pipe was formed on the side of the main slope for their use. Night skiing still continues as do the Bud Dow ski races though these races are now part of the annual Pinnacle Fest. This event also features live entertainment and cardboard sled races.

The Pinnacle has flourished over the years through the efforts of its devoted volunteers, who like the early originators, have been committed to its success in bringing winter sports to Pittsfield.

Pittsfield Driftbusters Snowmobile Club
Jim Dunphy

In the early 1970s snowmobiling was becoming a growing sport around Central Maine. It was, however, not organized at the time and along with that came many problems with the snowmobilers riding anywhere they decided to go. This made local landowners very upset because they were riding over small trees, water lines, and getting too close to their homes.

Then in the winter season of 1974/1975, a group of Pittsfield snowmobilers came together and had a meeting to talk about forming a Club. On March 25, 1975, the organization of The Peltoma Fish

and Game Driftbuster Association was officially listed as a Corporation. This included four officers: President – Alvah Wyman, Vice President – Walter Pelletier, Secretary – Beatrice Billings, and Treasurer – Janet Whitman. There were seven members elected as directors of the club: Elmer Morton, Edward Caruso, Allison Scribner, Theodore Thompson, Charles Philbrick, Robert Buzzell, and Reginald Haynes.

The Peltoma Fish and Game building located on Peltoma Avenue in town was going to be their club house. The mission statement of the club was to promote safe and organized snowmobiling and to establish a trail system for everyone to use with local landowners' permissions.

Today these practices are still in place. The club has grown over the years with an annual membership of 75 to 100 members. It currently maintains 90 miles of trails and several bridges in the local area. All of the trails are maintained by a 2004 Tucker Terra Trail Groomer. The snowmobiling season here in Pittsfield typically lasts for about 8 – 10 weeks from January to early March. For over 20 years (1991 – 2010) the club has supported Pine Tree Camp – a summer camp for handicapped and disabled kids/adults in Rome, Maine. Through the club's fundraising efforts, a $523,000 donation has been made to the Camp during that time period.

The snowmobile club currently meets every 3rd Wednesday of the month at 7:00 pm during the months of September through April.

Current officers are

President - Matt Huff	Trail Master - Lee Myrick
Vice President - Dave Thies	Safety Officer – Jim Dunphy
Secretary - Leslie Corrow	MSA Representative - Roger Dunphy
Treasurer – Jim Dunphy	Membership Chairman – Jim Dunphy

Original Pittsfield Public Library

By Terri DeNatale

Pittsfield Public Library with New Addition

By Milton Webber

From across the world, Dr. Syed Amir Gilani of the University of Lahore, Pakistan gives a working definition of culture: "the arts and other manifestations of human intellectual achievement regarded collectively." Dr. Gilani also lists its synonyms: "the arts, the humanities; intellectual achievement(s), intellectual activity; literature, music, painting, philosophy." Looking at Pittsfield's culture with his definition in mind, it is clear that the community is enriched by these aspects in many ways.

Pittsfield Public Library

Lyn Smith in collaboration with Don Hallenbeck & Ann McGowan

Like most Maine libraries in the 19th century, the Pittsfield Public Library began as a subscription library. Small collections of books were circulated in a town for a short period of time until the volumes were packed off to another village and replaced with a fresh lot. In 1894, the people of Pittsfield wanted a more permanent library, so they established one in the Osborn Block on Main Street. At that time, money allocated by the town to buy books was spent by the schools with only some actually placed at the library. The first librarian, Bessie Kimball, managed to keep the library going that first year on a mere $100.

By the year 1900, citizens wanted something more than a few books squirreled away in a back room for their library. The Carnegie Foundation was approached by Gordon Dobson and two others with plans for a larger, well-stocked library and received a grant of $15,000. The townspeople voted an additional sum of $10,000, and a trust from the estate of the late Robert Dobson provided $5,000. Once built, the library was to have an annual operating budget of $1,000. A lot on South Main and Railroad Streets, now Library Street, was chosen as the site. New York City architect Albert Randolph Ross was commissioned to design the building. Construction began in 1903 with a Waterville firm chosen as the major contractor and several Pittsfield firms hired for much of the interior work. At the same time, funds for a monument to Civil War Veterans were raised by the Davis Post of the Grand Army of the Republic with the front lawn of the library chosen for its location. Both the Soldier's Monument and the Library were dedicated on May 28, 1904. In addition to books purchased by the town, many were donated by clubs and individuals. Librarians were drawn from the ranks of retired teachers and it wasn't until 1975 that Pittsfield hired its first professional librarian.

Over time, the downstairs was finished to provide more space for public use with J. R. Cianchette completing a room that Girl Scouts used during the 1940s until 1960s. In the 1960s the Kiwanis Club made the other large basement area into a conference room. In the 1970s, the Jaycees finished the kitchen and downstairs bathroom. Through the efforts of Trudy Humphrey, the library was placed on the National Register of Historic Buildings in 1983. It was also that year that Tim Sample transformed the ceiling of the dome into a colorful mural titled *Reading - Gateway to Imagination.* The models used for the readers in the mural were members of the community.

In 2001, the library trustees began preliminary plans for renovation and expansion of the library. An extensive capital campaign was launched the following year to restore and expand the facility to better serve the growing demands of local residents. Construction of an addition began in 2008 followed by major renovations to the original building. The refreshed and expanded library opened in January 2010.

At the library, Russ Cox, artist and author, shares with children techniques of illustration

Advances in technology have broadened the services offered by the library with computers becoming a major presence. The library started circulating

86

books using a computer automated circulation system in 1995. Soon after, the card catalog, long indispensable to the library, was replaced with an online catalog of library materials. Patrons use computers to access the Internet, play games, do research, utilize desktop publishing, and communicate through email and social media. WIFI allows the use of the internet even when the library is not open. Patrons can access library resources from home for research or download books. Video conferencing is also available. The library offers written materials in print, audio, and electronic form. Many more items can be obtained from other libraries' collections through the interlibrary loan program.

The library serves as the area's setting for learning and entertainment, including thoughtful discussions and lively programs. On any given day, it is not unusual to find activity in every nook and corner of the building: adults doing research or scanning shelves for a novel or a movie; students tackling homework over computers; some very young patrons being read to in the children's area. In the Warren Community Room, children participate in story time, local crafters knit and chat, Maine authors share their work, magicians and scientists entertain and educate. The library often partners with other community groups.

Used by generations from newborns to nonagenarians, the library provides more than books. It is a gathering place to meet the educational, social, and cultural needs of the community.

Pittsfield Community Theatre

Jane Woodruff

For over a hundred years, Pittsfielders have been going to the movies. In 1909, Pittsfield had a new movie theater on Park Street where local talent was presented between films. Plots for movies at the Park Street Theater often were noted on the front page of *The Pittsfield Advertiser*. In the same year, mention was made of another movie theater being built in town - the one on Main Street where movies are still seen today. When it opened as Leger's Theater in 1915, it was the silent film era - the same era that Pittsfield-born actor Arthur Millett began his career. He was in over 100 films, but it was reported that his career declined with the introduction of sound. The theater became the Bijou in 1918 and a little more than a decade later, sound was added.

The Bijou Theater was extensively renovated by J.R. Cianchette who, in the mid-1950s, installed the rocking-style seats that are still in place today. The addition of a new marquee, air conditioning, cinema-scope screen and upgraded projectors - both movie and sound - greatly improved this theater. In the early 1960s, the Bijou was purchased and run by Glen Wheaton until 1971when it was closed. Vacant for several years, in 1975, Maine National Bank and Cianbro Corporation bought and donated the theater to a non-profit, the Pittsfield Community Theatre Association. At this time, the stage was expanded using hardwood flooring from the old Union Hall. Two years later, it was purchased by the town which still owns it today.

Over the years, various live performances by local groups and Maine artists have entertained audiences. From opera to Manson Essay readings to premieres of local cinema productions, this theatre has enriched our community. Tim Sample, Dave Mallett, Noel Stookey - to name a few - have taken to its stage.

There is nothing quite like an evening out with friends and neighbors, enjoying movies on the large screen and savoring buttered popcorn.

Performing Arts

Jane Woodruff

Drama under the leadership of Debra Susi of Maine Central Institute has come to mean that townspeople can plan on attending several performances each year seeing the best of what Maine high school students can produce. Year after year, her drama students have taken honors in regional and state competitions for their one-act plays. They have also participated with other organizations in local programs such as *Local & Legendary*, a Civil War

project where they produced a performance related to local history as the finale to a year-long project.

Deb Susi prepping Lexi LaMarre for *Local & Legendary* performance

Dean Neal with MCI band on Memorial Day

Similarly, Dean Neal has led his students to competitions where they have consistently taken honors for their performances in the Maine Music Educator's Association (MMEA) Jazz Festivals. Be it vocal jazz or jazz combo or jazz band, these groups of musicians, routinely impress the judges with their skills. Not only are they often performing successfully in competitions at a state level, they are doing very well in the Berklee College

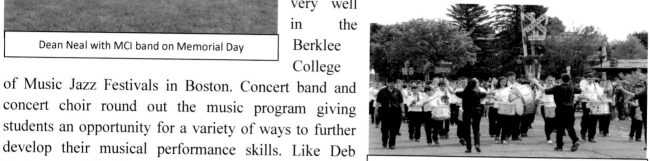
Marisa Weinstein with Warsaw Marching Band in Memorial Day parade

of Music Jazz Festivals in Boston. Concert band and concert choir round out the music program giving students an opportunity for a variety of ways to further develop their musical performance skills. Like Deb Susi, some of Neal's students participate in community-wide activities such as annually playing music near the Soldier's Monument on the library grounds for the Memorial Day parade.

Students come to Neal with a solid background in music performance skills as they have been taught by Marissa Weinstein over the course of their years as middle schoolers at Warsaw. In the fall of 2017, she was awarded the George N. Parks Award for Leadership in Music Education, which is an award given by the National Association for Music Education. Like the high schoolers, these younger students share their skills with the community and can be seen/heard in concerts or marching in the Memorial Day parades. Younger students - K to 4th grade- are introduced to music education by Marilyn Buzy. They, too, give back to the community as can be seen by their leading Christmas carols at the tree lighting ceremony in Hathorn Park. It is apparent that this early learning nurtured in the lower grades and challenged in the later grades has helped produce some very impressive musicians in our community.

Bossov Ballet Theatre

Natalya Getman and Elizabeth Audet

Natalya Getman, Artistic Director of Bossov Ballet Theatre (BBT) at MCI, came to the USA from Russia. After beginning her studies in classical ballet in Turkmenistan, her teacher, Musaeva, principal dancer and *National Artist* of both Turkmenistan and the Soviet Union, helped her transfer to the world famous Vaganova Academy in St Petersburg. Agrippina Vaganova created a system for teaching Russian Ballet that continues to be revered throughout the world, and to produce some of its finest dancers. More than any other art form, ballet requires a very physical transferal from one generation to the next that becomes deeply ingrained in every fiber of the mind and body. In this way, Vaganova passed her genius directly to her student Balikova, who in turn taught Getman's teacher, Musaeva. Now Natalya stands as the next in line to transfer this legacy to a new generation, right here in Pittsfield.

After dancing professionally in Moscow, Getman accepted an offer to tour the US, where she met her husband, and eventually came to settle. Even though she had the choice to work anywhere, Getman remembers her first visit to BBT and Pittsfield, "It quickly became very dear to my heart. Not only is Andrei Bossov, Founding Artistic Director of BBT, very talented, but he also demonstrated a precision and dedication to the beauty and logic of Russian classical ballet training that deeply impressed me."

Practice for a Tribute to Martin Luther King

In addition, the role that Maine Central Institute (MCI) plays in the continued support of BBT has, according to Getman, proved the keystone to its success, and another reason for her to move here, "MCI provides a very similar setting to the education I received back in Russia, where academics and dance were also integrated in a residential setting." Getman sees that this arrangement allows students to attend BBT from around the world, while contributing powerfully to their development as individuals and dancers. Like herself, these students not only bring a small piece of their own culture to the region, but help reveal Pittsfield to the outside world as something special. "My journey here was no small transition. There's no doubt that Moscow, my previous home, dazzles and inspires with its arts and culture, filling the soul with 850 years of tradition, architecture and history. However, I quickly came to love the warmth and kindness I found here." With her deep love of nature, Getman describes how, this too, shaped her response to her adopted home, "I can honestly say that in all my many travels, I never saw a place more beautiful than Maine. And I've come to observe that the people here in Pittsfield, with their emphasis on community and simplicity, reflect that same purity and strength found in its seasons and natural beauty. So, I knew this was the place where I could be most true to myself and my beliefs. "

Today, as Artistic Director of BBT, Getman considers it very important to maintain that thread of connection to her heritage, while recognizing the need to adapt to a new time and place. She explains how deeply she respects American culture, and how much strength she sees in American Ballet. "Not only the culture, but the speed of life here demands a different approach. The vision of the people, how they build their future, are all very different from my own experiences. So I knew I could not take a narrow approach. It is important not to become like *tomatoes stewing in their own sauce* as we say in Russia. Each season we need to grow and bring something fresh to the table." And that is why, she explains, she tries to meld two cultures in one: the excellence, artistry and strength that Russian ballet training represents, with the energy and freedom of her students.

According to Getman, this approach must be working. "If a restaurant opens, but no one likes the dishes, it will close that first year. This year, BBT turns twenty-two," she points out. "In the end, despite all cultural differences, everything comes down to this simple truth: If something is beautiful, it's *beautiful*. The audience doesn't have to be expert in technique, style, or country. If you can move them, you've succeeded. If your choreography has vision, and if, as a dancer, you are an artist as well as a strong technician - when all those ingredients combine, that's when the magic happens, that's when people love what they see."

And this beauty might be why others have described BBT as Pittsfield's 'gem'. "Like a gem," she explains, "we at BBT hold something rare and precious in our hands. Our desire is to preserve it in a beautiful setting, to pass from generation to generation." As BBT prepares to perform *Swan Lake* this summer – an ambitious ballet for even professional companies – Getman feels the responsibility to do justice to what many consider to be one of the most beautiful ballets in existence. "It's my job," she continues, "to preserve the purity of its choreography, and the message it delivers – to present the perfection it represents as a gift to our community, and to a new generation. And in such a way, I pass the torch that was given to me, and the old magic brightens a new day."

Mykayla Weinstein and Arjan Orr

Pittsfield Town Band

Gary Fitts

Music has long been an important part of the fabric of Pittsfield. Our local school system has been blessed with exceptionally talented and hard-working music teachers who have given rise to generations of gifted musicians. Dating back to the early 1900s, MCI's music program has been recognized as one of Maine's finest. Each year Ruth Plummer Cook, whose name adorns the recently replaced MCI Music Building, received well- prepared students from the area's elementary schools and transformed them into excellent performers. This tradition continues to this day.

THE PITTSFIELD BAND   (All Photos including Cover by Wakefield Studio)

One of the ancillary benefits of such a successful educational program was the significant number of local citizens who sought to extend their musical lives into adulthood. For some, that meant performing in bands, orchestras, and singing groups on a professional level. For an even larger number, it led to the establishment of and participation in a local "Town Band." The adult members brought in and mentored younger, school-age musicians, often including their own children, nieces and nephews.

The "town band" concept was not unique to Pittsfield by any means. Many Maine communities can boast of having had their own bands. However, in the middle of the 20th Century, Pittsfield's amateur musicians could hold their own with those of any small town in the nation.

The decades of the 50s, 60s and 70s certainly stand out for the large number of participants and the quality of their performances.

Many of those performances came in the form of Sunday evening Band Concerts held in the gazebo in Hathorn Park. Directed by well-respected local banker William "Bill" Griffin, an enthusiastic group of 25-30 musicians would entertain large audiences at these community gatherings throughout the summer months. There were several families who provided two generations of musicians to this effort and formed the backbone of the band in those years. The Quint, Jones, Wright, Fitts, and Higgins families all contributed several members, with Lewis Fitts succeeding Bill Griffin as the band's director in the mid-60s.

In addition to the Sunday concerts in the park, Pittsfield's town band also performed as a marching band. Each summer several weekends would be given to traveling to various festivals and celebrations all over the state of Maine and marching in their parades. From the Clam Festival in Yarmouth to the Potato Blossom Festival in Fort Fairfield, from the Lobster Festival in Rockland to the Sesquicentennial Parade in Bingham-Moscow, Pittsfield's marching musicians traveled the state playing the familiar marches of J. P. Sousa and wearing out many pairs of black dress shoes. Blistered feet were a small price to pay for the satisfaction of a job well done...and much fun and camaraderie. Many of those parade trips were turned into extended family camping weekends. Cars would be filled, and on some occasions, even a school bus would be commandeered to accommodate the musicians and their families. Tents would be set up, and community picnics would be prepared for the post-parade evenings. Impromptu jam sessions entertained many an unsuspecting campground on those nights. Lasting friendships were forged on such outings, and the memories are crisp over 50 years later.

In the mid-60's, when Lewis Fitts took on the directorship, sponsorship was sought in order to replace the classic, old wool uniforms of WW2 vintage design. The local American Legion Post answered the call and provided funding for sharp, new blue and gold uniforms with updated Shako hats. The new, modern look, combined with many hours of marching drills in the Northeast Shoe parking lot yielded a very fine-looking parade band indeed!

Concerts in the Park

The Pittsfield Summer Concert Series

Barbara Denaro

Yet another newly evolving tradition is the Holiday Lights in Hathorn Park Concert where schoolchildren from Vickery and Warsaw Schools under the direction of Marissa Weinstein and Marily Buzy perform Christmas Carols. This is followed with the lighting of the Christmas tree in the gazebo and a visit from Santa who gives out candy canes.

It all started with a small group of residents who met over lunch. An idea was formed to bring free concerts to the community. It quickly developed into weekly concerts at Hathorn Park from July through August in 2016. The goal was to provide local and free entertainment for the whole family in a safe environment while revitalizing the use of the gazebo at Hathorn Park.

Now in its third year, The Pittsfield Summer Concert Series continues to be fully funded by local business sponsors. All of the donations go directly to talented musicians and singers who perform at the gazebo. It is their generosity that makes each year a success.

Hathorn Park's gazebo was built in 1920s and dedicated to music teacher William Griffin who used it for band concerts. What could be more fitting than to use it again for community concerts! With the hope that music at the gazebo becomes a long-lasting tradition, bringing the community and surrounding towns together to reunite with friends and family during our warm summer nights is paramount!

Highway to My Hometown
c: Lee Southard

I had a red and white fifty-seven Chevy
My daddy left to me.
She'd do eighty-five between the bridges
down by the Tastee Freeze
then we'd park in front of the drug
store just to see who was around.

Chorus
On the highway to my hometown
I play oldies on the radio
Del Shannon and Bobby Darin
singin songs of long ago
from Jesse James to baseball games
All the dreams I lost and found.

Oh, it all comes back to me on the highway to my hometown.
I remember summer nights on Main Street with people everywhere.
The smell of hot dogs and onions sweet filling up the air.
Fishing on the river
'Til the 9 o'clock whistle sound.

Chorus

Now when I finally get there,
I'll take awhile to find the old school.
I'll make a left for the cemetery down that long avenue.
All my friends and family resting in that peaceful ground.
Oh, they all comes back to me on the highway to my hometown.

A Tear
by Deidre Heaton

Nights grow long and the sun sets early
The hardwood floors grow cold
Leaves start falling and the kids start running to school when the whistle blows.

Look outside my breath forms on the window
See those arrows moving south in the sky
Thoughts of you can't escape my mind and a tear rolls down from my eye.

Well, a tear rolls down from my eye.

Remember the cows out grazing in the fields, homemade ice cream, warm apple pie.
Christmas dinners with seven, fifteen, twenty, and a tear rolls down from my eye.
Easter egg hunts, pinatas, jelly beans, what more could a child ask for?
Campobello or Barney's penny candy and a tear rolls down from my eye.

Well, a tear rolls down from my eye.

Days grow short and time is moving on and I'm thinking 'bout kids of my own.
See that eagle soaring through the sky, does he ever feel alone?
Rocky mountains I can hear you calling, my heart is coming your way
But I've got so many things that I have left behind and a tear rolls down from my eye.
(Repeat verse.)

Yes, a tear rolls down from my eye.

Ken Cianchette and Barney McGowan at his Country Store on Sibley Pond. That penny candy can be seen in the barrel in the foreground.

My Childhood Town
By Clermont (Clum) Spencer

I was standing by the drug store
    one sunny April day
When they tore the east side of
    Main Street down.
As I stood there for a minute, I
    heard one merchant say.
"We're really going to have our
    model town."
I said, "I thought 'twas kind of sad
    to see those buildings go."
Never said they didn't need to
    be destroyed.
It's just that I remember
    most 49 years ago
When I was just a little boy.

Chorus
I remember the old Main Street.
    Still see all the stores
As they were when I first came
    to town.
Don't other folks remember
    or am I somehow
The only sentimental
    fool around?

I remember when the trains came
    with passengers and mail,
A conductor waved a lantern
    by the bail.
I still can see the platform,
    the baggage carts and all,
And those big ole road hogs
    steaming over the rails.
I remember an old friend of mine
    and the fun we used to have.
As we stood in front of Mayo's store
We'd watch the girls from Grammar

School, the prettiest in the world.
Their brothers' jeans and fathers' shirts
    they wore.

Chorus

Me they called the reverend, my friend
    they called the squire.
We were as close as brothers could
    have been.
We'd go down to the station and watch
    the tapping of the key,
And sometimes we'd deliver telegrams.
In my teenage years I'd go up to
    the Grange on Sat'day night
For box socials and other things
    like that.
I met a girl I used to think was cute
    as she could be.
And I wonder if she ever thinks of me.

Chorus

Now there's just the Grammar
    School and the old Grange Hall
And the legends no one can
    take away.
When you have succeeded,
    we have our Model Town,
Won't you give a thought for foolish
    folks like me?
All you saw was old buildings crashing
    to the ground
While I saw a lifetime of just memories.

Ballad of Moses Martin
Clermont (Clum) Spencer

Moses Martin came away from
    Norridgewock one day
Just to find a little turf to call
    his own.
On Sebasticook's fair shore
    In a place called Plymouth
Gore is where he settled in
    and made his home.

    Chorus
Now this was the good old days
    when a man was not afraid
To bend his back and labor with
    his hands.
The wife and children too had
    their own chores to do
From the housework to the birthing
    of the lambs.

They cut the trees and plowed
    the land.
The whole family lent
    a hand,
Planted crops and then they
    built a house and barn.
The raised horses. They
    raised steers.
Their every need was here and

    were thankful that they
Were all fed and warm.

    Chorus

They took honey from wild bees
    sugar from the maple trees.
Dried fish they caught from
    old Sebasticook.
Smoked their pork and
    corned their beef.
Made their clothes from their own sheep,
    made a living with our
Learning from a book.

    Chorus

Many stories going round, how they
    named old Pittsfield town,
But I have the only one that really fits.
    When Moses made it clear
How much he liked it here,
    Mrs. Martin said, "This
Really is the pits."

    Chorus

This ballad was written on the occasion
of the 175th birthday of Pittsfield.

Art in the Community

Jane Woodruff

Pittsfield is most fortunate to have art that has filtered out into the community. The town has an active

art curriculum in its schools. Beyond those projects that come home with the students, they have been placed out in the community. At Bud's Shop 'N Save, a large mural dons the back wall of the entry to the store. Produced by Vickery School's 3rd and 4th grade art enrichment students, it is a fitting tribute to the students' skills and to the products that are sold at this store.

In 2018, 8th graders at Warsaw Middle School had several showings of their art in the community for an experiential learning project called *You Be the Judge: Justice Through Art.* After researching various rights violations, they produced short essays and works of art related to their chosen topics. Mentored by Robert Shetterly, the artist of the series *Americans Who Tell the Truth,* they had a gallery showing at the Unitarian-Universalist Meeting House for the program *Speaking of Rights.* At the program, several students spoke along with Mr. Shetterly and Sherri Mitchell, Penobscot activist and lawyer, subject of one of his paintings.

Student-produced art from Maine Central Institute, along with that of members of the Sebasticook Valley Arts Alliance (SV AA), is shown annually at the Pittsfield Public Library. SVAA members also exhibit their artwork at the Sebasticook Valley Hospital and the Sebasticook Valley Regional Credit Union. Driving along route 152, one can literally see art out standing in the fields as Deb and Stan Short have an extensive display of metal art pieces. Art is truly out in the community.

Pittsfielders Create

Jane Woodruff

They wrote. They composed. They made music. They drew. They painted.

Some were born here. Some grew up here. Some were schooled here. Some worked here. Some were here for many years - some just a few, but Pittsfield claims them as her own.

Let's take a look at these folks who enriched the community and went out in the world to share their talents.

The Writers

Born in Pittsfield, **Hugh Pendexter** (1875-1940) became a prolific author known for writing historical novels, many of which were serialized in *Adventure Magazine*. Initially he was a teacher, then journalist before becoming a writer full-time. Pendexter would exhaustively research a subject before writing and would include the sources in his books.

In the 1980's **William Forstchen** was a popular instructor at Maine Cental Institute when he had his first novel *Ice Prophet* published. Now many years later, he is well-known for a number of series ranging from historical to science fiction. He has authored nearly fifty books, some of which have been on *The New York Times* Bestseller List.

Sanger Mills Cook wrote *Pittsfield - On the Sebasticook* which chronicles the history of Pittsfield from its origin to 1966 when it was published. The date of publication coincides with the centennial year of Maine Central Institute where he had been assistant principal from 1925 to 1942.

Author and Civil War expert **Dr. Thomas Desjardin** lives part-time in Pittsfield and is married to long-time resident Lori Ann Jordan. He has authored several books related to Gettysburg where he had worked as an historian at the national park. Perhaps best known for his knowledge of Colonel Joshua L. Chamberlain, Desjardin has written several books on him, been a consultant on documentaries as well as having consulted with actor Jeff Daniels in his role as the colonel in the movie *Gettsburg*.

Former *Central Maine Morning Sentinel* reporter **Ann McGowan** authored several books about the construction industry with the most noteworthy being *The First 50 Year History of Cianbro: the Constructors*. Her book documents the progression of Cianbro from its earliest years with the Cianchette brothers to near its current day as a large nationally known employee-owned business. Ann is also well known for her leading the campaign that lead to the substantial renovation of the town's public library.

Jolene McGowan '76 wrote a weekly column for the *Portland Press Herald* called *City Port Post*. In it, Jolene would reflect on topics of everyday living and at times would flash back on some of her earlier times living in Pittsfield. She is the founder of Matchstick Communications.

Former *Bangor Daily News* reporter **Brenda Thompson Seekins '67** has written several books for *Images of America*: one called *Around Great Moose Lake* and the other *Sebasticook Valley,* which includes Pittsfield as a subject. She also produced the book for Pittsfield's 175th anniversary - *Memories and Milestones* which provides glimpses of the town as it was. She currently writes articles for *Discover Maine* and assists people in writing their memoirs.

Wentworth Stone's story, **Sally Smith Bryant '61** recreated the children's story *Here's Juggins.* She spent her childhood in Pittsfield. She is the eldest daughter of Persis C. Smith, an avid reader, who inspired the community read named in her honor.

 Yet another writer growing up in Pittsfield and graduating from Maine Central Institute, **Arlene Frederick Beardsley '42** (1923-2017) wrote *The Sweet Apple Tree Farm,* a collection of stories about living on a farm.

Glenice Emery (1933-2005) wrote and had published three different collections of her poetry. Writing of her childhood and of nature, she would pen poems in the early morning before leaving to work at the Northeast Shoe Shop or San Antonio Shoe.

Wesley Burton '15 penned his first collection of poetry called *Where the Sky has No Stars.* It is described as being poems about depression, loss and the awakening of the soul.

Therese's Dream: Maine to Dafur: A Doctor's Story is the account of **David Austin**'s **'72** work in Africa with the Doctors Without Borders program as told through his emails to family and friends. Working in the Sudan, Democratic Republic of Congo and Djibouti, Dr. Austin recounts his experiences in these third world countries. He previously had worked two-week medical missions in Haiti and the Dominican Republic.

Douglas Fernald '67 researched and wrote the history of Detroit for its sesquicentennial. He has since had articles published in a number of magazines including *Down East Magazine.* Doug credits his beginnings as a writer with his drafting of his Manson Essay at Maine Central Institute.

History teacher **Shane Gower '93** penned the story of Lawrence (Larry) Dysart's success in a small town business from the days of the Great Depression to the early 1970's. *Caring enough to Succeed: The Story of L.A. Dysart's in Pittsfield, Maine* also gives a snapshot of the town in those years.

Yvonne (Lolly) Susi '68 best known for her acting and directing abilities was also an educator, playwright, and author. She wrote *An Untidy Career: Conversations with George Hall* and *The Central Book: A 100-year History of the Central School of Speech and Drama.* Her play *Gone to L.A.* deals with cancer which unfortunately Lolly succumbed to.

Spending her early years in Pittsfield, **Connie Baxter Marlow** photographed the mountain that her great-uncle Percival Baxter gave to the State of Maine. These are shown in the book *Greatest Mountain: Katahdin's Wilderness* and are combined with Governor Baxter's writings. More recently she has teamed with Andrew Cameron Bailey to write *The Trust Frequency: Ten Assumptions for a New Paradigm* in a self-help book they state leads to the high road to happiness.

Ernest (Ernie) G. DeRaps '48 teamed with his wife to write about their experiences working and living in lighthouses in Penobscot Bay. Ernie wrote *Lighthouse Keeper,* a journal depicting their family life while Pauline wrote her side of the story in *Light Housekeeping.* Their goal is to have this book in school libraries throughout the state.

Aaron Rosen '97 has written several books: *Art and Religion in the 21st Century* and *Imagining Jewish Art* along with numerous articles on these topics. He is currently a professor at Rocky Mountain College and visiting professor at King's College London. Dr. Rosen also has co-authored *Visualising a Sacred City:London, Art and Religion* and more recently a book for young people: *A Journey through Art: A Global Art Adventure.*

Poet **Arlo Quint '95** has authored at least a half-dozen books including such titles as *Photographic Memory* and *Drawn In.* Previously he had been the Managing Director of The Poetry Project at St. Mark's Church in New York City, an organization that promotes the reading and writing of contemporary poetry.

Courtney Cianchette Harvey '94 has created several books for young adults in a series dealing with the paranormal called the *Open Window* series. Teaching art by day, writing by night Courtney manages all this along with raising a family.

With his career in Navy Special Operations and his later work as a commercial pilot, **Willam H. LaBarge '67** was well suited to being a technical advisor to movies such as *Top Gun* and the television series *JAG.* He has authored several novels as well as the non-fiction book *Desert Voices: Personal Testimonies from Gulf War Heroes.*

Vicki Emery Sobota '82 writes historical fiction and romance novels under pen names Emery Lee and Victoria Vane. She has won numerous awards and just began a new Scottish series in 2017.

Douglas Quint '89 co-authored *Big Gay Ice Cream: Saucy Stories & Frozen Treats: Going All the Way with Ice Cream* with Bryan Petroff. Written in the format of a yearbook, they share stories of their experiences working from their ice cream truck along with recipes working from the easiest (freshman year) on up.

Returning with his family to his hometown, **Vaughan Woodruff '92** started a solar installation company known as Insource Renewables, Inc. and co-authored the *NABCEP Solar Heating Installer Resource Guide,* a study guide for installers used nationally. Vaughan also wrote the *Field Inspection Guidelines for Solar Heating Systems* for the New York State Energy Research and Development Authority and continues to write articles for national publications such as *Home Power* Magazine.

Johnathon Smith '04 had been known for his football prowess having played Division One football and in the NFL, but has since been working with advancing fitness in others. He has written a children's novel *Dare to Dream, Play to Win:Learning to Achieve Lifelong Victory* that emphasizes the importance of education and life-long lessons. He is working on an adult version of this book of the same title.

Known for his underwater explorations, **Barry Clifford '65** found the *Whyday*, a shipwrecked pirate ship. He has written of this discovery as well as numerous articles and books about pirates such as *The Black Ship* and *Real Pirates: The Untold Story.* His work has been featured many times on the Discovery Channel and by National Geographic.

Caron Butler '00 chronicles his early life of hardship and crime to his rise as a basketball star in the NBA in his autobiography *Tuff Juice: My Journey from the Streets to the NBA.* His life story is also told in the young adult book *Rising Above: How 11 Athletes Overcame Challenges in Their Youth to Become Stars.*

Madelyn Kenniston Given '62 shares her adventures in *Outstanding Feats by an Ordinary Woman* as she recounts running marathons on all seven continents. She also climbed the highest mountain in Africa and North America and in her travels encountered many different people and cultures.

Jessica Bane Robert '86 authored *Scarred Seasons,* a volume of her poetry, and has had her work published in a number of journals. She teaches writing at Clark University and owns a retreat center for artists and writers. Jessica is writing a memoir about growing up off the grid in Maine.

Donn Fendler '44 recounts his surviving for nine days in the wilderness after becoming lost on Mount Katahdin when he was twelve years old in his book *Lost on a Mountain in Maine.* He would visit schools and libraries sharing his story with children as this book has become a classic in Maine literature.

Debra Colby-Shafer has written *I Heard You: A Collection of Life's Truths* which is a collection of short stories and poetry. This is her third book.

In 2019 **Louis W. Clark** will mark his 50th year of music journalism that started in college but came into its own when he started writing for the *The Valley Times.* He currently writes "Music in Review" for the *Kennebec Journal.* He also is known for having taught art at Warsaw for 26 years.

The Innovators

Jill McGowan '78 has been designing and making distinctive, fine women's wear since 1994 beginning with the classic white shirt. The different shirt styles are often named after family members or friends and are sold worldwide. Her clothing making comes from an early age as she describes living in Pittsfield in the 1970s shopping with her mother and sisters for fabrics and patterns at Dysarts.

Peter Brooks '85 has conducted research in blood vessel development and discovered a specific compound and several similar to it that strengthen the effects of radiation and chemotherapy against tumors. He is a co-founder of Cell Matrix Incorporated, a biotech company. Peter has been an associate professor at several medical schools - NYU and USC.

Ralph Fowler '69 spent his career working in communications including working for Comsat at Earth Stations both in Maine and Pennsylvania. This experience made him very attractive to BBN which had a contract to build and maintain the first New England Internet connections between Harvard, MIT and BU. This project lead to the formation of what we now call the Internet. Ralph spent the majority of the rest of his career traveling the world educating people on the configuration and use of Internet routing equipment. Ralph credits his success to his upbringing in Pittsfield working at LA Dysart's and as an altar boy at St Agnes.

The Artists

Author/illustrator **Jean Hammond Watts '68** moved to Pittsfield at an early age and has loved painting since childhood. While teaching elementary school, she created two books of cartoons for teachers and parents of creative kids: *Off Hours* and *In Search of Perspective*. This led to her presenting at conferences for gifted and talented in several states. Since retiring from teaching, she has been happily painting watercolors and oils once again.

Known for being a professional cartoonist at thirteen, by seventeen **Gabe Crate '95** had written and illustrated for *The Tick*, a superhero comic satire. He has written over thirteen feature screenplays and co-written four short films as well as storyboarded five Super Bowl commercials. Along with his wife Kerri Parker, he has established Flophouse Productions for their film work.

Russ Cox both illustrated and wrote *Faraway Friends,* a children's book about the adventure of a small boy and his dog. He has illustrated numerous other children's books including *Freddy the Frogcaster and the Big Blizzard* and *Merry Moosey Christmas* and has taught and entertained children (and adults) with his drawing instruction at the town library.

Carol Ouellette is the illustrator for *Ripley - The Chrismas Tree Dog* written by Fredonna Ladd. Carol will be depicting Ripley in other adventures as this book is the beginning of a series about a real life dog.

Like her friend Jean Watts, **Marsha Hinckley Donahue** spent her early years in Pittsfield. She worked in galleries in D.C. and Portland before moving to Millinocket where she developed the North Light Gallery as well as co-founded the Katahdin School of Art. Her paintings depict the challenging landscapes of the Katadhin area.

Tim Sample is well-known as a Maine humorist and illustrator-writer of *How to Talk Yankee* and *Saturday Night at Moody's Diner*. His connection to Pittsfield is that he had a studio on Main Street in the 1980's and was the artist-in-residence at the Pittsfield Public Library where he painted a mural on the interior of the dome with six local residents posed reading various works of literature with the theme *Reading- The Gateway to Imagination.*

Penny Oliphant has lived and had a studio in Pittsfield for a number of years. She has drawn and painted rural scenes that reflect bygone times of which two are shown in Pittsfield's library. Recently she has changed media to photography and has published the book *Admit One.*

Terri deNatale's love of the outdoors is reflected in many of her paintings of rural landscapes. She may do a watercolor on-site or sketch the scene later returning to her studio to complete the painting. Her depiction of Pittsfield's library is hung in the lounge area of that building.

Milton Webber '71 depicts many familiar local scenes such as Maine Central Institute near his family home where he has a small gift shop and bed & breakfast. Working both in watercolors and pastels, Milt captures the familiar such as can be seen in his rendition of the library within the rotunda of the building.

Deb and Stan Short have teamed up to produce large metal sculptures that adorn their property on route 152. Deb sketches life-size figures on plywood that Stan uses to guide his construction in metal. Several of the animal sculptures have time capsules placed in them by local 8th grade students with plans for them to be opened their senior year.

Tim Rollins' '75 teaching art to at-risk middle school students in the South Bronx led an innovative style of combining lessons in reading and writing while students relate to the material and draw on the book pages that have been laid out on canvas. These students became known as became K.O.S.—Kids of Survival and their works became exhibited in multiple galleries. Tim's model has been replicated in many other cities in the U.S. as he and the K.O.S. had a traveling workshop to share their work and ideas.

While sculptor **Joe Query** is probably best known for his bronze sculpture of Joshua L. Chamberlain at Bowdoin, he may be best remembered in Pittsfield for his one-man show *An Artist in Our Midst* held at the First Universalist Church in the fall of 2014. This exhibit showed the range of his talents from some of his smaller sculptures in multiple materials to drawings in charcoal and pastels.

Living on the farm that has been in his family for generations, **Doug Frati '72** has his studio in the barn where he transforms old furniture into pieces of art. Previously known for his prints and paintings, Doug transitioned to this media using chisels to sculpt his animals and geometric designs in wood creating colorful folk art. Just two years after graduating from the Portland School of Art, his work became included in the Portland Museum of Art's permanent collection.

Barb Denaro's art is displayed on shirts and hats as she designed the logo for Pittsfield's bicentennial. One of her paintings is featured on the cover of the book *Where the Sky has No Stars*. At one time she had a graphic design business and did site plans for engineering firms, but now she wants to focus her creative work on her painting and sculpture.

Watercolorist **David Silsby '49** has painted some of Pittsfield's landmarks such as the train depot and MCI's Founders Hall as well as its activities such as the tug-of-war at Winter Carnival. He has generously donated some of his work to be auctioned to support the school's art and sports programs.

Some of **Joyce Raye's** work can be seen at the Depot and Town Office as she depicted various landmarks around Pittsfield.

Norman Clarke is known for his depictions of the cartoon egg and chicken that donned the Egg

Festival shirts for many years, but evidence of his work is also seen on the ski map at the Pinnacle lodge and the sign for Hathorn Park. He is an illustrator and has done many a sign and vehicle over the years. He also has done many paintings in acrylic and pencil. Some of which he has at home and many others are in the homes of friends and relatives. Norm's wit was showcased in weekly columns such as "Thanks for Listening" for *The SV Weekly,* "Just What I Thought" for *The Valley Times* and "From the Far East" for the Pittsburg, California weekly newspaper. He also co-edited "Chime Times" for the Edwards Company magazine.

The Performers

Born in Pittsfield, **Arthur Millett** (1874-1952) began working in silent films in 1914 and acted in one hundred sixteen films in his career. With the introduction of sound in 1927, his work was not credited on the more than sixty films he made after that time. He retired from the industry in 1940.

From Hawaii to London, **Lolly (Yvonne) Susi '68** had a career in theater that spanned acting to directing to writing until her untimely death. She also acted in television roles and movies in such films as *Dirty Rotten Scoundrels* and *The Jacket.*

Clermont (Clum) Spencer has written and performed *A Balladeer's Songbook* which has songs and stories of experiences of working in the woods and mills in the 20th century. He wrote the *Ballard of Moses Martin* about Pittsfield's first permanent settler for the town's sesquicentennial and had performed at Warsaw for part of the social studies class on Maine Folklore.

Singer, songwriter and humorist **Lee Southard '64** delights folks with his Downeast, down home routines in both Maine and Florida. Lee continues to be as proficient on the keyboard and trumpet as he was in high school at Maine Central Institute where his musical skills were a stand-out.

Bill Booth has made a name for himself in Europe, especially Norway, where he now lives and has recently been nominated for a Spellemannprisen (Norway's Grammy) Award for his latest album *Some Distant Shore.* He is a singer-songwriter with such a mastery of the fiddle and guitar that he captures audiences with his multifaceted talent and music. Bill has six solo albums to his credit.

For well over four decades **Rex Fowler '66** has successfully had a career with Neal Shulman as part of a folk-rock duo known as Aztec Two-Step. As a singer-songwriter he and Neal have produced nearly twenty CD's which showcase their harmonious style and reflect their years together as performers.

Dick Bryant '70 has been a musician based in NYC for many years where he plays solo, as well as with his band The Buckstops. He has been lauded for his first-rate songwriting, as well as for his driving guitar/harmonica stylings, and is proud to have his roots in Pittsfield where as a youth he was a member of the musical group Black Bananas.

Stephen Quint '72 has had a career as a professional French horn player in orchestras and for musicals as well as performing with the Hancock Wind Quintet. He played lead comedy baritone roles with the professional New York Gilbert and Sullivan Players. He has performed all over the continental US and Britain on tour with NYGASP as well as performing in regional opera companies. In 1985, Steve founded *Popular Opera of Pittsfield,* which brought highly original productions of G&S to Maine summer audiences for ten years.

Now living in Montana, **Deidre Heaton Corson '93** composes and sings folk/blues music. She also is the Executive Director North Valley Music School in Whitefish. Deidre wrote about living in West Pittsfield as a youth in her song *A Tear* in her CD *Lost Praire.*

Jess Tardy has performed both as a solo singer and as a lead with her rhythm and jazz band. She has written many of her own songs and has had several albums released over the years featuring her blend of country and jazz. Jess recently moved recently to West Pittsfield.

Sumner McKane '94 has combined live music, photography and history in what is called docu-exhibits producing *In the Blood* about lumbermen and *The Maine Frontier: Through the Lens of Isaac Simpson* about life in northern Maine at the turn of the century. He had toured and performed with various bands as the opening act for country stars such as Willie Nelson and Charlie Daniels.

Russ Copelin '01, known as Ukulele Russ, has performed in a number of different venues in the US, Canada and Australia. Working full-time as an entertainer for over ten years, he also has taught workshops on playing the ukulele. He now makes his home in Alaska.

Pete Witham '90 is the lead guitarist with his band The Cozmik Zombies. His song *Sunsets of My Mind* became well-known in 1999 after the Columbine incident as it speaks to loss, grief and hope. He has held a number of concerts to benefit the fight against hunger and Alzheimers.

Steven Dunphy '96 performs in Portland as a solo artist and has been seen locally at many different Pittsfield venues: the Egg Festival, MCI and the theatre. Previously with the Burnham Boys Band, Stephen plays oldies and country-rock music adept at both drums and guitar.

Jim Whitman, singer-songwriter, convinced his wife **Sam (Condon) '72** to join him on stage where they performed harmonic folk duos. Performing at venues throughout New England, they produced 5 different CD's of their music with the most recent one being *Twilite Motel*. They have retired from stage performances, but remain busy with Jim teaching guitar and Sam producing note cards using her photography and paintings.

Jared Sullivan '99 now known as **Riff Johnson** is pursuing a musical career as a solo artist and one-man band. He is self-described as a "musical encyclopedia" as he can play a multitude of songs on request and has written a number of his own songs.

Molly Gawler '03 is both a musician and dancer. Combining these two performance skills, she has developed her own dance company, Droplet Dance, that she choreographs, collaborates, and performs with other musicians. She is part of a trio with her sisters known as "The Gawler Sisters" as well and plays the fiddle and banjo while singing with the "Gawler Family Band".

Mollie Elizabeth Sharples '13, a Bossov Ballet Theatre graduate, received her Magna Cum Laude degree in Dance Performance from the University of Hartford's The Hartt School in 2017. Mollie is currently dancing professionally with Awaken Dance Theater, a contemporary dance company in New York City.

John Foss '54 played trumpet professionally in Tommy Dorsey's Orchestra and became known nationally when he was gagged and bound at the time of Frank Sinatra Jr.'s abduction. Foss was able to free himself and alert the police. Sinatra was returned several days later to his family after the ransom had been paid.

Anna Parker '66 is known for her acapella singing especially with the Sweet Adelines, a women's barbershop group, for which she has also arranged music. Besides teaching voice and piano, Anna has been an organist and music director in several churches in the past.

Jean McGowan '87 may be remembered as writing a weekly column in the *Central Maine Morning Sentinel* with her mother Ann called *Like Mother, Unlike Daughter*, in the mid '90's where they debated topics from their differing views. People may not know that Jean also composed and released a CD named *"Itch"* with songs that describe the many conflicting roles a woman encounters.

Steve Peterson with his banjo in hand led the Union River Band for over 10 years playing in New England, New York and Canada. At one time this band was considered the top blue grass one in the state and received a highlight review from *Bluegrass Unlimited Magazine:* "... Union River Band once again dramatically reminds us - as artists like Alison Krauss and Dan Tyminski already have - that fine bluegrass music is simply fine bluegrass music, no matter which side of the Mason-Dixon Line it comes from."

Matthew Stein '93 toured one year with the Union River Band as guitarist and lead vocalist and is featured on the band's second recording *One More Day*.

Drew Field '68, technical and artistic director at Dallas Opera, attributes his career in the performing arts as beginning with his participation in MCI's one act plays directed by Anna H. Furbush. Other venues where he has been technical director include opera houses in Santa Fe, Boston, and Central City, CO.

The Resistance is a rock band that has been going strong since 2010. The band is comprised of Sierra Carey on lead vocals, **Jerad Smith '12** on guitar, Matt Mower on bass, and Amber Sinclair on drums. They have played all over the state of Maine and have worked extremely hard to be the best group of musicians they can be while taking honors in several statewide music competitions. Sharing their musical beginnings and journeys are Richard Bryant, Steve Peterson, and brothers Stephen and Douglas Quint.

Black Bananas

Richard Bryant

Five Pittsfield teenagers banded together in 1967 to celebrate and to explore the music explosion that swept through popular culture during that wondrous, raucous decade. Inspired by Dylan, Beatles and Stones - Bill Booth, Dick Bryant, Doug Frati, Marjorie Jones, and Tom Mayhew pooled their self-taught musical skills to form the Black Bananas.

There were gigs to be had – the Congregational Church teen center, high school events, a talent show or two, and even TV exposure on Frankenstein's Country Jamboree way over in the big city of Bangor. Add Manson Park campfire singalongs, and these young folks – armed with guitar, flute, harmonica and enthusiasm – were able to hone their musical skills, and even to think about opportunities that might beckon beyond the rustic confines of Central Maine.

Fast forward to 2018, and Bill is a Grammy nominated musician based in Oslo, Norway, while Dick's harmonica can be heard wailing in many New York City bars. Marj taught music her whole professional career, and Doug is a celebrated visual artist who always keeps a guitar handy. Tom's great singing can be heard around campfires and kitchens across North Carolina.

But it all started in Pittsfield, where the band reunited in December 2017 to perform before a packed house, bringing back the 60's (and some lost youth) to an exultant audience.

Peterson Bluegrass Farm

Stephen Peterson

So, when I decided to get serious about my music, I sought out and found two very accomplished and talented people – Billy Thibodeau and Nancy Merrill - who were equally responsible for our sound and our continued success performing, writing and recording. It all came together when I bought the old Archibald place in West Pittsfield, named it the Peterson Bluegrass Farm, and began making bluegrass music. 1998.

Remembering now how it all went down, there was a higher purpose in motion beyond the bluegrass band itself, and we all knew we were making happen something bigger than that. The Bluegrass Farm was a place to showcase musical talent, but we all had young children and the Farm was providing a safe and wholesome venue where families and children could come and hear good acoustic music and provide a stage where the youngsters were encouraged to play. We had many family and friends gatherings - we truly wanted to inspire, promote, and encourage musicians at any level and any age (just as long it was an acoustic instrument- the only "rule"). We still do this once a year - the day after t-day. Folks bring a bluegrass instrument, some leftovers and we pick well into the evening each fall. Union River in our name - to bring people together and celebrate families and music - all sounds a little like a commune and a little hippie, but it's what we did.

Popular Opera of Pittsfield

Stephen Quint

ARE YOU AWARE that from 1985 – 1995 Pittsfield had its own opera company? Professional singers came up from New York and stayed at the Quint summer house ("camp") on Sibley Pond. We had less than a week of rehearsals and gave from 2 – 6 performances, being careful not to conflict with the Skowhegan Fair. Local singers had weekly chorus rehearsals June and July. We had an orchestra. Doug Frati, my old friend and MCI class of '72 classmate, designed and built the sets. I organized everything, raised money, directed the productions, and played a role. It was the first time I had done anything like this. It seemed like it would be fun.

We performed the comic operas of Gilbert and Sullivan. Victorian author and composer dudes. Their operas have crazy plots, a lot of very funny dialogue – in English – catchy tunes, and having been written in the late 1800s, were in the public domain. Meaning they are free to perform. No fees. A vital ingredient for their continued popularity with low-budget opera companies.

Colby Tomas with Stephen Quint as characters from the universal horror movie *Frankenstein*

Our first production was *The Mikado*, which in the 20th century was the world's most popular English language stage piece. For the title character, who doesn't appear until halfway through act 2, I contacted Maine celebrities Eddie Driscoll (WLBZ's resident comic genius) and author Stephen King. They both laughed at the idea but Eddie had no actual stage experience and was not interested and King would be in North Carolina directing *Maximum Overdrive* (he knows now he would have been far better off artistically playing the Mikado).

After much consideration and consultation I decided to call the company "Popular Opera of Pittsfield," with its catchy acronym, POoP. My runner-up title was "Heart Of Maine Opera," which also has a dandy acronym. The Pittsfield Community Theatre was a tricky little stage for a production with 29 people in costumes. There was no space in the wings, and of course nothing like a dressing room or even a place to put your stuff. Cianbro was happy to supply a trailer for makeup, wigs, and dressing. Bathroom needs had to be met by walking 60 yards to the Elks Lodge.

Every summer our productions got more elaborate and we finally had to move on from the movie theatre. We performed at Lakewood and in opera houses in Camden, Rockport, and Waterville. We changed our name to the more high-falutin' Maine Opera Theatra (MOThra) in an attempt at some lameass dignity.

Ten years seemed like a good time to stop. The main thing I've taken from the POoP/MOThra experience was the joy and utter hilariousness of getting the Mainers together with the New York men, women, and others. It was very intense and exhausting work. And fun!

From Musician to Entrepreneur to Author

Douglas Quint

Douglas Quint spent his first sixteen years locked in a bedroom room reading comic books and practicing the bassoon. He was born and raised in Pittsfield, a town in Central Maine known best for the annual Egg Festival. Escape was imminent. At age 17 Doug sacked high school, grabbed his bassoon and took off for New York City.

Doug with Buster visiting his mother Mary in Pittsfield

The next twenty-something years of Doug's life were spent shackled to a desk making thousands of bassoon reeds. True, he wandered the halls of Manhattan School of Music and the Juilliard School - eventually earning degrees from both joints and learning a bunch from Frank Morelli - but the scars from all that reed-shaving are the most lasting impression.

After graduating from Juilliard with his Master's Degree in bassoon performance, he ran around the world tooting his own horn with ensembles including the Orpheus Chamber Orchestra, the Boston Pops. and other such little bands. He also worked as the orchestra manager at Juilliard until the day before he was fired (saw it coming). One day in early 2009 a very queer thing happened: a Big Gay Ice Cream Truck appeared. Doug turned this weird notion into one of the most successful dessert businesses around. Big Gay Ice Cream has two shops in New York City, one in Philadelphia, and more on the way. Doug is the co-author of *Big Gay Ice Cream Book,* a collection of stories and recipes published by Random House. He has cooked on television alongside Paula Deen, talked about cupcakes on Cooking Channel's "Unique Sweets" and judged on Top Chef. He has seen the

Go-Go's in concert 63 times and divided his life between his work in New York City and his home in Freeport, IL.

IMAGES OF PITTSFIELDERS
by Tim Sample

Spencer Havey & Martha Kleinschmidt

Hannah Norris & Oscar Gerry

Marion Small & Stephanie Sample

David Bois

113

MAINE CENTRAL INSTITUTE, PITTSFIELD, ME.

One Room Schoolhouse

Mrs. E. B. Cronkite, West Pittsfield

Maine Central Institute

Postcard Published for the Libby Pharmacy Pittsfield, ME

Schools educate community's youth, but also are gathering places for its townspeople. They help weave the fabric of the community together.

Pittsfield Schools Today

Gayle Middleton and Jim Hammond

Those of us who grew up in the MSAD 53 school system may remember a different kind of learning. At five, you entered kindergarten (for a morning or afternoon session) to learn colors, letters and shapes. Today, students enter the system in preschool and leave kindergarten as readers. Elementary school used textbooks and "dittos". Today, it is novels and Google Docs. In middle school, it was not uncommon to sit in rows, silently, while the teacher wrote notes on the chalkboard, which you then studied and rewrote for a test. Today, students are more likely to be investigating themed topics through what are called "expeditions." Questions are posed and groups of students listen to experts in the field, do actual field work related to the topic and delve into a variety of readings where the student must decide what is important enough to note. Instead of a test, the end product may be a comprehensive project that shows mastery of varying skills. Showing mastery is also the basis of "standards-based learning," which the state has mandated. Students now have a list of standards, based on critical skills and must show that each has met that standard. For parents (and teachers) who grew up with an "A, B, C, D" report card, switching to 1, 2, 3 and 4 with a 3 meaning the student has met the goal, is a major mind shift. Manson Park and Vickery School shifted to standards-based learning several years ago, so students who went through recently are already comfortable with the new system. Education in Pittsfield, from the days of primers and ferules, to personal iPads and digital portfolios, is constantly evolving. Today the world is at the students' fingertips which makes us feel a little less like Mayberry and a little more Star Trek.

While the programming has changed quite a bit, many of the faces in the district are still very familiar. Sue Nile just can't stay away from school! Several times a year, she can be seen right in front of Vickery Elementary School with Michelle Carr, who teaches first grade. You can't miss them - they're

fully decked out in yellow "smiley" clothes, waving at the busses. But much of Sue's involvement with MSAD #53 is less obvious. She's been known to spend time in the gardens around our buildings, weeding whenever she sees that it's needed. She's still on the Children's Benefit Fund Committee, which she once chaired. She joins the Vickery students in October for their annual Food Walk to the Pittsfield Food Pantry, an event she spearheaded when she was a teacher in the building.

Sue Nile is not the only person who has chosen to stay in the school district where they had already spent a good deal of time. In fact, Vickery's Principal, Sarah Allen, spent her entire public-school career in the district. While she didn't initially plan to be a teacher (she majored in history and psychology as an undergraduate), she fell in love with teaching special education after teaching for a time in Korea, and then acting as a long-term substitute at Vickery. Sarah returned to the district officially in 2004, as a special education teacher for grades 3 and 4. In 2012, she was in the office accepting her position as Assistant Principal as her mother was in the same office completing her paperwork to retire. Sarah's mom ended her career as a State Director for Special Education, based in MSAD #53.

Missy Noonan, third- grade teacher, also spent all of her public-school years here. She and Tammy George, who now teaches second-grade, were members of the last class to spend 9th grade at Warsaw, before it moved to MCI. Missy has many great memories of her time as a student. She was cast in the lead part in her second-grade musical, and still remembers many of the songs! She remembers hatching eggs in the fourth grade with Mrs. Susi. There was dancing at Warsaw to a playlist created by the art teacher, Lucky Clark, and a trip to Quebec with the French Club. Missy's mother worked in the Warsaw office while she attended there.

While Tammy taught for 2 years elsewhere before coming to Vickery School, Missy has been working here since 1990, all but one of those years in the third-grade. She is currently teaching in the room where she had fourth grade language arts with Mrs. Howland. Both of them agree that they are exactly where they wanted to be - in the community where they grew up and where they can teach with former teachers and former classmates. Missy notes that there is a "great sense of community [here], with a staff that always goes the extra mile so all students get what they need."

Sarah Ross ('99) is another teacher who never wanted to be anywhere else. In fact, she never applied for a job elsewhere. While she did not get the ½ time Kindergarten job for which she first applied, she was asked to interview for a full-time special education position, which she held from 2003-2010. In 2010, she became the Reading Interventionist at Vickery, and in 2015 added Title I Math Coordinator to her duties. For Sarah, her favorite moments as a student, and as a teacher, are the events that gave the students a chance to dress up and be someone else - the times "you could be a little bit more of a risk taker."

Warsaw Middle School also has deep roots in the community. The current principal, Sherry Littlefield, grew up here in Pittsfield. Teachers Ronny Rollins, brothers Scott and Jim Hammond, Frannie Oviatt Rogers, Jenn Cummings Saucier, Jordan Kennedy, Liz Anthony, Cindy Taylor and Aaron McCannell all grew up here as well and have come back to roost. The school offices have Roberta Hicks, Lori Wyman Glidden and Carol Anthony - all local daughters - taking care of business. Custodian Matt Bennett grew up here as well. A community school where teachers are former classmates of parents, who remember the middle school personally, can serve the students with an eye to both our past and our future. So many of our staff are simultaneously alumni, parents and community members, making them deeply invested in the Pittsfield school experience.

Founder Oren B Cheney

Maine Central Institute

Pam Dorman

Maine Central Institute (MCI) was founded in 1866 to prepare students for study at Bates College which, at the time, was a seminary in Lewiston. MCI founder Oren B. Cheney chose Pittsfield as a suitable location because of the town's industrial prosperity and its desirable location that "was east of the Kennebec and in central Maine" (Kemp M. Pottle, The History of Maine

Central Institute, 1961). With Cheney's efforts and those of church and business leaders – Rev. Ebenezer Knowlton, Going Hathorn, Rev. Nathanial Weymouth, Rev. Lot L. Harmon, Rev. Aura L. Gerrish, Rev. William Stinson, and Jesse C. Connor – the Maine Legislature approved the School charter in February 1866, and classes began that following August for the "51 gentlemen and 32 ladies" enrolled as the first MCI students (Pottle).

In those early years, students attended lectures in public spaces and private homes throughout Pittsfield. For the first two years, MCI offered only a fall and a spring term with two similar courses of study – college preparatory and a Ladies' Course (Maine Central Institute Catalogue, 1867). Over the years, MCI modified its curriculum to fulfill the academic needs of students pursuing post-secondary studies or vocational training. Today, MCI provides a safe and nurturing atmosphere for students to acquire knowledge, self-esteem, social responsibility, and the critical thinking and communication skills necessary for global citizenship and lifelong learning.

Bates senior Arthur Givern was MCI's first headmaster, and Ellen Knowlton, the daughter of founder Ebenezer Knowlton, was the first teaching dean (called a preceptress). For many years, MCI's first administrators were Bates upperclassmen who worked at the School for a year before graduating from college. It was George Files who, upon graduating from Bates, became the first headmaster who was a college graduate when he led MCI, and Files served as headmaster from 1869 to 1873 (Pottle).

In 1868, construction of the MCI campus began atop what was formerly a sheep pasture outside town. The Institute Building (later renamed Founders Hall) consisted of six large rooms on the first floor (Pottle). The second floor (later refurbished and named after MCI trustee and state governor, the Honorable Llewellyn Powers) and third floor were completed later, and an unfinished fourth floor provided access to an impressive bell tower. Henry W. Lancey donated the bell that was added in 1877 (History of Our School, 2010).

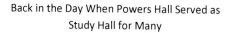
Back in the Day When Powers Hall Served as Study Hall for Many

Founders Hall is used to this day for classes and offices, and Powers Hall is where the Bossov Ballet Theatre (BBT), MCI's pre-professional ballet school, instructs students and holds rehearsals for its many performances.

MCI was one of the few schools in Maine to offer teacher training, and the School's first graduate, Maria Simons of Pittsfield, successfully completed studies in 1869 to pursue a career in teaching (Pottle). By 1900, 600 students had graduated from MCI, and most of the early graduates became teachers, lawyers or doctors – and nearly all of them attended Bates College. To prepare students for rigorous college studies, MCI established the Manson Prize (later renamed Manson Essay) after local physician and school trustee, John C. Manson, MD. The Manson Essay competition remains a scholarly milestone for MCI students. Manson's family gifted their family home to MCI in 1944, which the School uses as the Head of School's residence to this day.

As the student population grew, the need for extracurricular activities and a wider range of courses increased as well. Popular activities like Girls Glee Club and MCI Orchestra were formed in 1907, and over the years, performing and visual arts programs have sustained their popularity with students that have led to many student achievements at the state and national levels to this day. Performance activities like music, drama, and art became courses of study, and for many years were housed separately throughout the campus. In 2017 and after the largest capital campaign in the School's history, MCI's music programs (formerly in the Ruth Plummer Cook building) joined the School's drama and visual arts programs in the JR Cianchette Building and, combined, became the Performing and Visual Arts Center. The center enables these programs and students to collaborate and share leading edge technological resources.

Award Winning Vocal Jazz Group - Caravan

In 1893, MCI introduced sports programs to students: tennis, baseball, football (in 1899), and track. George M. Parks, a distinguished alumnus of the Class of 1885 and devoted trustee, contributed a large sum of money for the development of an athletic field with a cinder track (History of Our School). Parks

Gym was built in 1936 and named after Parks in recognition of his generous gifts to MCI. Although MCI constructed the larger Wright Gym in 1987 (thanks to the contributions of the Perley Wright family, Cianbro Corporation, alumni and friends), Parks Gym is used to this day for school meetings, community gatherings, sport practices, and performances.

For many years, MCI students practiced sports and played games at Manson Park. The School added two new playing fields in 2015 which enables students to practice and host games on campus throughout the school year.

The 20th century represented economic stability for MCI due in part from the growing influx of students coming to MCI from outside central Maine and the United States and from Maine's reimbursement of student tuition to towns without high schools. In 1909, MCI entered into its first contract to educate students from Pittsfield, Detroit, and Burnham (Pottle).

MCI transitioned to a boarding and day school in 1903 when it purchased a local boarding house from Benjamin Bowden, added another story, and renamed it Cedar Croft Hall that it used it as a girls' dormitory. Many male students lived off campus in private homes while other students commuted daily by train. Enrollment at the school before and during World War I increased dramatically, making it necessary to provide more space for residential students. In 1911, MCI constructed a new girls' dormitory named Weymouth Hall. The construction of Weymouth Hall made it possible for male students to board in Cedar Croft Hall until 1927 when the wooden structure was destroyed by fire during the Christmas break. MCI's alumni began a capital campaign to raise funds for a new dormitory, and by October 1928, Alumni Hall opened to students. At MCI's 1987 summer reunion, Alumni Hall was rededicated and named Stanley/Alumni Hall in recognition of former Headmaster Edward Stanley. Today, MCI houses students in four student residences: Rowe Hall (built in 1961), Stanley/Alumni Hall,

Nye Hurd Honors Dormitory (for honors students), and Manson Hall (built in 1966) (History of Our School).

By World War II, MCI enrollment declined as young men opted for military service in defense of their country. It wasn't until the 1950s that MCI was able to expand its campus to include a Quonset hut donated and erected by JR Cianchette in 1950 for industrial arts instruction, built the JR Cianchette Hall of Science in 1958 for science and home economics, and constructed the William H. Powell Memorial Library in 1959. Powell Library resulted from a gift by the late judge's family and, at the time, the Powell gift represented the largest gift in MCI's history. Powell Library is a beautiful building equipped with classrooms, a full-service library and media center, and the Hazel Monteith Earle Memorial Language Department (History of Our School).

Ella Night – A Revisioning of the Early Prize Speaking Contest for Freshman & Sophmores – Now is Open to All Classes. It is named in honor of Ella Powell who made the Powell Library possible.

In 1962, Johnson W. Parks (nephew of George M. Parks) donated to MCI the Parks Homestead, a 200-acre farm on Hartland Avenue. MCI transformed the property into a nine-hole golf course that opened to the public as the Johnson W. Parks Golf Course. Thirty years later, MCI sold the golf course in 1996, but J.W. Parks continues to be an important part of student life: the MCI golf team practices and plays home matches on the lush green fairways, and the course has been recognized by the National Golf Foundation as one of the finest nine-hole courses in New England (History of Our School).

Weymouth Hall was restored in 1982. Once a dormitory and dining room, today Weymouth Hall provides much-needed office and classroom space to the School. In 1992, the former Bryant House on the school campus was renamed in honor of its long-time residents, Ralph and Edna Cianchette and their children (Carl '37, Norris '40, Clair '41, Kenneth '42, Ival '44, Marilyn '47, and Alton '48). The building is a meeting place for alumni, friends and guests of the School as well as offices of Admissions and Institutional Advancement.

In the winter of 2001, the Quonset hut was razed and Cianbro Corporation constructed the 26,000 square foot, three-story Chuck & Helen Cianchette Math & Science Center. Cianbro was also a significant contributor to this project and their in-kind gifts in memory of Alton "Chuck" Cianchette were significant (History of Our School).

In early 2005, MCI purchased the Shorey House building on Main Street across from Manson House. The property enabled MCI to provide more faculty housing and increase the number of adults who supervise in the dormitories. In 2007, MCI completed the Trustee Memorial Student Center using funds from MCI alumni and friends. The center houses the Patterson Student Lounge, Savage Family Dining Room, the Jeff Hazell Kitchen, Furman Recreation Facility, Kinney Conference Suite, and the Merrill Bank Dining Server. The dining room seats 250 people and is also the location of many events and gatherings (MCI-school.org).

Lunar New Year is celebrated with Asian Students hosting a dinner with their dormmates.

MCI's history comprises several snapshots of the generosity of alumni and community leaders over the past 152 years: its picturesque tree-lined campus is alive with students on their way to the Chuck and

Helen Cianchette Math & Science Center, the William H. Powell Memorial Library, Weymouth Hall, Founders Hall, the Joseph R. Cianchette Hall, or to MCI's two gymnasiums. With the dedication, love and pride of many, MCI has prospered in preparing students for the future.

Schools Repurposed

Jane Woodruff and Melissa Flewelling

A thirteen-year old teacher? Hard to imagine, but Ann Gould was that age when as one of Pittsfield's first teachers she instructed students in the home of her uncle, Moses Martin. As the town's population grew, so did the need for schools. Over the years the educational system became more centralized with larger school buildings in town replacing the neighborhood and rural one-room schools.

Yet some of these older schools survived and were transformed. They became a home, a store, an office building, an apartment building, a factory. Many of the one-room rural schoolhouses were destroyed by fire or neglect but several remain standing today. On the corner of the Snakeroot Road and Route 100 stands an old schoolhouse that was renovated to become a single-family residence. On route 2, a building that has functioned as an antique store had its earliest beginnings as a school.

In town, the former Riverside School, which had been built in 1890, was repurposed several times. In 1959, it became a factory for Churchgoods and later Faithcraft which provided religious items for C.M. Almy. Years later, it would be totally remodeled and become the apartment building it is today.

The grammar school on North Lancey was built the same year as the library and Catholic Church in 1904. It would serve generations of children until its closing at the end of the school year in 1983.

Vacant only one year, its classrooms and lower level area were completely renovated in stages into a number of varying sized offices. Over the years. it has housed a variety of businesses including some that returned students to this building including Headstart. Six former tenants grew their businesses and moved out into the community into larger spaces with those tenants being Tax Pro, Northeast Planning Associates, Northeastern

Environmental Services, Loretta's, RJD Appraisal, and Maine Federation of Farmers' Markets. It continues to serve as an incubator for small businesses.

The Hartland Avenue School is in transition and from its owner, Melissa Flewelling, it is learned that it has been a part of the Pittsfield community for over 120 years.

In March 1897, the Pittsfield townspeople approved the building of a new school to relieve overcrowding at the Riverside and Lancey Street Schools. It was a new, modern design by prominent Bangor architect, Wilfred E. Mansur, which included sewer connection specifically approved by the town.

Classes began winter term 1897. It is interesting to note that the terminology of the day was such that the Hartland Avenue Intermediate School, first taught by Myrtie Hanson, and the Hartland Avenue Primary School, first taught by Bessie Maxfield, were considered separate schools housed in the same building.

Over time, the Hartland Avenue school building housed various grade levels, but generally the lower, primary grades. Over time, every effort was made to conform the building to meet changing safety criteria. Eventually, perhaps the mid-1950s, the Hartland Avenue School closed. About 1965, it was opened as a school for special needs students and was named The Marie Bradford School, after the town nurse.

The Marie Bradford School closed sometime in the 1970s, and the building sat unused again. In the 1980s, it was repurposed with multiple offices to serve the school district administration. As repairs became more dire and costly, and the school budget got tighter, SAD 53 chose to close the building and move administrative offices to Vickery Middle School. The Hartland Avenue School was sold to private owners in 2012 after several years on the market.

As of 2018, the new owners have not completed renovations, which include opening the two main rooms to their original size and height. The hope is that the Hartland Avenue School building, which has long been involved in educating the Pittsfield community -- albeit sporadic -- will continue to be a part of Pittsfield's future.

Hathorn Sunset

By April Smith Stock

Hathorn Park

By Mark Schumpert

Manson Park in Winter

By Mark Schumpert

Pittsfield is fortunate to have many green spaces with her numerous parks and recreational fields.

Seven Parks, A River and Some Woods

Jane Woodruff

The River

The Sebasticook River with its wildlife drew the natives and Pittsfield's first settlers. It became the source for power generation years ago as it still is today. In the past, industries bordering its shores disposed of raw materials, chemicals and sewage treating it as a watery dump. With the Clean Water Act of 1972, this stopped and with the cessation of dumping has come the return of wildlife over the years.

The river coursing through the center of town provides habitat once again for any number of birds and animals. Quite unlikely is the annual return of a pair of loons each spring at the time of ice out on the Mill Pond. These loons thrill townspeople with their calls and in summer the parading of their newborn chicks.

Come spring also is the return of canoeists from MCI to the river and Mill Pond as they take to the waterways for their physical education classes. No matter the season fishermen are drawn to the water as they can be seen casting lines along the edge and in winter drilling holes through the ice to drop their lines either at Mill or Sibley Pond.

In the early 1900's Captain Parsons with his boat, the *Winthrop,* would ferry people from the Waverly boat landing area up the river to the Ringwood Pavilion for picnics and dances. In the 1980's Ringwood would serve as a campground for the general public. This boat launching area now serves kayakers and canoeists who ply their paddles on this same portion of the river and Douglas Pond as did earlier recreationists.

Pinnacle Park

Pinnacle Park, best known for its ski season, attracts people year-round as it is the boat launching site for Douglas Pond, a well-known site for viewing wildlife particularly wading birds and waterfowl. Bird watching huts are located near the summit of the Pinnacle and evidence from turtles leaving shells near the base attest to its being a natural habitat. Mountain bikers and hikers enjoy views from it as it is one of Pittsfield's highest points of land.

The Pinnacle has long drawn children to its slopes for sledding in the winter and hiking other seasons, but since the winter of 1954-5, it has been the home to local skiers as the Kiwanis developed it as a ski slope. Hundreds and hundreds of people have learned to ski on its slopes and MCI fielded class B alpine ski champion teams in the 1960's. With a headwall, suicide trail, jump landing, bowl and main slope, it sports more variety of terrain than would be expected from this hill of gravel. Many children have learned to skate on its rink that lies at the base of its lodge.

Over the years the Pinnacle has been host to a number of activities including an MCI Alumni Concert, Girl Scout Day Camp, Easy St. Coffeehouse, Cub Scout sled races and numerous reunion parties and wedding receptions. It continues to serve as a vital recreation area and hosts the annual Kiwanis Easter Egg Hunt and the annual Pinnacle Fest.

Hathorn Park

But for Clyde Martin, Hathorn Park might not have been. Ceaseless in his efforts to convince townspeople to have land set aside for a park, in 1921 he sought money from the town to purchase what was at that time called the Haskell lot providing the citizens raise an equal amount. And that they did.

In just six weeks 173 residents committed more than $5000. The park was to be named after the late Going Hathorn who was one of the "first men to take an interest in developing the Town of Pittsfield." This

land had been the site of his former estate before passing out of the family with its buildings subsequently being moved to various sites in town. A landscape plan was devised by W. J. Dougherty of Portland. The following year the Pittsfield Band built a new steel bandstand for a cost of $944.36 which has been in use ever since. The Business Professional Women's Club donated playground equipment and townspeople donated trees in memory of loved ones.

As in the past, folks have come forward to donate time and money for the development of this park. Named Legge's Diamond after beloved MCI science teacher and sports enthusiast/coach Paul Legge, the baseball field at the south end of the park has been the site of Little League games for decades. The smell of hot dogs and popcorn waft through the air as parents manage the concession stand. Basketball is played year-round - even in winter - as youth shovel snow off the court to be able to shoot hoops. The adjacent playground is busy with little ones as they swing, climb and spin on the playground equipment.

A series of summer concerts are held weekly throughout the summer and in December a Christmas concert led by school children for Holiday Lights in Hathorn Park fill out the musical calendar for the year.

On the west side of the park, the weekly Farmers' Market is held from May to October providing direct access to local produce. Nearby the cupola from the Hathorn Stable has been returned to near its original home amidst flower planters lovingly cared for by members of the Pittsfield Garden Club.

Manson Park

Mary Ann Lancey Manson became immortalized with the gifting of land for a park in her memory by her lawyer son John W. Manson. Mrs. Manson was a sister to Isaac Lancey of Lancey House re-known and wife to Dr. John C. Manson, the originator of the MCI's Manson Essay. This largest and second oldest park in Pittsfield lies adjacent to the Sebasticook River with its first parcel of land given by her son to the town in 1926. In 1935 a baseball diamond was developed known as Lancey Field. The park would expand with the later acquisition of greater acreage bequeathed to the town by her son at the time of his death in 1941. He also provided trust funds for its maintenance and care to be overseen by a five-member committee.

In his will, he elucidated that "I desire it to be improved, beautified and, if necessary, enlarged, to be used somewhat, not principally, as a sport field to which the students at Maine Central Institute shall be welcome; to be used especially as a garden, walk, and playground for all the people who desire to use it." And enlarged it was - by additional land given over the years by multiple donors: Lancey Milliken, Sonia Call Bartlett, Eva, Connie and Ronello Brown.

Known for his having designed the Capitol Grounds in Augusta, Carl Rust Parker of the famed Olmsted Brothers firm was the landscape architect selected to design and make recommendations for the park's development. Design elements promoted by the Olmsteds were incorporated in the design such as attention given the site's natural scenery to promote a restorative environment using its topographical features and plants indigenous to the area. The original plan was never fully realized as the proposed skating rink and five hundred seat outdoor amphitheater were never developed; however, the little children's playground, ball fields and winding paths in a natural setting were actualized. It would take the impetus and funding of the Pittsfield Kiwanis Club to add the planned features of a public swimming pool and tennis courts all of which have subsequently been replaced in recent years. Later additions to the park include the

snowmobile bridge which crosses the river giving access to what is called "Paradise", a wooded area with several trails.

Playing fields have hosted a variety of sports over the years from pee-wee soccer to MCI's sports teams. While no longer home field to many of MCI's fall sports, it does still provide facilities for baseball and tennis. Multiple exercise stations throughout the park were added by Patrick Hapworth as part of his Eagle Scout project.

Large scale events such as the annual Egg Festival, Scout Jamboree, and Bike Maine have occurred over the years.

This park is well-used and well-loved seemingly meeting John W. Manson's hope and vision for this land.

Remembrance Park

An Eagle Scout project helped prompt the development of Remembrance Park. A dilapidated store on the corner of Sebasticook Street and North Main had been torn down leaving a vacant lot. In the fall of 1988, Vaughan Woodruff began working with Town Manager D. Dwight Doherty and Cianbro engineer Tom Ruksznis to develop and implement a plan that would transform this land into a "mini-park". Raising money and building benches as well as preparing and seeding the land with fellow scouts all were part of the requirements for Vaughan's attainment of Eagle Scout.

The park remained unnamed until 2003 when the Town Council formally named it Remembrance Park with the intention that it would be a special place for memorial plantings in remembrance of loved ones. Situated overlooking the Sebasticook River, this park provides a peaceful view of the river with its loons as well as easy access for fishing.

Veterans Park

Like Clyde Martin tireless in their efforts for a park, Arthur Dewey and Ruth Walker researched and assembled the list of the eight hundred and fifty-seven Pittsfield veterans that are honored in one of Pittsfield's newer parks. They also raised over $19,000 for its construction. Mr. Dewey's concept for this park was sparked by his witnessing the children waving flags he had given them during the 2000 Memorial Day parade. Just one year later, Veterans Park was in place and dedicated.

In contrast to several of the other parks, a local citizen was enlisted to design the park with the town's public works department completing the landscaping. Trees were donated and a granite bench by E.D. Call and Son was given. Built near the site of famed Colonel Walter Morrill's stable, this park offers a green and restful setting on Main Street. Each Memorial Day the parade stops at this park to lay a wreath in remembrance of these veterans.

Stein Park

Dilapidated commercial buildings on what was once called Park Street were torn down in the 1970's as part of a Community Development Project. The Pittsfield Garden Club approached the Town requesting that this area be turned into a park. They obtained a site plan from Dr. Lyle Littlefield of the University of Maine - Orono which they then presented to the Town. The Arts Club gifted money for the transformation of this area to become what was originally known as Mill Pond Park.

Dana Woodruff helps Dr. Stein ready for the Dedication Ceremony

In 1986, it was rededicated and named after Dr. Ernest W. Stein, a well-loved local physician. Arguably, one of Pittsfield prettiest parks, it overlooks the Mill Pond and has become the showcase for the Pittsfield Garden Club with the floral displays that reflect the artistry of these tireless volunteers. A split rail fence and arbor donated by Walpole Woodworkers enhance the beauty of this park. The watering trough now serving as a planter comes with its own history. Originally located on Hartland Avenue, it was lost for a number of years when it was spotted at

Julia's Auction House and kindly returned to town. It now serves as one of the centerpieces of this park.

Fendler Park

A factory. A slaughterhouse. A trailer park. Fendler Park has been the site of many things before its gifting to the town by Ryan and Tom Fendler for the development of a park in memorial to Barbara, Ryan's wife. In 2006 along with the Fendlers' generous gift, a grant and countless hours by local

volunteers transformed this land into a welcoming park bordering the Mill Pond. While the mills are gone, a millstone - reminiscent of Pittsfield's past - was recycled for use as a fountain as the centerpiece of the town's newest park. The Carla Hunt Bertrand Memorial Garden adds color and contrast to this green space sprinkled with gingko trees and many shrubs.

Peltoma Woods

At the south end of town, an area known as the Peltoma Woods or the Town Farm Property rounds out the public green spaces in town. Though technically not yet a park, it serves as one with its meandering trails through the woods to the river and access to the home-site of Pittsfield's first settlers, the Martins.

Pittsfield is most fortunate to have these woods and five of its parks strung along the river like green gems on a blue necklace.

Rail Trail

Jane Woodruff

Previously a spur of what was to become Maine Central Railroad, the Sebasticook and Moosehead Railroad (SMR) initially ran from Pittsfield to Hartland. Built in record time in just ten weeks in 1886, it

was intended to reach northward along the Sebasticook River to join the Monson and Athens Railroad. Monson was known as the gateway to the Moosehead region and exporter of slate, but its railroad only operated between it and Monson Junction; thus, becoming known as the smallest railroad in the United States. It was unfortunate that these two spurs never met, and the dream of accessing the Moosehead region by rail never materialized. Meanwhile, the SMR would extend to Harmony in 1912 making access to the recreational area on Moose Pond known as Castle Harmony available to out of state patrons.

Track with train shown in red in this ca. 1944 aerial photo

In the 1950's known by locals as the Harmony Squirtgun, the SMR would stop near the crossing of Somerset with one of its engineers jumping from the train to run to Lloyd Elias's neighborhood grocery store to buy a six pack of beer. The origin of its nickname is up for dispute, with one theory being it was such a short run to Hartland of only eight miles. The other was that it was named for its steam engine. Children from this area often walked the tracks as a short cut to the street leading to Maine Central Institute (MCI) despite being warned by police that this was supposedly "illegal."As the need for rail service declined in this area and with the subsequent

closing of the Pittsfield-Hartland branch in 1983, discussion ensued as to its potential use. Homeowners were interested in extending their property to include adding the shoulders of the railroad bed. Use as a conduit for high fiber optics was also discussed but never realized. In the end with its closing and subsequent removal of rails and ties nearly 100 years later it would become accessible as a favored trail for a number of recreational enthusiasts: hikers, bikers, snowmobilers, cross-country skiers, ATV and horseback riders. As in the 1950's, it would also become a route to MCI as well as the Vickery-

Warsaw school complex. What had been built as a railroad to access recreational areas had itself become one.

Recreation Facilities: The Pool and Playing Fields

Paul Bertrand

In 2008-2009, the Kiwanis Swimming Pool, made with asphalt in 1953, was removed and replaced with a new concrete pool. The new pool is 50' x 70' with a wading area and is handicap friendly. Also replaced were the bathhouse and the equipment building.

In early 2000, land was given to Warsaw Junior High for a new football field. At the same time, a water line was installed and a storage facility built. Also, a softball field with dug-outs was added.

In 2010, at Hathorn Park the Legge Diamond infield was rebuilt, new planks installed on the bleachers with help from the Boy Scouts. The basketball court was resurfaced, new backboards installed, new picnic tables, and new bleachers were added. A few years later, the children's playground was replaced with new equipment.

In 2015, the tennis courts at Manson Park were removed and replaced with four new courts. This was a joint effort with Manson Park and Maine Central Institute (MCI). Endowment by Ronello Brown made this possible. These new courts are able to accommodate players from the youngest to the older players. One court will accommodate "Pickle Ball" for seniors.

At MCI, the football practice field was rebuilt with new field hockey and soccer fields built as well as an extra practice field. A water line was installed and new irrigation equipment purchased.

Editor's Note: Businesses and many individuals volunteered countless hours to make these facilities possible. Leading the effort on many of these projects was Paul Bertrand for whom the pool is named.

Pittsfield Recreation Department

Suzy Morton

The Town of Pittsfield has much to offer families including the Pittsfield Recreation Department which certainly enhances the overall community experience for everyone. We are fortunate to have facilities and funds designated for recreation purposes in Pittsfield. The Rec Department offers four seasons of athletic programs and recreation activities for individuals in the town of Pittsfield and the surrounding communities. This department also manages the Paul E. Bertrand Community Swimming Pool.

The shared goal of our sports programs is to teach the basics of a particular sport to beginning athletes. And then to continue to work and teach students about a sport until they are on a middle school team. Primarily we offer athletics to students in kindergarten through 6th grade. Volunteer coaches strive to communicate the importance of the rules, teamwork and good sportsmanship to all participants as well as encourage knowledge and growth as an athlete.

Currently, our fall sports include soccer, football and field hockey. Our younger students start out learning the basics and play in small scrimmages. The older athletes are placed on formed teams that travel throughout our area playing teams from other towns. The travel opportunities increase awareness and competitiveness for future athletic programs.

In the winter season, we offer basketball and cheering. Students have the option to learn their sport during practices, games with other Pittsfield Rec teams as well as hit the road on travel teams. The basketball travel teams generally play in exciting weekend tournaments throughout central Maine in March to conclude their seasons.

Spring is a busy season for the Pittsfield Rec Department. The younger students start out in T-Ball and Farm League. They learn the basics of the game and the rules. Teams play quick games against each other in an effort to put their skills to work in game situations. The older students play softball or Little League. The action becomes a bit more intense as these teams are in structured leagues such as the Sebasticook Valley Little League. They practice locally and then travel to play fast-paced games with local competitors.

During the summer months Pittsfield Rec manages the Paul E. Bertrand Community Pool. It was rebuilt around 10 years ago and is now a remarkable facility. People from all over are amazed that we have such an outstanding feature in our small town.

The Pittsfield Rec Department hosts a variety of summer programs for the duration of 6-8 weeks such as arts and crafts, sports programs like soccer, basketball, tennis, field hockey etc. We offer swimming lessons and daily open swim times at the community pool. In addition, we work closely with JW Parks Golf Course to offer golf lessons as well.

The Pittsfield Rec Department enlists the year-round aid and assistance of primarily volunteers. We are so fortunate to have such compassionate citizens. These volunteers constantly step up and encourage the positive growth of our young individuals through their dedication to Pittsfield. The Pittsfield Recreation Department sincerely appreciates all our volunteers and their commitment.

The Pittsfield Recreation Department has grown, evolved and expanded throughout the years. We will continue to strive to offer more for our citizens in the future as well as look for ways to improve and enhance the overall Rec experience. Please visit our Facebook page at Pittsfield Recreation Department for up to date information.

Johnson W. Parks Golf Course

Michael Dugas

In 1962, Johnson W. Parks donated the land on which the golf course and the Pinnacle ski slope now occupy to Maine Central Institute. It was in 1964 that MCI was convinced to establish a golf course on the property. With the help of math teacher, John Dana, a design was rendered. Many of the local people including, Sanger Cook, John Dana and several of the founders of Cianbro helped in the construction project. After two years of construction, the course opened to public play in 1966 as our records indicate.

In the early years, the course was a tool for community gatherings and a benefit to the employees of MCI. John Dana became a member of the PGA of America and was named the first Head Golf

Professional to the club. JW Parks has had only three PGA Head Professionals in its 54 years of existence. Duffy McCallister succeeded John Dana and Michael Dugas is the current PGA Head Professional.

In 1995, the board of directors at MCI felt it was best to not be in the golf business and focus on education. It was at that time that the course was put up for public sale. During the early winter months, Tom Gordon reached out to Michael Dugas about a possible purchase of the facility. Michael and his wife, Dawn Kitchin Dugas, were living in West Palm Beach, Florida at that time. Stan Kitchin, Dawn's father, was willing to help with the purchase of the course and bring the business into the Kitchin and Dugas families.

The first years: The clubhouse was gutted and a new grille room and function hall were created. As time went on, the clubhouse was expanded again in 2002 to include the kitchen area moving into the golf shop. The golf shop was then moved to the garage that is attached to the house. The next project happened in the year 1998 when the driving range was constructed across the street on the old Pittsfield town dump. This was a major enhancement to that property and a great addition to our facility. In 2000, the facility took on another major project, a full irrigation system. This project started in the fall and was finished the following summer with the help of many members and friends. You will find the facility to be quite different today than it was back in the day. We hope that you find it more enjoyable and player friendly.

Junior Golf: JW Parks has always been a strong supporter of junior golf. Many of our juniors have gone on to become PGA Golf Professionals. We have also hosted many High School State Champions as individuals and teams at MCI. We also are home to the only Maine player to win the New England High School Championship, Gavin Dugas in 2015. We still very committed to the development of junior golfers and their access to the course.

Community: JW parks has been a great venue for local organizations to raise money for their causes or just come together in fellowship. Through the years, over $500,000.00 has been raised for community efforts while providing an enjoyable activity for those involved.

Vacationland Skydiving

Brad Fisher

Locals know when to look skyward upon hearing the sounds of a plane climbing, climbing and then the silence. A motor starts again and suddenly there are skydivers free-falling before deploying their beautiful, colorful parachutes that allow them to drift to earth.

Operating out of the Municipal Airport in Pittsfield, Vacationland Skydiving offers first-time students training and tandem skydiving where they are securely fastened to a professional United States Parachute Association (USPA) licensed skydiving instructor. Off in the airplane for a quick 20-minute ride up to 10,500 feet above the beautiful Central Maine region, the student then experiences free-fall, soaring for 45 seconds through the clear blue skies, and then a calm and tranquil scenic canopy ride safely back to the drop zone – landing in front of friends and family.

The skydiving season lasts from May to October and with over 2000 jumps per season, Pittsfield residents vicariously can enjoy this beautiful sport.

Sibley Pond

Gary Fitts

On the western boundary of Pittsfield lies a body of water that has provided recreation, solitude, and a soul-nourishing natural setting for its inhabitants and visitors for over 150 years. Known today as Sibley Pond, this 380-acre, spring-fed jewel is divided down its middle between Pittsfield and Canaan. It

currently boasts 106 "camps" and year-round homes, most of which belong to local families who have been connected with the Pond for generations. Many have also been vacation havens for folks "from away." The Pittsfield side of Sibley Pond, its Eastern Shore, is blessed with a natural shoreline that is ideal for family recreation. With its shale covered rock bottom, gradually deepening water, and general lack of weeds, young and old alike have enjoyed swimming in its clean water and have reveled in the almost nightly displays of spectacular sunsets. I'm not unbiased in my observations. I'll admit to that readily. My family has been a fixture on Sibley since my Grandfather, Lewis R. Fitts purchased a camp on the Pittsfield shore in 1938. The camp was built in 1911 by a professor from Bowdoin College. The fifth generation of Fittses is now enjoying being on the Pond. Ours is only one of the many families who have seen multiple generations grow up appreciating this place. The Greeleys, Scotts, Quints, Graffs, Nelsons and others have been friends and neighbors spanning the 107 years our camp has been there.

Many of those in my generation, Baby Boomers, grew up spending our entire summers filling our days with outdoor adventures shared with our summer buddies. There were hours and hours of swimming and playing in the water while our Moms kept a somewhat relaxed watch from the beach. Underwater breath-holding contests, cannonball splashes from the docks and floats, collecting freshwater clams from the bottom (note: always return them to the water quickly, and NEVER leave a pail full under the porch overnight!), and endless rock skipping contests were daily activities. When the "dog days" of August brought extra heat and humidity, it was no problem to find some buddies to join in a walk down the camp road

to visit the little country store on the corner on Route 2. Popsicles never tasted better, and a

plunge into the pond would take care of the inevitable sticky, bare bellies.

As we got a bit older, much time was spent on top of the water in our various watercraft. My first boat was an ark of a wooden rowboat, courtesy of my maternal grandfather, Abel Webb. She was a heavy beast, and she required several days of soaking to swell the boards of her hull together to staunch the freshwater flow, but she was mine. With a boat, we could travel the Pond on our own. What a sensation of freedom! Four boys (me, my brother, and two cousins), fishing poles, a can of freshly dug worms, a batch of PB&J sandwiches, and we were set for the whole day. Don't drown, don't hook your little brother, and be home in time for supper were the only rules I remember. Summers on the Pond were the best! Winter days spent on Sibley Pond were also a pretty good time. Skating on a cleared-off patch in front of the camp was such fun, and cries of "flag up!" would echo around the pond on most winter weekends. We loved watching the trucks and Jeeps driving across the ice to favorite fishing spots in the days before snowmobiles became the vehicles of choice. Bonfires to warm up chilled toes and thermos bottles of hot chocolate were a standard treat out on the ice.

There were a few lessons to be learned in those years on the Pond. Some were more pleasant than others. Certainly, many of the skills relating to water sports were fun to acquire…learning to ride the aquaplane and water skis, learning to handle an outboard motor in order to graduate from oars, and catching and cleaning fish for example. Other skills pertaining to land-based activities were also fun…target shooting with BB guns, building tree forts in the woods, whittling with our jack knives, all good stuff. On the darker side of lessons learned; we discovered the pitfalls of playing in poison ivy, the retaliatory fury of a hornet swarm whose nest was shredded by thrown rocks, and the unpleasantness of shooting one's younger brother between the eyes with one's BB gun…while playing "Army" in the woods. We also learned to build toboggan runs that didn't cause you to go airborne before hitting the ice.

Whether it was idyllic summer days filled with swimming, boating, fishing and playing in the woods, or crisp, clear winter days of skating, tobogganing, and ice fishing … it would be difficult to find a better place to have spent one's childhood than the shores of Sibley Pond.

Suited Up

Firefighters Photo – Date, Photographer unknown

Current Gear Photo by Jane Woodruff

Fire. Police. Ambulance. These are a few of the essential services that townspeople have come to rely on for their well-being. Services like the post office and the airport have become indispensable. All of these providers promote and maintain the welfare of the community.

Pittsfield Fire Department
Bernard Williams and Jane Woodruff

It has been thought that the Pittsfield Fire Department originated in 1894, the same year that water lines and hydrants were laid out on both sides of the Sebasticook River joining at what is now Dysart's; however, it is likely that it actually might predate this time. Firefighting must have occurred as early as 1881 or before though the so-called "great fire" unfortunately took many of the buildings on the west side of Main Street as well as some on Park. Over the years, a number of buildings on Main Street burned including the famed Lancey House as have other structures throughout town though not without great effort by the fire department to save them.

Assistant Chief Reginald Haynes Fireman's Coat & Super Chieftan Safe-T-Helmet Displayed at the Historical Society's Museum

The first identified fire chief or chief engineer as he was called was David M. Parks known for his strength and popularity having been voted in as chief in around 1900. At that time, there were three "companies" with No. 1 being located at would be later known as the Shoddy Mill, No. 2 at the Pioneer Mill, and No. 3 at the Waverly Mill. A company would be comprised of 10 firefighters, a captain and lieutenant. These companies were organized for the protection of the mill and later became the town's department. The mills erected water towers to supply the sprinkler systems within the structures and if needed, flooded a given floor. Originally a driven pump filled these towers and at least the Waverly Mill was later converted to an electric pump. The Pioneer Mill was erected in 1864, the Maple Grove (Shoddy Mill) in 1884, and Waverly Mill in 1892.

Many may recall the box code in the 1950s when the air driven whistle at the town hall (Union Hall) would blast out a sequence of numbers which one could look on a chart to identify the fire's location. School children as late as the 1980s would listen hopefully for six blasts of the whistle to indicate "no school" as it did on April 1st in 1987 alerting townspeople of what was to be the "flood of the century." Over the years, people would start to follow scanners to learn of fire locations. Today's firefighters receive alerts on their cell phones and have pagers with each town having its own specific tone.

While the equipment and requirements have changed over the years, what has not is the relief seen when the flashing, red fire trucks rush to the scenes of accidents and fires - be it one or several of the engines or the rescue truck with its extrication equipment. The now antique 1936 Seagrave City Ladder, as it was known because of its 45-foot ladder (also known as a Bangor ladder) rests in the fire station available for show. The Bangor ladder was actually designed in Bangor. A ladder builder watched longer wooden ladders collapse at their joints. He added the poles to the ladders close to the joints to stabilize them. These proved fairly popular for many years with New York City Fire Department owning at least 200.

As with all things, firefighting has evolved with new technologies and equipment. Fire engines have been developed to incorporate safety standards in all vehicles and have some that are available only on a fire apparatus. Gone are the rubber coats and long boots. The newest turnouts are made from Nomex (a fire-retardant material) with removal liners that consist of an insulating layer, a vapor barrier, and a face cloth layer that assists in donning by being somewhat slippery. Boots now have steel shanks for puncture resistance, insulation for heat protection, and either a steel or hard covered toe. Nearly all helmets are made from some type of plastic although leather helmets are still available, but at a significant price difference. Helmets have suspension system face shields and thermal protection for the ears. Gloves are from several kinds of leather with a thermal barrier and a moisture barrier.

Training used to consist of being elected to the department and receiving a coat and boots (that might or might not fit), an aluminum helmet, and a pair of plastic coated gloves. The first time the whistle sounded you responded and got on the side or tailboard of a vehicle to ride to the scene. Upon arrival, you did whatever was requested including taking the nozzle into the building if you were on the first apparatus. Training was by doing with little, if any, structured training on basics. Today, an applicant has to have a doctor's statement that he or she is physically able to perform the duties of a firefighter and a Pulmonary Function Test to ensure that he or she can wear a self-contained breathing apparatus (SCBA). Prior to being allowed to enter a building fire, there is an 80-hour course (which takes closer to a 100 hours) that must be taken and passed. There is training on specific department procedures, many which must be redone yearly. Hazardous material incidents require specific training depending at which of the levels you respond at. Everyone must have at least the Awareness Level, which is basically a "not to do" level except call for help. Nearly everyone is at the next level, the Operations one which allows for some emergency rescues and allows members to decontaminate

Testing of "Dry Hydrant" Located at the Mill Pond

patients that have been subjected to the hazardous material. The Technician Level allows for entry and actual stopping of leaks in valves or vessels. Confined Space Training is required if someone is trapped in a space which is designated as such. Our Water and Sewer Department has several of these spaces and therefore requires us to maintain this training. The push from all levels above us is to have all members at a nationally recognized certification of Firefighter 1 and 11. This training requires in excess of 300 hours of training and testing. The classes are such that if a person misses a class it is extremely hard to make up.

Today's department has a roster for a Chief, Deputy Chief, four Captains (Health and Safety Officer, Training Officer, Maintenance Officer, and a Chaplain), four Lieutenants, 20 Firefighters, 5 Public Safety Traffic Flaggers (Fire Police), and 5 Juniors. It would be great to say that we have members to fill the slots but, as with many departments, we are needing help.

As of today, the department apparatus consists of a 1986 Ford/ Pierce 1000 gallon a minute pumper (GPM) with a 1000 gallon tank; a 2003 Pierce Dash with a 1500 GPM pump, a foam system, and a 1000 gallon tank; a 2018 Pierce Enforcer with a 1500 GPM pump, foam system, and a 1000 gallon tank; and a 2007 Ford with a 350 GPM pump and a 350 gallon tank. This apparatus also carries our extrication tools (cutters, spreaders and rams) and the system to operate them.

Pittsfield Police Department

Tim Roussin with Jane Woodruff

Employing a night watchman and police, when necessary, is noted in the *Pittsfield 1904 Town Register.* When the police became a full-time department of the town is not known. Today, there are 6 full-time officers with an additional 6 budgeted reserve officers to provide 24/7 law enforcement coverage for the town.

"To protect and serve", the motto for the Pittsfield Police Department, simply states their duties but does not reflect the diversity of their responsibilities. Charged with providing safety to community members, this has become increasingly complex over the years. In the past, this often meant "stopping" people for traffic violations and dealing primarily with "locals." With the ever-changing and growing population, the drugs freely flowing into the area via the interstate, and increased and wider criminal activity, your police department has had to change its enforcement methods to fit the times.

Today's police force interacts with a variety of agencies as they may do record checks for the Department of Health and Human Services or criminal ones for the Federal Government or mandated reporting to Child Protective Services. A complaint may be radioed from the Somerset Communication Center to an officer who then can access more information on the laptop in his cruiser before addressing the situation. In the case of domestic disputes, two officers are sent. Besides local streets, they patrol routes 2 and 100 and are called at times by the State Police to assist them in accident scenes on the interstate. In addition to law enforcement, they help townspeople who are locked out of their homes or provide safety education in the schools.

For emergencies call 911. For non-emergency situations, people should use the number 487-3101.

Sebasticook Valley Hospital

Bre Graffam

Aerial of SVH Taken in the Early 1960s

"It is a symbol of dedicated citizenry not built without sacrifice and without effort on the part of many; it will do much to alleviate suffering and pain, and all concerned should be truly proud" said Governor John Reed at the grand opening. Sebasticook Valley Hospital (SVH) opened its doors during the winter of 1963 in Pittsfield. Planning began several years earlier as a grassroots effort to bring a hospital to the region. Local service organizations, physicians, businesses, and individuals all worked together to raise funds and develop plans for the facility that would be built on land that Mr. and Mrs. Luther Leighton donated.

While the hospital was state-of-the-art in the early 1960s, over the years, advancements in healthcare drove the need for change so that these developments could be brought to the region. New equipment was purchased and eventually a need for a major construction project became evident. A Capital Campaign was put into place and plans began in the late 1980s culminating in a $4.5 million construction and renovation project which was completed in 1993.

As the practice of medicine and healthcare continued to evolve, additional services were brought to SVH such as specialty services, surgical procedures and home health. In 2000, with the help of a cohesive community, a helipad was built allowing for patient transport by LifeFlight of Maine. In emergency situations, every second counts. The helicopter can transport a patient to a tertiary hospital such as Eastern Maine Medical Center in approximately twelve minutes. To drive this distance, it could take greater than thirty minutes. Also in 2000, SVH found it once again needed to expand to meet the demand for services in evolving medicine. The Outpatient and Women's Health Center resulted from a feasibility study with community input which drove the design for the $1.2 million expansion. This design features a private entrance and waiting area for the Women's Center. This area is geared to services for women that include digital mammography services, lymphedema therapy, ultrasound, and bone density services. Today we proudly serve our communities with quality healthcare, specialty services, surgical procedures and state-of-the-art testing. In 2018, after a very successful capital campaign, SVH purchased a 3D mammography unit. Each year, SVH raises funds through its various hospital and community events to infuse money into the Nancy Stone Fund which provides breast cancer screenings and services to women who are underinsured or uninsured for these life-saving efforts.

In the early part of this century, SVH formalized its relationship with Eastern Maine Healthcare Systems (EMHS) by becoming a full member. SVH continues to maintain its all-volunteer, community represented board of trustees. SVH works collaboratively with EMHS and entities within the system to provide the highest level of care with efficiency, professionalism, and compassion. SVH is grateful to have the strong backing of a System. The system continued to grow and now serves much more than just the eastern part of the state which means EMHS was no longer an invigorating name for the system. In October 2018, EMHS proudly became Northern Light Health.

Over the years, changes in treatment options occurred – including an increased emphasis on outpatient care through same day surgery. This added additional surgical procedures and reduced the number of post-surgical inpatient stays. With new advances in techniques and laparoscopic surgeries, operations that previously required a lengthy stay and intense post-discharge recover periods are now preformed routinely on an outpatient basis. For instance, in the 1960s a cataract operation required a patient to be immobilized for up to a week and today, the surgery can be performed as a "no-stitch" procedure in the morning with the patient discharged home within just a few hours and back to everyday activities within a few days.

SVH is committed to providing primary care services as well as specialty services. Primary care offices are located in Clinton, Newport, and Pittsfield. These offices offer same-day care with open lab services, diabetes and nutrition counseling and specialty services.

SVH Family Care Staff Readying for the Annual SVH Breast Cancer Awareness Walk

SVH has a very robust community health division that works closely with Healthy SV and has secured several million dollars in grant funds over the last decade. Some of which includes federal tobacco settlement grant funding distributed through the state Bureau of Health to implement programs that help prevent tobacco usage, increase physical activity and improve nutritional habits. Other grants have helped establish dental health services, substance abuse prevention among youth, community wellness programs and food insecurity.

A number of areas have experienced growth which required an expansion of the SVH peri-operative or surgical areas. With over a dozen surgeons providing services, the hospital added a second operating room, an endoscopy area, and seven recovery areas to accommodate patient volume.

In 2012, the Campaign to Modernize SVH began and updated various areas throughout the hospital during an 18-month period, beginning with the upgrade of the hospital parking and walking areas, the inpatient wing expansion, and much needed upgrades to the hospital's heating and cooling systems. Eventually, the modernization efforts encompassed changes in various patient areas throughout the hospital. In July of 2013 the new inpatient wing opened to patients. The expanded inpatient care area offers large patient rooms with private bathrooms for each patient, fifteen private rooms, and five semi-private "super suites."

One thing that hasn't changed is that SVH is committed to providing quality, affordable healthcare to its patients. The staff all work together to make this possible and their efforts do not go unnoticed. SVH proudly accepts awards and recognition for this outstanding work. To name a few:

- Top Performer on Key Quality Measures by the Joint Commission on the Accreditation of Hospitals
- Most Wired by the Hospitals and Health Networks
- Designation by the Health Information Management Society as a Stage 6 Hospital
- One of the top ten critical access hospitals in the United States for clinical excellence by the VHA
- Workplace Wellness Excellence – Platinum – by Well Workplaces of America
- All three SVH Family Care offices received the highest-level certification as a Patient Centered Medical Home from the National Committee for Quality Assurance
- Recognition as one of the best rural healthcare hospitals in the United States by The Leapfrog Group
- Best Places to Work in Maine, 2015, 2016, 2017

Over the years, SVH has been recognized many times for excellence by AVATAR International, an industry leader in healthcare quality improvement services:

- 2002-2014: Exceeding Patient Expectations
    o Best Overall Performer
    o Most Improved: physician offices
    o Best Inpatient Meals

Throughout the years, the success of SVH, a small critical access hospital, has been attributed to the support of its communities, stewardship of its volunteer board of trustees, an active Auxiliary, and very dedicated leadership, staff, and volunteers. With its vision to be the healthcare leader in our communities, SVH is poised to continue providing quality patient care for many years to come.

Hometown Health Center

Carolyn Higgins-Taylor

Sebasticook Family Doctors, known as Hometown Health Center since August 2016, began serving patients in Pittsfield on October 1, 2008. Hometown is a Federally Qualified Health Center (FQHC) with a mission to provide compassionate, comprehensive, affordable and accessible health care to people of all ages, regardless of economic status.

Dr. Flanigan, who was practicing in Pittsfield at the time, wanted to join the FQHC and make the transition from private practice. It fit Hometown's mission to continue to serve the patient population and to bring services close to home for the patients in the area. Over the years, Hometown has seen an estimated 3,500 people.

Hometown is a safety net for the community, serving patients who may otherwise not be able to afford medical care. It provides a vast array of services at its four locations, including medical, dental, behavioral health, lab services, a sliding-fee scale, medication assisted treatment for opioid dependence, prescription assistance so patients can get medications at a much-reduced cost, care management, and certified application counselors to assist with the Health Insurance Marketplace. Hometown also offers the Kibble Club so patients who are struggling to feed their pets can get supplemental pet food and supplies. There is also a community garden, managed by staff and volunteers, that in the 2017 season, grew and harvested 2,500 pounds of produce for the community to help increase the nutritional value of their diets.

Hometown also participates in unique events for the betterment of the community. Give Kids a Smile Day provides free dental care to children who do not have insurance. Every August, for National Health Center Week, Hometown holds weeklong activities at all locations. And there are free public suppers during the year.

Hometown Health Center has received the designation as a Patient Centered Medical Home (PCMH) from the National Committee for Quality Assurance, which is a private, not-for-profit organization dedicated to improving health care quality. As a PCMH, Hometown uses a team approach to a patient's care based on their physical, mental and behavioral health care needs. In other words, Hometown cares for the whole person, not just the physical side of someone. The providers take the time to understand a patient's individual needs, values, and living preference.

Hometown has a strong presence in Pittsfield and a commitment to serving the community, including, providing dental hygiene services at MSAD53 and the school-located vaccine program at MCI. Pittsfield is a very community-oriented town, a standard that is embraced by Hometown, which gets involved in activities throughout the year, including the Egg Festival, HealthySV coalition, the summer concerts and anywhere else it can provide support.

It is important community members know that Hometown Health Center is always ready and eager to help them and support them by reducing barriers to medical care and assisting them with navigating the maze of health care. Hometown is not just a medical practice, but a neighbor and friend.

Skills, Inc.
Emma Gallimore

Families Band Together to Support Loved Ones with Intellectual Disabilities

In the 1950's there were very few options for people with intellectual and other developmental disabilities. There were no day programs, no programs offering job training skills and many people lived in institutions.Families wanting to keep their loved ones out of institutions were on their own.

And so, all over Maine, groups of families banded together to create a framework of support for their loved ones, especially their younger children. One such group founded The Sebasticook Association for Retarded Children, which became the governing body of the Marie Bradford School on Hartland Avenue in Pittsfield. Over the years, the children grew older. Public schools started introducing special education classes. The now-redundant, Marie Bradford School, closed and parents reorganized to form Sebasticook Farms, a support program for their children, now adults.

Creating Employment Opportunities
The group purchased Lawrence Acres in Saint Albans. They turned the big farmhouse into a home where people could live, work and be a part of the local community. The need was great and they quickly expanded their network.

In the early 1990's Square Road Workshop in Athens moved to old Ford Garage in Pittsfield, near Manson Park. Throughout the 90's this program provided work opportunities. Participants picked and packed literature and products for EST, they cleaned the offices of Cianbro, stained wood handles for tools sold by Johnny's Selected Seeds, and assembled candle wicks, packed bulk floats and lucid kits, and replaced gaskets on spigots for C.M. Almy.

Evolving to Survive

By the early 2000's, the board at Sebasticook Farms brokered a merger with Ken-a-Set, which shared similar values and a familiar origin story. It formed in 1971 when the Upper Somerset Association for Retarded Children merged with the Greater Waterville Association for Retarded children. Almost 30 years later, on July 1, 2005, Ken-a-Set and Sebasticook Farms became SKILLS, Inc.

The word SKILLS was an acronym for "Somerset, Kennebec, Individualized, Living and Learning Supports" but it was also a one-word mission statement. The goal of the newly minted SKILLS was to support adults with developmental disabilities to build the personal, social, and job skills they needed to thrive in the world.

Over the years, Pittsfield Community Supports expanded opportunities for people with intellectual disabilities to include community support services along with employment opportunities. They moved out of the Ford Garage and into the old Berry's Pharmacy on Main Street, then to a warehouse facility owned by EST, to the basement of the First Universalist Church basement and then finally to their current location at 460 Hartland Avenue where the restaurant "Wrights Emporium" used to be.

After a fire at that site, Cianbro helped with the teardown and disposal of the building. We rebuilt Pittsfield Community Supports where we continue to support members of the Pittsfield community.

Today, SKILLS encompasses 16 residential homes, four center-based community support programs, an electronic waste recycling facility in Waterville, and a thrift store in Skowhegan which are all spread throughout Somerset, Kennebec and Penobscot counties.

Pittsfield Municipal Airport

Caleb Curtis

From horses to airplanes. Many do not know that the site of today's Pittsfield Municipal Airport previously was the home to harness racing. In 1893, Colonel Walter G. Morrill of Civil War fame and Medal of Honor winner purchased the Pittsfield Driving Park, improving it and installing the road that is now called Harrison Street. Renamed Union Trotting Park, he hosted harness races, one of which featured women drivers, a first in Maine. A few years later in 1898, balloon "ascensions" were held there.

As harness racing declined and with it the Union Trotting Park, the land changed from a racetrack to a runway - several in fact. J.R. Cianchette and the Kiwanis Club were instrumental in convincing the town to seek a Federal grant to upgrade what had become a landing field. In 1942 with the substantial financial assistance of the Federal Government, 4000 feet of runways were built and a year later a training program for Navy cadets was instituted. Cadets stayed on MCI's campus and stories have it that instructor Rosswell Furman taught cadets bomb drops with bags of flour. The runways were ultimately given to the town but remained under Federal control.

In 1979, an 1800-foot seaplane taxiway south of one of the runways was constructed. In 1985, the shorter runway was discontinued. About 15 years ago, the airport benefited from a significant Federal Capital Improvement program with the town only having to match at a 2.5% level. The runway was dug to a depth of 4', good fill spread, and high-quality sealant applied to the new pavement. A few years later, the main ramp and tie-downs were improved. Given the 35 to 40 miles per hour crosswinds, these tie-downs afford security for the nearly two dozen airplanes that are kept outdoors at the airport. Including those housed in the hangers, there are forty planes, one helicopter and seven twin engine planes that are based in Pittsfield.

Caleb Curtis, Dustin Costigan, Jon Gould, Dan Delano, Ed Porter, Fred Delano

Today Curtis Air and the Town work together to oversee the airport operations. Caleb Curtis, who has been working there since the mid-'90s, provides a variety of functions in his role as fixed base operator. He partners with other companies for plane rentals, posts notices on weather conditions, sells fuel, rents the hangers, does plane maintenance and repairs as well as annually inspects planes which take anywhere from 6 to 40 hours.

Curtis Air also provides fuel, a lounge, phone and accessible restrooms for pilots and passengers, charter flights, as well as repair and maintenance services for planes. Central Maine Aviation, run by Charlie Surprenant, operates the aircraft rental and flight instruction business out of the airport. On average, he has about ten students learning to fly.

Every year during Saturday of the Egg Festival, local pilots team together to donate their time and their airplanes to give free young eagle rides to children. This is Maine's largest Young Eagle event with about 100 youth being given a ride every year.

The future is bright for the Pittsfield Municipal Airport. New hangars will be built soon to store more planes. Stop down at our town's airport and find out what makes it so special. It truly is one of Maine's most active small airports.

Pittsfield's Post Office

04967

Glen Wellman on His Delivery Rounds

"Neither snow nor rain nor heat nor gloom of night stays these couriers from the swift completion of their appointed rounds." Popularly believed to be the motto for the Postal Service, it is actually a quote from *The Persian Wars* by Herodotus, but it might well describe one of Pittsfield's early postal workers - Etta May Nelson. For 3 years, she never missed a day delivering mail by wagon or sleigh along her 17-mile route in the early 1900s.

Pittsfield actually had two post offices in the early 1800s - one in West Pittsfield and one in East Pittsfield. Down to one post office by the late 1880s, this business would change locations multiple times along Main Street until its current location on Central Street where it has been since early 1966. Delivering mail 6 days a week, carriers brave the weather to bring those letters and packages to residents' homes unless, of course, one rents a postal box giving one the excuse to meet and greet neighbors at the post office. There was one special Christmas when Postmaster Judy Mann decked out with a Santa's hat did those late deliveries surprising many of her customers.

On June 19, 2019, the Pittsfield Post Office will be using a specially designed postal seal for that day only to designate and celebrate the 200th birthday of the town's incorporation.

Pittsfield's Cemeteries

Peter Snow with Jane Woodruff

Carr - Wilson - Weymouth - who knew there were so many cemeteries in Pittsfield?

Everyone could probably name the Village Cemetery on Peltoma Avenue and maybe even the one on Route 2, but these other three, most people would be hard put to locate them or even know they existed. Another relatively unknown fact is that even the Village Cemetery didn't start there. According to Sanger Cook's *Pittsfield on the Sebasticook*, the original burying ground was at Hathorn Park, later changed to east and south of what is now the Unitarian-Universalist Meeting House and finally re-located once again to its current site when gravel was needed for the construction of the railroad in 1854.

Carr Cemetery, located on Route 100, has a number of unmarked graves with numerous headstones unfortunately lost. Each spring, slates lift out of the ground and from the way they are lined up, it is surmised that they identify gravesites as slates were used in the past when folks couldn't afford gravestones. The two oldest gravestones, similar in shape to those seen in Arlington, are for two Revolutionary War soldiers.

Powers Cemetery on Route 2 is thought to have been a dump at one time as a car top and other debris have been found when staff have been digging gravesites. This cemetery is the location of the grave of Llewellyn Powers, former Maine Governor (1896 - 1900). Also found here is the private tomb of the Higgins family, one of Pittsfield's oldest families.

Wilson Cemetery, located just off Route 2, has 15 unmarked graves. This small cemetery was desecrated in the 1940s when unknown vandals plowed it over to use it for grazing sheep. The bottoms of stones are still being found.

Weymouth Cemetery has only 12 gravesites of which one is for then 22-year-old John, a Civil War veteran, for whom a memorial stone is being sought. This small cemetery is located off route 100 near the Burnham town line.

Sexton Pete Snow by the marker of Pfc Burns Knowlton for whom the American Legion Post is

Village Cemetery, in the area known as the old section, is adjacent to the river. Here lie many of Pittsfield's early leaders and many of its Civil War veterans. Stones read like pages from a history book on Pittsfield with names such as Martin, Manson, Lancey, Haskell, Hathorn to name just a few. Across the street is the 1904 tomb which surprisingly has a fireplace and chimney. Today, it is used for equipment storage while its grassy exterior is home to groundhogs and foxes. Deer also frequent the cemetery where nearly 700 are interred. In the spring, local cub scouts put out over 440 flags in their holders on the graves of veterans here and remove them in the fall.

All of these cemeteries are lovingly cared for by sexton Peter Snow and his staff.

HER INFRASTRUCTURE

Lagoons

Photograph by Jane Woodruff

From Yourdictionary.com we learn the definition of infrastructure is "the basic facilities and installations that help a government or community run, including roads, schools, phone lines, sewage treatment plants and power generation." Often taken for granted until things don't work, these departments are basic to our town and how it runs.

Pittsfield Public Works Department

Steve Vance with Jane Woodruff

The year was 1819 and at the town's first meeting on July 19th, $1000 was raised for highways. In today's dollars that would be equivalent to nearly $19,000. At that time, the town voted to pay 17 cents per hour, be it oxen or men to work on the highways. Horse-drawn wagons with water were used for dust control on Main Street. Fast forward to the 1950s and by this time, the town had a highway department. Oil was spread on country roads for dust control and torches that looked like cartoon bombs lit construction sites.

Steve Vance & Dave Connors Install
Fence Donated by Walpole Outdoors

Today's "highway" department now named the public works department is responsible for not only roads and streets, but parks, town buildings, and street lights. Many of the numerous tasks vary with the season as this four-person department literally takes to the streets. Come spring, they must repair damage to roads caused by plows and frost. Crews can be seen patching potholes or running the street sweeper to take up the sand left after snow and ice storms. Or they might have to be repairing culverts and filling sinkholes. Equipment that has been "mothballed" over the winter has to be serviced readying tractors and mowers for summer work.

Summer brings its own needs as the crew readies the town pool for opening or takes to all of the parks except Manson for mowing and trimming. What roadside brushwork that didn't get completed in spring is worked in as time can be made available. Dirt roads are re-worked to be crowned for water drainage or gravel added when worn down to the base. This work continues into fall with the additional task of needing to put up sand for winter. While the roads are snowplowed by private contractors, this department is responsible for sidewalk plowing, sanding, and snow removal.

Interspersed throughout the year, any maintenance needed on town buildings such as the municipal one, the library, the theatre or the bathhouse is done by the town crew. Shelves needed, lights changed on Main Street, damaged trees removed ... these are just a few of the duties added to their work list. The diversity of jobs and skills needed to work in this department are impressive and hopefully well appreciated by its townspeople.

Pittsfield Water Department

Scott Noble with Jane Woodruff

Scott Noble Listens for Water Flow at Shut Off Valve

The bicentennial marks another birthday. It is 125 years since the Pittsfield Water Department laid its first pipes with water being delivered through them for the first time on November 30, 1894. Originally, a group of businessmen proposed to have a water system installed, but the town voted to take over the charter to have it as a municipally owned system. Six and one half miles of pipe were laid that first year compared to now nearly 30 miles of pipe. They also installed sixty-two hydrants compared to today's one hundred fifty-eight hydrants, some of which are those original ones. Additionally, they put in 2 drinking fountains and 2 watering troughs, one of which now serves as a planter in Stein Park. The standpipe atop the Pinnacle served as the water tower for the town for nearly 100 years until its demise in the late 1980's. It finally was cut in sections with a torch as it resisted efforts to be toppled by snapping cables meant to pull it down.

Over the years, the wells changed from one location to another moving from near what is the site of the

town garage on Waverly to Peltoma near Cianbro's equipment yard to its current site just over the town line in Burnham. Today's wells are 8" in diameter by 35 feet in depth and 12" by 42 feet. Department head Scott Noble describes these wells as having a "magnificent recharge." Served by two water towers - one on Grove Hill and one on Phillips Corner - the town with this gravity-fed system affords sixty-pound pressure to its citizens that use somewhere between 300 to 400,000 gallons per day. The water is tested daily for chlorine, fluorides and phosphate residuals. Monthly, it is tested with samples sent to the state for fluorides, chlorine and e-coli. Annual tests are done as well for other contaminants determined by the state.

Actually, the department is considered two departments: water and sewer. To handle the town's sewage two lagoons nearly 35 acres each were built in 1975. Designed by local resident and engineer William Ball, these lagoons are the largest municipally-owned lagoons in the state. By design, the settling time is estimated to be 180 days. This all-natural system is unique as it has no mechanized parts or chemicals used. It did not have its first dredge until 2009. With the water pressed out, 1200 dry tons of waste were shipped to the Old Town landfill - one-third of what had been expected to be removed.

Pittsfield is fortunate to have Scott Noble and Chris Pelletier in this department as both are experienced dowsers. Scott described their being able to locate water sources with about 90% accuracy. This is an especially needed skill as the department was without written plans of the water system which they have been developing.

Pittsfield Transfer Station

Don Chute with Jane Woodruff

Don Chute Oversees Transfer Station Operations

Burn and dump. That was how waste was dealt with in the past. In 1954, landfills came into use where it was then burn and bury. The burn came from the combustion of decomposing organic materials and the bury was what occurred with the rest of the waste. This was a time remembered by some where a trip to the "dump" might be more than just leaving one's garbage, but a time to "pick" for treasures or shoot rats.

Faye Cummings and Deanna Tilton along with other volunteers run the Reuse

In 1984, things changed radically as this "landfill" was closed and it became a transfer station. By 1986, recycling began. Wood was segregated from demotion debris and garbage and the first baler was purchased for recycling cardboard. For 5 years garbage was "transferred" or rather trucked to White Mountain Transfer Station in NH. A second baler was purchased in 1988 and with the buying of two more balers 4 years later, newspaper, white paper, and plastic were added to the recyclables.

David Lessard and Jim Handley at the paper baler while Dave Whitman works the plastic baler.

Buildings were added and by 1999 electronics began being recycled as Pittsfield's transfer station became a multi-sort recycling facility. For 10 years Pittsfield's garbage was sent to Penobscot Energy

Recovery Company (PERC), followed by 5 years of being transferred to the Norridgewock Landfill, then for 7 years again to PERC and now back to Norridgewock.

Besides being paid for the recovered recycled materials is the saving on "tipping fees"; that is, the avoided costs of not having those items sent to the landfill. As an example, for the ton of recycled cardboard to be paid $110 and avoid a $65 tipping fee means an actual saving of $175. Another source for saving disposal costs is the opening of the Trash to Treasure Reuse Center or what is known as the "free store." Rather than toss items, townspeople are encouraged to donate them to the Reuse Center where others may pick them up on Saturdays for free. Volunteers staff the center on Saturdays from April through October where they weigh selected items to determine poundage rescued from being thrown in a landfill.

Waverly Avenue & Pioneer Hydro

Christopher M. Anthony with Jane Woodruff

For many years, Chris Anthony worked as a general contractor for both residential and commercial customers with his former company Anthony Construction Inc. Doing a variety of jobs, he put in foundations, did bridge repairs, and renovated the first floor of the former Grammar School to name a few.

Hydro Station at Pioneer Dam

In the early 1980s, he built his first hydro power station at the Waverly Dam. Securing a lease from the town, he started generating three-phase alternating current which under optimal conditions can produce 400 kilowatts/hour. At this same site nearly one hundred years ago, Pittsfield Electric Light & Power Company supplied town-owned electricity. In contrast, Chris's station generates power which is fed to the Independent System Operator - New England. ISO is a Federal government corporation and a clearinghouse which then sells this power to large scale businesses.

In the late 1980s, Chris then built a second power station at the Pioneer Dam. This hydro station can generate up to 220 kilowatts/hour. As might be expected, the optimal conditions for power generation are in springtime. Chris inspects his hydro stations daily checking for any leaks, mechanical or electrical problems as well as sighting the dams. Daily readings are taken. As Chris says, "It is the most interesting job I've ever had". He has no plans for retirement.

Town Government

Kathryn Ruth

On January 22, 1970, Pittsfield voters decided to change to the Town Council form of government. This

would mean that a number of steps would need to take place. During the Board of Selectmen meeting on April 18, 1970, Selectman George Newhouse made the motion which was seconded by Paul Susi, Jr. to plan a Special Town Meeting to change the Town Charter to allow representatives of districts to be elected from the district and not at large. The first Town Council Meeting was held on January 14, 1971. Many actions were taken shortly thereafter as the new government was organized. For example, at the February 3, 1971, Council Meeting, the following orders were made: (1) a Finance Committee of three to be elected from the council membership; (2) an Ordinance Committee of three be elected; (3) all warrants for the disbursement of monies for the town to be signed by the Mayor or Chairman of the Finance Committee; and (4) the Mayor and Chairman of the Finance Committee were authorized to execute all necessary legal documents for the Town Council. On February 11, 1971, the Town Council's first Town Budget hearing was set for February 25, 1971. Many of these same types of actions take place today on a year basis many decades later.

Union Hall – Site of Town Meetings and Town Business

Today's "Town Hall" or Municipal Building & the Fire Department

Note that what remains of Union Hall is basically from the granite line down.

Business Establishments in Town

Type	No.	Type	No.
Agricultural Impl.	1	Hotels	1
Imports	1	Ice Dealers	1
Airport Construction	1	Insurance Agents	7
Automobiles Access.	2	Jewelers	2
Auto Repair and		Junk Dealers	2
Service Stations	9	Laundries	2
Banks	1	Lawyers	6
Barbers	4	Libraries	1
Beauty Shops	8	Light and Power	1
Blacksmiths	1	Livestock	4
Bridge Construction	1	Lumber	1
Building materials	2	Lumber Mfrs	1
Canners	1	Meats	1
Cemeteries	4	Milliners	1
Chemicals	2	Newspapers	1
Churches	5	Oils and Lubricants	3
Cleaners and Dyers	2	Optometrists	1
Clothing Dealers	4	Osteopathic Physicians	1
Coal Dealers	4	Painters and Decorators	4
Confectionary and		Paper Dealers	1
Ice Cream	8	Photographers	2
Contractors	3	Physicians	4
Carpenters	7	Plumbers	4
Excavating	1	Plumbing Supplies	1
Masons	1	Printers	1
Road	5	Pulpwood Dealers	2
Daries	4	Radio Equipment & Serv.	1
Dentists	2	Real Estate	6
Department Stores	2	Restaurants and lunch	
Dining Room	1	rooms	5
Druggists	2	Road Construction	2
Electrical Contract.	1	Schools	5
Express Companies	1	Shoddy Mfrs.	1
Florists	3	Shoe Dealers	2
Fuel Dealers	4	Shoe Mfrs.	2
Funeral Directors	2	Social Agencies	1
Furniture Dealers	2	Stenographers	1
Gas (Bottled)	2	Theaters	1
General Store	1	Tire Dealers and rep.	3
Gift Shop	1	Trucking	1
Grain Dealer and		Undertakers	2
Traders	2	Woolen mfrs.	1
Granite and Marble		Yarn mfrs.	2
Works	1		
Grocers	17		
Hardware Dealers	2		
Hides, Skins	1		

Business Establishments in Town

Maine Studies – 8th Grade

Pittsfield Grammar School

1948

PITTSFIELD at WORK

They came to farm. They started businesses. They harnessed the river. They built a town. Over the years the small family farms gave rise to larger ones with a focus on single products like eggs for which Pittsfield became famous. Today Pittsfield has several large farms but these are committed to dairy. In recent years there has been a renewal in farming as the influx of young people have come to develop small specialty farms.

The industrial part of town remains in what was formerly called East Pittsfield although it has expanded from near the river's edge to include the Industrial Park. Closed are the wool, shoe and electric signal factories of a few years ago as these buildings await new occupants and industries. What has remained are the construction and engineering industries as well as manufacturers of church vestments and wood products.

Gone are the shoe, women's and men's clothing stores as well as many other retail stores of yesterday that lined Main Street in the 1950-60s. With the exception of Renys, retail shifted to the Somerset Plaza as Craig Hardware led the move from Main Street. The railroad had helped prompt the economic development of the town center in its current location in contrast to the previously developing West Pittsfield which was along the stage coach route, now Route 2. Just as the railroad influenced the location of businesses, the opening of Interstate 95 just off Somerset Avenue shifted retail business away from downtown to this area which became known as the Somerset Plaza. Over time even retail businesses in this mall declined as people took to the interstate to reach larger shopping areas in Bangor and Waterville.

Neighborhood grocery stores became a thing of the past with the arrival of larger grocery stores centrally located on Main Street and later the plaza.

The loss of the famed Lancey House that drew people from away for its cuisine and charm was supplanted by the Carriage Inn and Restaurant later known as the Woodbriar Inn on outer Somerset Avenue. Unfortunately, like the Lancey House and many other business establishments, it too was lost to fire. Today travelers have the option of staying at the Pittsfield Motor Inn or at a bed & breakfast: The House Next Door.

Health services, once performed by the local family doctor at the office often attached to the home, now are performed in rural health care centers with fully staffed offices with doctors, nurse practitioners, assistants and clerical staff.

The financial services originally limited to the 1st National Bank have expanded to include several bank branches, a credit union and personal financial consultant service.

Gone is the town's newspaper and scant coverage is now provided by local dailies as they no longer supply reporters to cover local news as in the past. Today many people now rely on social media and a weekly advertising paper.

Let's take a look at those businesses that are here today.

THE MANUFACTURERS

Walpole Outdoors

Thomas Gates

Walpole Outdoors was started in 1933 by a farmer in Walpole Massachusetts that wanted to keep his workers employed during the Depression. From these humble beginnings, the company has continued a steady growth over the last 85 years. In the 1950's, it was decided to get closer to the Cedar lumber in Maine. This brought the company to the Pittsfield area. In the early 2000's, it was decided to move all of the manufacturing operations to Pittsfield. This was done to take advantage of the space available and large labor force. The company now occupies 4 buildings in the Industrial Park along with a facility in Detroit and a sawmill in Chester.

From a company just making wooden fence, Walpole Outdoors has evolved into a company that can take care of beautifying any outdoor space. In addition to the Cedar fencing that has been offered through the years, there are Lantern Posts, Mail Posts, Lattice Panels, Trellis Systems, Railing Systems, Outdoor Showers, Storage Buildings, Pergolas, Outdoor Kitchens, Window Boxes, Planters, Outdoor Furniture, Bird Houses, and Garden Ornaments. All of these items are offered in traditional Cedar and Cellular PVC.

Today Walpole Outdoors has grown into the premier Cellular PVC manufacturer in US and one of the leading Landscape Design companies. Walpole Outdoors employs approximately 100 people in Pittsfield. Walpole's generous donations have enhanced Stein Park with their split-rail fences that border the Mill Pond and the large flower garden and the arbor that offers a place for climbing plants along with the custom lattice panel at the library. Walpole Outdoors is looking forward to many more years of growth and being an active participant in the Pittsfield community.

CM Almy

Michael Fendler

Mildred Bragg, Thelma Lancaster, Jackie Donnelson and Rosalie Shaw Stitching at the "new" Pittsfield facility in 1962

New York City based C. M. Almy & Son, Inc., founded in 1892 and owned by Donald Fendler, purchased Pittsfield's Riverside School on North Main St. in 1959. His son Ryan who had started a small shop at the Fendler farmhouse in Palmyra managed the Pittsfield school building renovation and conversion to a textile cutting and sewing shop for Almy's church and clergy customers. In the late summer of 1959, Ryan moved the manufacturing start-up to the "new" Pittsfield facility which was incorporated as Church Goods Manufacturing Company, and served as its President until his retirement in 1986.

Church Goods Mfg. grew quickly, adding products that Almy had previously subcontracted to local New York City area contractors and volume increased as Almy used increasingly effective direct marketing to acquire new customers. By the mid-1960s, with the space becoming tight and the two-story old schoolhouse hindering operational efficiency, Church Goods contracted with the Cianchette Brothers to build a new modern single-story

building across the river on a lot that had most recently been used as a gravel pit and named its new street Ruth Street in honor of Ryan's mother. It retained the Riverside schoolhouse as a warehouse and shipping facility. Almost as soon as the building was finished the Fendlers realized it was too small and they increased the building size by 30% in 1972.

Almy had gradually acquired other church goods companies in the early 1970s and by the mid-decade

Melissa Mayhew, Sandy Luce, Tracy Gilbert and Diane Gould Busy at Work at the Ruth Street Facility

started to struggle to retain reliable suppliers for its church metalware product line. So, Church Goods expanded again in 1976, adding to its Ruth Street building and converted the old schoolhouse to a metalware manufacturing shop, fabricating church metalware using machining, spinning, polishing and electroplating operations and working with local people to develop new skills in metalworking. Since the new metalware shop would be owned jointly by Donald and his sons Ryan and Thomas, they incorporated this operation as Faithcraft International, which sold its products to CM Almy and to other church supply retailers. By the early 1980s, with the metalware operation proving its value, the companies decided to make a final move from the well-used old schoolhouse and the Ruth Street building was expanded again to add additional warehouse space and a new church metalware fabrication and restoration shop. In addition, in 1982 Ryan and Tom acquired all of their father's stock in the company. By the mid-1980s Ryan and Tom were ready to retire and in early 1986, sold their combined C.M. Almy, Church Goods and Faithcraft companies to Stephen and Michael Fendler who consolidated the companies to the single C.M. Almy name and they continue to function as its President and Vice President today.

Currently, CM Almy has three locations. No longer in New York City, its home office houses its marketing, product management, finance, sales and human resource operations in Armonk, NY. It has a retail showroom in Old Greenwich, CT and its Pittsfield facility serves its manufacturing, warehousing/materials management, and information technology support functions. Since the mid-1980s, Almy has acquired two additional smaller companies in order to sustain its growth and it launched an entirely new candle product line in January 2017.

In Pittsfield, C.M. Almy manufacturing uses a wide variety of textiles, metals and plastics, sourced from suppliers worldwide, to make many different products for churches, clergy and, now, the general public. Its church and clergy products include liturgical vestments and sanctuary appointments, choir robes, clergy apparel and church supplies. Although liquid fuel candles have been part of its product line since the early 1990s, Almy recently made a strategic decision to expand beyond its traditional customer base to develop a new line of candles that it markets to the general public under the brand Lucid Liquid Candle Works. Almy sells products through its almy .com and lucidcandle .com websites and markets through the use of catalogs and distributes the Lucid Candle product line through retails stores nationwide.

C.M. Almy employs approximately 80 people in Pittsfield today and makes literally hundreds of different products. In addition, its skilled people refurbish deteriorated church vestments and metalware usually restoring them to like-new condition. Current operations place a strong emphasis on safety, quality and customer service while focusing on product development and innovation. Almy people are dedicated to its mission: "We create superior products of beauty, quality, and function, for life."

Innovative Specialties

Josh Miville

Nitro Trailers was formed in the spring of 2013 by its current owner Chad Dow.

Chad began his learning at a young age like any ordinary kid, working in the garage and on many race cars at local stock car tracks learning the ins and outs of fabricating, welding, fit and finish. As his skills grew throughout his high school career, he applied for a job at a high-quality trailer manufacturer and began his welding career on aluminum trailers.

Throughout the seven years there, Chad started at the bottom of the ladder and rapidly worked his way to the custom fabricator position, one of two positions in an 140 employee environment. After achieving multiple perfect attendance awards and in 2008 the MVP award, the company closed its doors in 2009. The recession took a toll on the company and left Chad on the outside of a once successful business. Deciding which way to go from there was an easy decision. With the passion for perfection and enthusiasm to work, he then formed his own fabrication shop as Innovative Specialties. He had been thinking of a trade that he could specialize in and aluminum products came to mind instantly after all his years of aluminum fabricating. With the help of many family members and friends the company has grown leaps and bounds throughout its young career.

Chad chose Innovative Specialties for its name for all the unique custom work we do that is second to none. Dealing with many top recognized trailer dealers throughout the state, a relationship was formed with many that put their trust in Innovative Specialties to do work for them. Building numerous custom trailer products and doing countless repair work, the company had the idea that maybe it should build a high-quality aluminum trailer. With the encouragement of dealers, friends, family, and customers it was decided it was time to form NITRO trailers.

Hancock Lumber – Pittsfield Mill
compiled by Erin Plummer

Established in 1848, Hancock Lumber Company is a sixth-generation, family-owned business operating a land company, a sawmill division, and a network of retail lumberyards, home design showrooms, and a truss manufacturing facility. Led by their 522 employees, Hancock has four times been selected as a 'Best Place to Work in Maine' and was recognized as the 2017 national ProSales 'Dealer of the Year'. Four of their locations have received OSHA's highest safety certification, earning SHARP certifications at their Casco, Bethel, Pittsfield sawmills and Bridgton lumberyard. The company is also a past recipient of the Maine Family Business of the Year Award, the Governor's Award for Business Excellence, and the MITC 'Exporter of the Year' award.

Hanging on the wall in the company's main office in Casco Village is an original copy of a handwritten contract dated October 4, 1848, for the construction of a new mill for the grand sum of $840. In the original contract of 1848 between N&S Decker and Ambrose F. Wright, the agreement reads, "*Nathan*

and Spencer Decker agree to pay to the said Wight for building the said mill and dam the sum of Eight hundred and fifty dollars, one hundred in two months and the remainder when the work is completed..."
It is only by mere circumstances that Hancock Lumber exists under this name and is not called Decker Lumber. Nathan Decker originally began the lumber business in Casco Village in 1859, around the same time he married his wife, Hannah Stuart Hancock.

Hannah was the widow of Sumner M. Hancock who had died, leaving her with a baby boy, Sumner O. Hancock. The couple lived in Casco village and Nathan raised Sumner as his own; in fact, the child's name always remained "Hancock". Sumner O. Hancock inherited the Decker fortune as there were no other children. Eventually, the family chose to rename the business Hancock Lumber, as it remains today over 170 years later. *Family Business Magazine* recognizes Hancock Lumber Company as the seventy-first oldest family business in America.

When Hancock Land Company began their legacy in 1848 by purchasing a 400-acre timber stand in Casco, Maine, trees throughout the forest were harvested and hauled to the Crooked River. When manufacturing became an integral part of the business, steam engine portable mills powered were established, which traveled to harvest sites to collect trees. To this day, Hancock Land and Lumber companies remain the largest harvester and seller of timber in southern and southwestern Maine. It takes 80 -100 years to grow an Eastern White Pine Tree to maturity, so despite the company's 170-year history, Hancock Lumber has only been through two harvest cycles in its lifetime. Hancock Lumber relies on natural regeneration to perpetuate growth and success of its Eastern White Pine tree forests.

Today, Hancock Lumber Company is one of the largest, most dynamic, and vertically integrated lumber companies in New England, with 530 employees. Our sawmill division is the largest manufacturer of eastern white pine, with our Pittsfield mill being one of our three sawmill operations. Hancock distributes its world-class pine boards throughout the state at its retail lumberyards, across all of North America, and around the entire globe. Working directly with our customers, we analyze the markets to understand what pine products will work best by region and customer base. Working closely with our distribution partners, we customize and co-brand product resources and manufacture proprietary grades and patterns, as well as provide field support for the end users. Hancock Lumber: six generations of continuous operation—growing trees, keeping Maine green, manufacturing renewable and sustainable eastern white pine products, and providing building materials and first-class customer service to builders, architects, and homeowners alike. Learn more, please visit HancockLumber .com

Russell Coulter, Gov. John McKernan, Rep. Olympia Snowe, Dave Hancock, and Toby Hammond at Hancock Lumber Company's opening in 1990

Sonoco
Dan Boreham, Bob Ballard & Bethany Knowles

The Sonoco Pittsfield Plant began operations in the summer of 1982 as a satellite of the Lowell, MA facility. The original Pittsfield location was a 20,000 square foot building and employed five people. Of the original five, three remain today (Steve Debeck- senior Maintenance Mechanic, Ron Poulin, Account Manager, Bob Ballard, Production Manager). In 1998, the plant was relocated to its current facility, a 96,000 sq. foot building, and employs approximately 30 people.

For many years the Pittsfield plant was predominately servicing the Maine paper mill industry. As this industry declined, the Pittsfield team had to make a difficult choice ('Get busy living or get busy dying'). Over the last +5 years, the plant has 'stretched' its conventional production thinking, and as a result, has expanded into additional packaging segments. With this new mindset, the Sonoco Pittsfield team has been recognized on numerous occasions for outstanding contributions and innovation. Most recently, in 2017 the team was chosen for the prestigious "Customer Satisfaction Through Excellence Award."

In addition to being a leading packaging plant, the teammates at the facility took it upon themselves 2 years ago to become good community citizens. A volunteer team, the Engagement Team, holds events throughout the year to raise money and donations for local charities and events. The entire Sonoco Pittsfield team has supported various local charities including the Pittsfield Food Bank, MSAD #53 Children's Fund and donations of school supplies for local school children, the Skowhegan Area Animal Shelter, John Bowman Lacrosse Rebounder Wall, Pittsfield Youth Sports, Sebasticook Valley Elk Lodge Scholarship/Charities Fund, Steve's Cup Golf Tournament benefiting the Harold Alfond Cancer Care Center, and to the Red Cross Hurricane Relief Fund. This is all done by the employees themselves. The employees are looking forward to surpassing their charitable contributions from 2017 in the coming years.

Founded in 1899, Sonoco is a global provider of a variety of consumer packaging, industrial products, protective packaging, and displays and packaging supply chain services. With annualized net sales of approximately $4.8 billion, the Company has 20,000 employees working in more than 300 operations in 35 countries, serving some of the world's best-known brands in some 85 nations.

For 2018, Sonoco has been selected to the prestigious list of Fortune's World's Most Admired Companies, ranking first in the Packaging category. Additionally, among its industry peers, Sonoco ranked first in nearly every single area – including Innovation, Use of Corporate Assets, Social Responsibility, Financial Soundness, Long-term Investment Value, Quality of Products/Services and Global Competitiveness.

ENGINEERING & CONSTRUCTION

Cianbro

Alan Grover

Cianbro was founded by the Cianchette Brothers of Pittsfield, Maine, upon returning from service in

Cianchette Brothers - Carl, Alton, Kenneth and Ival

World War Two. The company is now one of the nation's largest, most diverse and successful construction and construction services companies. The firm operates in more than 40 states coast-to-coast, in five markets, and employs more than 4,000 team members. Cianbro continues to maintain a strong link to Pittsfield, with the Corporate Headquarters still located in the town where the business was born. Throughout the community, townsfolk see a complex of construction-related facilities, including a fabrication and coatings shop, an equipment repair facility, logistical support, human resources offices, a state-of-the art workforce development center, and a fully-equipped wellness gym. Furthermore, some of Cianbro's current senior managers hail

from the same hometown as the Cianchette Brothers, including Chairman of the Board Pete Vigue, Chief Executive Officer Andi Vigue, and Cianbro's Vice President of Engineering Frank Susi. The company also maintains a workforce of more than 400 team members in Pittsfield.

During its 69-year history, Cianbro has planned, managed and constructed technically complex, historic and environmentally sensitive projects for a wide variety of public and private clients. A total commitment to safety combined with an innovative team of construction professionals has enabled Cianbro to build a durable reputation for completing projects safely, on schedule and within budget. Among the Cianbro projects that have gained regional and national headlines in

Penobscot Narrows Bridge

recent years include the Petrodrill semi-submersible deep sea exploratory drilling rigs which the company brought to Portland Harbor to assemble in 2002; Neptune - a 660 megawatt sub-sea cable developed by Cianbro to transport DC power from New Jersey to Long Island in order to stabilize the power supply; the landmark Penobscot Narrows Bridge which became a visually pleasing replacement for the crumbling Waldo-Hancock Bridge in the mid-2000s; the National Air Force Memorial in Arlington, Virginia – a gleaming steel icon honoring the United States Air Force upon the skyline of the nation's capital; the Motiva Modules Project at the Cianbro-developed and Cianbro-built Eastern Manufacturing Facility in Brewer, Maine – an unprecedented effort to construct 52 refinery modules to be shipped via ocean-going barge to Texas with the help of two million Maine work hours that brought 100 million dollars into the local economy; the Maine Power Reliability Program which modernized Central Maine Power Company's bulk power system from 2010 to 2015 and became the largest construction project in Maine history; and the Sarah Mildred Long Bridge Replacement Project between Kittery, Maine and Portsmouth, New Hampshire – one of the biggest and most complex bridge projects in the region's history.

Cianbro is 100 percent employee-owned through the Employee Stock Ownership Plan (ESOP) where each team member shares in the risk and success of business. The move to establish employee ownership at Cianbro was completed in 2005, with the purchase of all of the outstanding shares of stock owned by company founders Bud, Ken and Chuck Cianchette. As owners, team members work more safely and productively to ensure the successful completion of each project. This commitment is reflected in Cianbro's vision and mission. Cianbro's vision is to be the best employee-owned construction company in the world. The mission states, "Cianbro will safely provide quality construction services, on time and at a competitive price. Through innovation, efficiency and our can-do spirit, we will develop people, satisfy customers and grow shareholder value."

Another key attribute of the company is its status as an open shop / merit shop contractor. Teamwork, dedication and innovation are what differentiate Cianbro from its competitors. Cianbro applies a robust can-do spirit in the workplace, implementing creative solutions for client's needs on a wide variety of projects. The company's diversification encompasses geographic diversity with an established service territory that spans the United States, including operations and support services facilities in the New England, Mid-Atlantic, North Central, South Central and Pacific regions. Facilities include equipment yards, enclosed shops, fabrication and coating shops, deep-water marine, and modular manufacturing facilities. A key acquisition for Cianbro in recent years includes the organization's wholly-owned subsidiary, Starcon International, a Texas-based refining and petrochemical services firm with expertise in the food processing, metals, paper, and power industries.

Cianbro is now among the top 100 contractors in the nation, based on revenue. The organization is the largest contractor in the state of Maine and is the state's fourth largest company. Cianbro's disciplines include civil, structural, mechanical, electrical, instrumentation, fabrication and coating. The firm offers construction services in several different capacities, under a variety of contractual methods, from the conceptual stages of design through implementation, all the way to start-up activities and turn-key operations. Additionally, as shown through exemplary regulatory compliance, environmental stewardship is at the forefront of Cianbro's projects.

Cianbro's top priority is the health and safety of its team members. The company has an ethical obligation to ensure that every team member goes home in better condition than when they arrived. Cianbro's Healthy Lifestyle Program helps to educate and guide team members toward realistic, sustainable lifestyle changes.

On the job, Cianbro ensures that risks are eliminated or mitigated, which not only protects life and limb but also improves production quality and boosts productivity. The company has been recognized nationally for its safety and wellness programs, including being named the "Healthiest and Safest Company in America" by the American College of Occupational and Environmental Medicine.

Nationally, while earning accolades for health and safety, the company has also accumulated recognition for excellence in the field as a recipient of the Associated Builders and Contractors' (ABC) Contractor of the Year Award, ABC's Excellence in Construction Awards, and Associated General Contractors' Build America Awards.

No matter how much success comes to Cianbro – which might be seen by some as a temptation to move to brighter city headquarters – Pittsfield continues to be the preferred home town of The Cianbro Companies. Nearly seven decades after the firm was founded in the pastoral central Maine community, company leaders view Cianbro's loyalty to Pittsfield as a symbol of the virtue of "remembering our roots." The company has long held that giving back to the communities where the team lives and works is a matter of integrity. Whether the task at hand is helping to improve the local academics at Maine Central Institute, quietly ensuring that the necessary upkeep of the community's infrastructure is accomplished, or even just putting up festive lights in the trees at Corporate Headquarters during the holiday season – Cianbro and Pittsfield enjoy a relationship that shows every sign of continuing well into the distant future.

NES/NIS/NSS

Bobbie Goulette

Northeastern Environmental Services (NES) was founded in 1989 by Michael and Ruth Vigue, providing asbestos insulation and lead paint abatement to primarily industrial and educational clients, such as paper mills and universities.

Shortly after, in 1990, Northeastern Insulation Services (NIS) was founded as a need to provide those clients with re-insulation services of piping, tanks, ductwork and boilers. This provided our clients with a seamless transition from one activity to the next.

Often scaffolding would be needed to access tanks, piping and ductwork that needed repairing, abating or re-insulation. Seeing this need, Northeastern Scaffolding Services (NSS) was founded in 2004.

NES/NIS/NSS has survived and thrived for 29 years by offering diverse, reliable and dedicated complimentary services to its clients.

NES/NIS/NSS works along the East coast, traveling as far south as South Carolina, with projects in Maryland, New York, Massachusetts, New Hampshire and Maine. Identified below are some of the larger scale projects performed by each company:

NES
* Star Enterprise oil terminal in Portland, Maine;
* Eastland Woolen Mill Superfund Clean-up in Corinna, Maine;
*Katahdin Paper Mill demo in Millinocket, Maine;
*Eastern Fine Paper demo in Brewer, Maine;
*Bangor Auditorium demo, Bangor, Maine;
*Maine General Medical Center renovations, Waterville, Maine; and
*several complete renovations of dormitories and classrooms at the University of Maine in Orono.

NIS
*Amethyst Oil Rigs in Portland, Maine;
*plant expansions at Huber Lumber, Easton, Maine
*McCain Foods, Easton, Maine;
*Dragon Products, Thomaston, Maine;
*Motiva Oil Modules in Brewer, Maine;
*expansion of Sebasticook Valley Hospital, Pittsfield, Maine;
*Tissue Machine installations at Woodland Pulp & Paper, Baileyville, Maine;
*Several projects at Portsmouth Naval Shipyard and
*Currently the #1 PM expansion at Sappi Fine Papers, Skowhegan, Maine.

NSS
* Lehigh Portland Cement in Maryland;
*Expansion at Huber Lumber, Easton, Maine;

*Tissue machine installations at Woodland Pulp & Paper, Baileyville, Maine;
*Eastern Maine Medical Center Expansion, Bangor, Maine; and
*Currently the #1 PM expansion at Sappi Fine Papers, Skowhegan, Maine.

NES/NIS/NSS has a team of 35 permanent employees, all cross-trained to perform the various different services offered to its clients. Cross-training allows for team members to operate together as a team, focusing on providing our clients with a seamless transition from one activity to another, without sacrificing safety. Currently, NES/NIS/NSS has an industry low Experience Modification Rate (EMR) factor of .65. This is exceptional when clients require a rate of 1.0 or below.

Kleinschmidt Associates

Brenda Seekins

R. Stevens Kleinschmidt, Ph.D., hydraulic engineer and former professor at Harvard University, founded Kleinschmidt Associates in Pittsfield in 1966. Dr. Kleinschmidt was respected for his

knowledge of hydropower engineering and his practical approach to problem-solving. His legacy of expertise in hydropower issues and practical, solution-oriented approaches remain key components of the organization today. In 2016, Kleinschmidt celebrated its 50th anniversary.

In early 1970, Steve offered a partnership to Richard F. "Dick" Dutting. A graduate of Tufts University and Northeastern University with degrees in civil engineering, Dick proved to be more than an engineering partner who shared Steve's passion for practical down-to-earth approaches to engineering challenges. Having worked as an engineer for many companies, Dick knew what the company needed to build a robust engineering consulting firm, so while Steve took care of the engineering work, Dick focused on day-to-day operations of managing the office. He recruited and interviewed employees, developed benefits programs, invoiced clients, and made sure the bills were paid. Dick hired Eloise Reilly as office manager. By 1974, Dick and

Scientist Brandon Wright Taking Water Elevation Readings

Steve welcomed GNP engineer Robert Liimatainen to the company. Much of the early work came from Cianbro, like projects for the town of Pittsfield, Bangor Water District, Irving Tanning, and various paper mills. During the first 10 years, the company continued developing its core strengths in hydro projects like dam repairs, pumping station design, and wastewater/sewerage treatment jobs. By the end of 1975, Kleinschmidt and Dutting employed eight full-time employees who were poised and ready to take the company into the next decade and in new directions as it continued to grow.

178

The services have expanded over the years in response to the changing needs of industry coming to work in harmony with the environment. In the 1980s, the company expanded into environmental and licensing services. In the 1990s, Kleinschmidt recognized the opportunity to expand its client base

beyond hydro and developed an Ecological Services Group to branch out into new areas. This group has become nationally known for ecosystem assessments, individual habitat and river restoration projects, watershed management, water supply reservoir management, dam removal, fish studies, and siting and impact studies for wetlands and other habitats.

In the 21st century, the firm recognized the growth potential in other renewable energy resources, especially the Marine Renewable industry, which includes offshore wind, wave, tidal and hydrokinetic energy. The firm also recognized the similar challenges from hydro around the regulatory, environmental and engineering requirements for successful deployment of these "new" renewable energy products. Today, the team is an advocate for the industry as a whole, helping clients develop and deploy these emerging technologies.

Bill Cunningham meets with Andy Qua & Steve Knapp of Kleinschmidt Associates to review site plan for boat launch for Fendler Park

Insource Renewables

Vaughan Woodruff

The company was originally founded as a sole proprietorship by Vaughan Woodruff in 2008 in Bozeman, MT. The company was originally named Yankee Solutions and was primarily engaged in the design and installation of solar heating systems and energy efficiency consulting. Woodruff relocated his business to Maine when he moved back to his hometown of Pittsfield in 2009.

Once in Maine, it took nearly a year to establish the business as full-time employment for Woodruff. As he was considering hiring the company's first employee, an opportunity arose with Kennebec Valley Community College (KVCC) to lead the training of the northeast region of the Department of Energy's Solar Instructor Training Network (SITN). Woodruff continued to moonlight as Yankee Solutions as he served as the lead solar thermal instructor for KVCC from 2010-2012.

SITN was funded by the U.S. Department of Energy, through which Woodruff was responsible for helping technical schools throughout the northeastern United States integrate solar heating technologies into their trades and engineering programs. When federal funding ended in 2012, he returned to full-time contracting and re-branded the company as Insource Renewables.

Insource Renewables pairs with the Amish company Backyard Buildings to make a solar shed

Shortly after this transition, Insource Renewables brought on its first two employees and expanded into solar photovoltaics (PV) and mini-split heat pump technologies. From 2013-15, five key permanent staff members were added. In 2015, a former service station and convenience store in Pittsfield was renovated as a new warehouse. In February 2015, the company was selected by the Town of Freeport to lead Maine's first formal Solarize program which garnered extensive publicity and reinforced Insource Renewables commitment to community-centered energy solutions. Solarize Freeport received statewide recognized for its success, and Insource Renewables gained significant earned media and name recognized as a result. In 2016, there was a similar effort - Solarize Mid Maine in the greater Waterville area. In 2017, the company was the lead for Greater Bangor Solarize.

In late 2016, Woodruff approached the company's employees to inquire about the interest of restructuring the company from a sole member LLC to a worker's cooperative. In 2017, interested individuals collaborated to develop by-laws for the new cooperative and incorporated the new business, Maine Solar Cooperative, Inc. The transition was completed in 2018. Upon conversion, Insource Renewables is prepared to receive additional recognition as a Certified B-Corp.

In addition to our installation and service work, Insource Renewables has been highly visible in Maine's solar policy discussions. Since 2015, solar has been a highly politicized industry in Maine and Woodruff's role as the state industry's trade association representative has led to significant earned media and has further strengthened Insource Renewables' name recognition across the state.

previously known as Leon E. Gordon, Inc. and Gordon Construction Corp.

Russ Collier

This is a picture of the tank for the first hydroseeder in Maine behind the office on Hartland Ave. The finished product was powered by 5 separate engines and it was difficult to find out which had run out of fuel first. Soon after Leon built this he bought an early Finn hydroseeder.

The predecessor companies to hydrograsscorp.com have been in business since 1947, located on Hartland Avenue. Leon E. Gordon Inc. was founded by Leon Gordon. The succeeding company, hydrograsscorp.com, continues to operate today under the ownership of Leon and Dot's son, Tom.

Dot and Leon were well-known fixtures in the town for many years. Leon E. Gordon, Inc. was focused on installing rip rap, an early erosion control technique for drainage swales, also specializing in guard rail construction, granite curbing and sodding. As the erosion control technology and awareness grew, Leon built the first hydroseeder in Maine and soon after purchased one of the first commercially-available hydroseeders, manufactured by Finn Corp., which becomes important later in the history of this company.

In 1963, with Leon's health failing, Tom Gordon left college prematurely to come home and run the family business. Tom was an active part of the work crew and the company accountant. As the interstate highway system expanded he built the business, which was the largest hydroseeding company in Maine, to one well-known regionally, and the most reliable company in the business. In 1973 Leon E. Gordon, Inc. became Gordon Construction Corp.

Through the years Tom maintained close contact with the Finn Corp. which supplied the company with hydroseeders. In the early 1980s, the company contacted Tom to see if he would be interested in distributing the Finn hydroseeder throughout New England. Tom eventually relented which resulted in the formation of a new and separate company in 1980. Hydrograss Corp. would focus on providing equipment and materials to the erosion control and landscape industry throughout New England.

Then there were two companies, focused on the same industry from different angles; one Gordon Construction Corp. focused on providing the service and the other Hydrograss Corp providing materials and equipment. In 1988, Tom appointed long-time employee (since 1972) Russell Collier as President of Gordon Construction Corporation. Tom remained as CEO of Gordon Construction and president of Hydrograss.

Leon Gordon Using Early Mechanical Sod Cutter with Son Tom as a Young Boy Standing 2nd from left

In 1995, the Finn Corp. developed a new and revolutionary piece of equipment called the Bark Blower that would change the face of the landscape industry. Both Gordon companies continued to flourish. In 2007, Gordon Construction was sold; the market had changed. Russ Collier became President of Hydrograss, and the company name was changed to hydrograsscorp.com. Today hydrograsscorp.com maintains three locations scattered about its Finn territory, which includes all of New England and most of New York; Pittsfield, Maine, Pittsfield, NH and Albany, NY. Currently employing 18 people, it is frequently recognized as Dealer of the Year in its distributorship.

Northeast Skywagon
Frank Woodworth

Started in 2008 by Frank Woodworth, Northeast Skywagon is a Pittsfield construction business that focuses on earthwork and site preparation for commercial buildings. Certification by the Maine Department of Environmental Protection also allows work in environmentally sensitive areas. Work is performed primarily in the central Maine area.

AAA Energy Service

Dave Barden

Since 1983, AAA Energy Service has performed service, preventive maintenance, design build, as well as bid and spec work in the HVACR (heating-ventilation-air conditioning-refrigeration) industry. There are three offices. The home office is in Scarborough, Maine and covers southern Maine. The Pittsfield office covers central, eastern, and northern Maine from Rockland to Gardiner to Rumford North and East. The Auburn, New Hampshire office covers New Hampshire, Vermont, and Massachusetts.

The Pittsfield office has technicians that live in the Bangor to Waterville areas. There is a 24-hour 7 day a week on-call rotation to provide full coverage in the heating, air conditioning, and refrigeration fields no matter what time of day or night it may be when a need arises.

Full-coverage preventive plans as well as test and inspect maintenance plans are provided. AAA Energy Service can provide construction work from complete facilities to one unit replacement.

AAA Energy Service's fast service and competitive prices make it the best choice for your HVACR needs.

LEGAL, FINANCIAL & BUSINESS SERVICES

Alfred Bachrach, Esq.

Alfred Bachrach

Teaching brought Fred Bachrach to Pittsfield, but lawyering has kept him here. Wanting to live in Maine, Fred accepted a social studies teaching position at Warsaw Middle School in 1972 while his wife Mildred (Millie) completed her master's degree in nursing. In the fall of 1973, Fred began his 3 years of study at the University of Maine law school in Portland while Millie stayed home and continued her job at Kennebec Valley Mental Health Center.

Fred worked summers between law school terms at an Augusta law firm and took his first job there after passing the bar. A year later, the firm had sold. He opened his own law office on Main Street in

 Pittsfield in 1977. This office was on the second floor of the building housing Renys. In 1980, when Mr. Reny decided to expand the store, Fred found that he was once again in transition. He actually had to climb down a ladder to move his files during his last day on Main Street as the exterior stairs to the second floor had already been removed. He relocated his office to the Somerset Plaza where he rented space opposite what was then the racquetball club.

In 1984, Fred bought the Elias property on Somerset Avenue and moved his office once again. The flood of '87 brought water lapping at the curb in front of his office the night before, so he moved his files up onto desks and tables to what he thought was safety. Having to go to court the next day, Fred returned to town to see people in canoes and motor boats on Somerset Avenue. Getting to his office by canoe, Fred waded in chest deep water to find his floating files, which later took weeks to dry.

Fred works primarily with civil cases including probate, family law, real estate transactions, estate planning, child protective and corporate work. He has had the able assistance from his long-term paralegals Rena Hodgins and Lorna Lincoln. Pittsfield area residents have been fortunate to have him serve their legal needs for over forty years.

"Lawyers Above the Bank"

Burky & McCarthy, Attorneys at Law

Barbara J. Pomeroy with help from Kim Post and Rick McCarthy

Attorney Elton Burky bought his first home in Pittsfield in 1968, next to the Pittsfield Public Library on Main Street, where he first began his practice of law in Pittsfield as a solo practitioner in 1969. He sold that house in 1973, relocating his law office to the second floor of the bank building on Main Street in the early 1970's, where the firm of Burky & McCarthy remains to this day.

Attorney Richard W. McCarthy, Jr., known to almost everyone as Rick, has been practicing law on Main Street in Pittsfield since he joined the partnership of Elton Burky and Michael Wiers on September 14, 1987, as an associate attorney. He graduated from the New England School of Law in Boston, MA, in May 1987 with the degree of Juris Doctor, after obtaining his undergraduate degree at the University of Maine at Orono. He grew up in Skowhegan, the son of Richard W. (Sr.) and Judith McCarthy.

The partnership of Burky & Wiers existed from 1985 to 1995, when it became Burky, Wiers & McCarthy, with offices in Hartland, Pittsfield, and Greenville; then on April 1, 1997, the partnership of Burky & McCarthy was formed when Attorney Mike Wiers left the partnership to be a solo practitioner in Hartland.

Burky & McCarthy continued as a partnership, with offices in Pittsfield and Greenville, until Elton Burky's retirement from the practice of law in September 2014.

Today (2018), Rick McCarthy operates his law practice as a solo practitioner, doing business as Burky & McCarthy, with offices in Pittsfield and Greenville. He enjoys collegial relationships with the many members of the Maine Bar practicing in the greater Central Maine area, particularly Mike Wiers in Newport and Fred Bachrach in Pittsfield. He is a longtime member of the Somerset County Bar Association, a new member and Vice President of the Piscataquis County Bar Association, and he continues to be a member of the Maine State Bar Association, the American Bar Association, and the American Land Title Association, as well as the Sebasticook Valley Chamber of Commerce. Rick McCarthy's varied practice of law includes many years of experience with family law including child protection, divorces, parental rights, adoption, probate and estate planning, real estate matters, and corporate law for small businesses, landlord/tenant disputes, and other general matters. Attorney McCarthy is pleased to be able to provide notarial services to his clients and the communities his practice serves, through his experienced and knowledgeable staff: Pittsfield office secretary/paralegal, Barbara Pomeroy, is a Notary Public and Dedimus Justice; and in the Greenville office, Kim Post and Ann Murray are both Notaries Public.

Northeast Planning Associates, Inc.

Michael Lynch

I moved to town in 1966, as an infant, and grew up in this wonderful community. After studying at Maine Central Institute and the University of Maine, where I earned an MBA, I joined NPA and ultimately moved my office back to Pittsfield in 1992, so I would have the opportunity to work in my hometown. Founded in 1959, NPA is a Registered Investment Advisor firm offering financial planning services in more than 30 offices across New England, and overseeing more than $3 billion dollars in brokerage and advisory assets (as of January 2018). I have built my personal practice around retirement planning for individuals and businesses in more than a dozen states, but I'm happy to still call Pittsfield home.

In 2015, I was honored with the Joyce Packard Community Spirit Award for my work with several community-oriented projects. I believe it is vitally important to give back to this community of which we are a part – and I try to do that in any way I can.

RJD Appraisal

Bob Duplisea

RJD Appraisal is a municipal assessing firm incorporated in the State of Maine, located in Pittsfield. Founded in 1983 by Bob Duplisea, RJD Appraisal has performed over 60 re-evaluations in Maine over the last 35 years. Currently, this company performs the assessing duties for over fifty communities in Maine offering full-service tax map updating including drafting, printing, and tax billing services. In

addition, it provides commercial and personal assessments, and assessments using several computer-assisted assessment programs. It employs eight full-time assessors, all with Certified Maine Assessor certification, as well as two part-time employees.

Pittsfield has always been an important part of the lives of the employees of this company. Bob is the second of four generations of MCI graduates. In fact, all but one employee are graduates from MCI. RJD Appraisal is located at 300 Waverly Street.

Bangor Savings Bank

Robin Chase

Bangor Savings Bank, with more than $3.7 billion in assets, offers retail banking services to Maine consumers as well as comprehensive commercial, corporate, payroll administration, merchant services, insurance, and small business banking services to Maine businesses. The Bank, founded in 1852, is in its 166th year of service to the people of Maine, with 54 branches and on the web at bangor .com. The Bangor Savings Bank Foundation was created in 1997. Together the Bank and its Foundation invest more than $1.7 million per year into the community in the form of nonprofit sponsorships, grants and partnership initiatives. Proudly serving the Pittsfield community for more than 19 years! Visit your local branch at 138 Main Street, Pittsfield.

Sebasticook Valley Federal Credit Union

Melinda Nyman

The year was 1953 when a group of hard-working employees at Northeast Shoe Company banded together to form Maine Aire Federal Credit Union (fun-fact—the name "Maine Aire" was actually the name of a shoe that was made there). *The purpose of the credit union, as stated in the Bylaws was, "To promote thrift among its members, by affording them an opportunity for accumulation of their savings; and to create for them a source of credit for provident or productive purposes."* A Credit Union is a non-profit financial institution that is owned and operated entirely by its members. It has an all-volunteer Board of Directors that oversees the credit union. There are no stockholders—only shareholders (the members of the credit union). The initial field of membership was the employees and immediate family members of Northeast Shoe Co. Inc., and the employees and immediate family members of the credit union. Some of the shoe factory employees that were instrumental in establishing this credit union were, Everett Houston Jr., S. Aubrey Dunton, Scott Smith, Virgil Small, Frank Bennett, Russell Haynes and Cecil Peppard. They were all "incorporators."

The first President was Clarence Hilyard and the first Vice President was Robert Young. Marie Walker was Clerk-Secretary and Christine Ward was the first Treasurer. The credit union was located right at

the shoe factory. Having it right on site made it convenient for the employees who worked long hours and had a difficult time making it to a bank between 9:00-3:00 ('banker's hours'). The employees were able to deposit money into their accounts, cash their checks and apply for loans without leaving the building. Eventually, the credit union moved offsite to the home of Ken Shaw on Sebasticook Street.

In 1968, Maine Aire Federal Credit Union, changed from being a SEG-based (serving only Northeast Shoe Co.) to a community-based credit union. Membership in this credit union was open to anyone that lived, worked, worshiped or attended school in the towns of Pittsfield, Detroit, Burnham or Palmyra. The name changed to People's Regional Federal Credit Union in 1972. In 1974, the towns of Hartland and St. Albans were added. The offsite operation moved from Ken Shaw's house to a trailer on Sebasticook Street until a new building was built in 1976. When operations moved to the new building, assets totaled just over $1 million, having grown from just $19,000 in assets in 1964. The credit union had grown to just over 2000 members. The years from 1976 to 1998 brought many changes including adding Newport in 1984 and in 1993 a new branch of the credit union opening on Rt. 7 in Newport. In this time period, membership grew to 6,335 members, while assets grew to over $16 million in 1998.

In 1998 the credit union began a new era - new leadership, an expansion at the Newport branch and a new building for the main branch, and new location in Pittsfield. Jim Lemieux was hired in 1998 as President/CEO of Sebasticook Valley FCU. With Jim at the helm and a dedicated staff and board of directors to help him, this credit union has grown from $16 million in assets in 1998 to over $100 million in 2018. The membership grew to over 11,000 in 2018. This growth was spurred by many new products that were introduced—from Visa check cards to online banking and e-statements, mobile banking, online account opening, and lending. Some other changes during this time period: the name changed from People's Regional Federal Credit Union to its current name, Sebasticook Valley FCU to better identify the name with the service area. Sebasticook Valley FCU became very involved in the Maine Credit Union's Ending Hunger in Maine Campaign starting around 1990. Locally, the staff, members, and sponsors have raised well over $100,000 in SVFCU's Ending Hunger in Maine Campaign. 100% of that money has been given directly to food pantries and local food initiatives in the communities of Sebasticook Valley. SVFCU has served the members of the Pittsfield and surrounding communities for over 65 years, and looks forward to serving them for many, many more!

People's United Bank

Founded in 1842, People's United Bank is a community-based, Northeast regional bank with national businesses spanning the country. People's United and its subsidiaries provide Commercial, Retail, Wealth Management, Equipment Finance, Brokerage and Insurance services, with branches throughout its footprint including Connecticut, New York, Massachusetts, Vermont, New Hampshire and Maine.

In Maine, the bank has more than 130 employees and 27 branches throughout the state, including a branch at 27 Main Street in Pittsfield, one of the state's oldest buildings dating back to 1889, as

recognized by the Pittsfield Historical Society. People's United Community Foundation, the bank's philanthropic arm, has supported more than 100 non-profit organizations in Maine, focusing on community and youth development, and affordable housing.

2017 marked an important milestone for People's United, its 175th anniversary. It was in 1842 when the bank, originally named Bridgeport Savings Bank, accepted its first deposits—amassing $97 in the first week. This success is attributed to the collaborative efforts of its employees and commitment to the bank's guiding principles, including providing an exceptional customer experience, building lasting relationships, having an impact on the communities where we live and work and returning value to shareholders.

As part of the celebration, the Foundation awarded a special anniversary grant of $175,000 to Junior Achievement USA, to be allocated among seven Junior Achievement chapters across six states, including Maine. Since 2009 Greenwich Associates has granted People's United 42 awards in Middle Market Banking and Small Business Banking, including eight National and four Regional Excellence Awards, and one Best Brand Award for Ease of Doing Business received since 2016.

Clients and their businesses are at the center of everything we do. We continually invest in our people and technology, enabling us to provide high-quality products and practical solutions that matter most to client's long-term success.

 Whether it is financing, cash management, card payment processing or business insurance, we deliver value to your business in the areas that matter most. Let's discuss your business needs. Stop by or give us a call.

United Insurance – Pittsfield

(formerly Lehr Insurance Agency)

Beth Smith

Today, United Insurance has 14 local agencies throughout Maine and New Hampshire and nearly 150 insurance professionals. We take great pride in our communities and honor the history we have helped create over the years. The United Insurance – Pittsfield office (formerly Lehr Insurance Agency) traces its roots back to 1873 when Parks Bros Insurance Agency was founded by Lewellyn, Warren, and David Parks. The agency was eventually purchased by Charles and Earle Vickery, (father and son).

In 1950, the agency merged with Willard W. Lehr Jr. Agency (former Sanger M Cook Insurance Agency (founded in 1943) and was incorporated under the name of Vickery & Lehr, Inc. In 1954, Earle Vickery retired and sold his 50% interest to Willard Lehr Jr. In 1960, the Stone Agency was purchased (formerly Sidney F Jones Agency – est. 1916). Burton Hammond came with the purchase and the name was changed to Lehr/Hammond Agency, Inc. The agency moved from 59 Main Street to 6 Hunnewell Square in 1962. This was a newly constructed building owned by Willard Lehr Jr. The Maurice E. Gould Agency was purchased that same year.

Burton Hammond retired in 1970 selling his interest to Willard Lehr and the name was changed to Lehr Agency, Inc. Michael Gray joined Lehr in 1979 after working several years for the General Adjustment Bureau. In 1981, the agency moved to a new, more spacious office in the Cianbro Building located at Hunnewell Avenue The agency purchased the Kenneth A. Hughes and Son Agency (which had offices in both Pittsfield and St. Albans). Three years later, the Preston B. Chadbourne Agency in Harmony was purchased and in 1985 the Kenney Agency in Unity Agency was purchased, further increasing the agency's size.

In 1987, Douglas Chadwick joined the agency with 12 years of insurance experience. Mike and Doug purchased the agency from Willard Lehr in January 1994. In 2007, United Insurance purchased the agency from Mike and Doug taking on the name United Insurance Lehr Agency. Mike Gray retired in December of 2010 and Doug Chadwick retired in December of 2011. In June of 2015, United Insurance moved out of the Cianbro building on Hunnewell Ave and into Somerset Plaza which remains our current home. Today, Beth Smith manages the Pittsfield office. Chris Condon, CEO of United notes, "Though time has marched on, United has stood by its values which include community and providing unique insurance solutions to individuals and business. We are proud to celebrate Pittsfield Bicentennial!"

FOOD & RETAIL

Bud's Shop 'n Save

Dean Homstead

Bud's Shop 'n Save in Pittsfield opened for business on January 22, 1959 by owners Frank (Bud) and Tina Homstead in the building now owned and occupied by Cianbro Institute. This building located on Hunnewell Avenue was built by the local contractor Joseph R Cianchette, Sr. and leased to the Homsteads for their new supermarket. A few years later, the building was sold to John Morse of Bath, Maine. Over many years the store experienced growth and was expanded in 1968 to accommodate more items and customers.

Originally, the store opened as Bud's Red & White and later transitioned to the name Bud's Shop 'n Save. To cause excitement about the store opening within the community, Bud Homstead hired a plane to throw paper plates out of the window with special deals printed on them. People all over town chased down these paper plates. This promotion turned out to be a great success and everyone had a great time. This promotion would not be an option in 2019.

In the early days, there were other unique promotions. One such promotion was the watermelon sale right off the railroad box car. The railroad would bring the boxcar up from the South and would drop it off next to the store where customers would purchase them.

On June 14, 1988, Bud's Shop 'n Save relocated its business to the Somerset Plaza in the former IGA location. As the business continued to grow a major expansion to the store was completed in 2010 to its current size. Bud's Shop 'n Save in Pittsfield was part of the small chain of stores owned by the Homsteads with other locations in Newport, Dexter and for a short period in Wilton. Bud and Tina Homstead owned the company from 1953 to 1985. Dean Homstead and Dan Hill owned it from 1985 to 2002 and in 2002 Dean Homstead became the sole owner.

Throughout its history, Bud's Shop 'n Save has been locally owned and operated and has been a strong supporter of local farmers, producers, and distributors. The company has also been very supportive of local communities, schools, and organizations.

Today, the company employs approximately 75 people from the communities that it serves. Many of these employees have been employed at Bud's for decades with some having worked forty and fifty years. This type of longevity provides a great store culture and a family atmosphere that customers recognize, appreciate and enjoy. Bud's Shop 'n Save is a full-service grocery store selling groceries, meat, produce, deli, bakery, general merchandise, health and beauty care products and alcoholic beverages. Its services include lottery tickets, money orders, and utility payments.

Vittles Restaurant

Kathy Phelan

We are Vittles Restaurant and we set up our business in May of 2011. We are family operated by Kathleen and Robert Phelan and son, Richard LeRose. We chose Pittsfield to start our business because of its location in the center of town. It fulfilled the criteria we were looking for, centrally located, in a historic building and walking distance from local businesses. We wanted to be a cheery spot for our patrons to gather and establish roots that would allow us to grow and flourish. We have kept our promise to serve "good food", healthy, local and fresh. We cater to individuals with dietary restrictions and allergies and take pride in our ability to remain committed to serving Maine products first.

We have participated in joint ventures with SVH to promote healthy eating and cooking with an

after-school children program and the Bossov Ballet for a special dinner/ballet event. We have worked with MCI students on their senior projects and employ interns from local culinary schools. We employ local students and have been a "first job" for many. Vittles promotes integrity, a work ethic and accommodates our students' extra-curricular activities as they learn the balance required in life. Our college students work around their schedules changing semester to semester and receive references for their next job.

We have retained the feel of the original building and have many customers especially during MCI Alumni Weekend who join us with their friends to reminisce and we have become part of their weekend celebration.

Richie's Pizza

Richard Bellows with Jane Woodruff

Richie's serves more than pizza. A variety of take-out items are available ranging from sub-sandwiches to dinners. One item of note is the donuts. A few years back, a local radio station had a call-out to folks to name their favorite place to buy donuts. While Frank's Bakery in Bangor and Hillman's in Fairfield were mentioned, as Dick Bellows, owner of Richie's, tells it, "We slammed them."

Open at 5 AM every day except Sunday, which opens an hour later, his staff are busy making these fresh donuts and serving breakfast sandwiches to their early customers. Richie's remains open until well after the typical supper hour as they are available to their customers until 8 to 10 PM dependent on the night and season. Richie's employs six people with some having worked there for decades.

Most people don't realize that the name Richie's came not from the Richard in Bellows name but his brother-in-law Gordon Richards from whom he took over the business in 1974. Originally located on the corner of Sebasticook and North Main Streets, Richie's was relocated to its current location when Dick built his restaurant on South Main Street in 1976.

Family has been involved in this business over the years as his children have worked there. His daughter originated the name "Belly Buster" for one of their signature sandwiches which has all the fixings of a combination pizza heated on a submarine roll. His son works with Dick in providing locally-grown beef and other meat products that are used in the restaurant as well as sold on the premises.

Grandpa's Specialty Smoked Meats

Mike Raven with Jane Woodruff

Why Grandpa's? Mike Raven honors his grandfather with the naming of his business. As a child, Mike

learned the techniques from his grandfather that he uses to render meat to become specialty smoked meats - meats such as kielbasa, dogs, ham, sausage, bacon. Buying meats from the local area, he then processes them up to three weeks followed by an all-day smoking process. He and his wife Linda also prepare their own homemade barbecue sauce, their own mayonnaise, and coleslaw. When asked about the results, Mike replies, "The proof is in the taste."

For several years, he had been "smoking meats" and selling to a limited market. In June 2017, he and Linda opened Grandpa's Specialty Smoked Meats in a newly built shop adjacent to their home on West Street making their gourmet-type food available to the general public. As their motto says, they provide "down-home cooking in a small place with big taste."

Dysart's Travel Stop

Stephanie Valente with Jane Woodruff

Built in 1926, the Karam building on Main Street has a diverse history. It housed a Nash dealership and Shell station as well as the Post Office for forty years. In subsequent years, it became many things: the Citgo station, a video and carpet store, the Pool & Spa place, a pick-up location for dry cleaning. On December 5, 2007 it finally became what it is today: Dysart's Travel Stop. As Stephanie Valente, manager for Dysart's, likes to call it: "the center of downtown." Purchased from Rae and Charlie Philbrick, it continued to offer Citgo products but it was more than just a gas station as the Philbricks had added a deli run by Gail Ross.

Catering more to in-town folks, it does not draw many travelers off the interstate given its location away from the highway. But Dysart's is a stop - a stop for regulars. With its deli still

Steph Valente, Gail Ross & Lottie Killam by Dysart's Deli

run by Gail Ross and the availability of a convenience store, it attracts its "regulars": students from MCI and Warsaw, employees from local nearby businesses and civic committee members.

Besides being a community gathering place it is a community helper. Stephanie related how Dysart's and Bud's have helped each other over the years in times of power outages. In the ice storm of '98, Bud's lost power and was faced with the potential loss of many food items, Corner Citgo (now Dysart's) came to their rescue when these items were transferred there for sale and storage. Similarly, in the recent wind storm in October of 2017, they were able to return the favor when Dysart's lost their power.

Maine Federation of Farmers' Markets
Leigh Hallett

The Maine Federation of Farmers' Markets (MFFM) runs statewide programs that help sustain Maine farms, connect market farmers, strengthen farmers' markets, and widen access to locally-grown food for all. MFFM was founded in 1991. After 20 years as an all-volunteer organization, in 2012 it was incorporated, with market farmers from around the state joining the new Board of Directors. First based in Portland, then Freedom, the Federation finally settled in Pittsfield in 2014.

Pittsfield is an excellent home base for an organization like MFFM that serves the entire state. It's less than an hour from Augusta, and its central location makes it as easy to get to Houlton or Milbridge as to Portland. With a long agricultural heritage, the Pittsfield area is also home to many experienced market farmers, including Tom Roberts of Snakeroot Organic Farm, Heather Donahue of Balfour Farm, and Hanne Tierney of Cornerstone Farm, all of whom have served on the MFFM Board of Directors.

POPonOVERs

Cafe and Baked Goods

Nancy Monteyro with Jane Woodruff

Nancy and Dekk Monteyro are living their dream of operating a cafe and bakery. Along with their cafe, POPonOVERs, came operating an ice cream business as well. In a two-week period after making the decision to take the leap from a secure, corporate job, they had re-opened Big Bill's in July of 2017. By the third week in September, the Monteyros had POPonOVERs open and running six days a week.

Nancy MacGown Monteyro was born and grew up in Pittsfield and returned to her family's farm with her husband Dekk to raise their three children. As she so aptly stated, "Every Mainer comes back and I am one of those." With her strong attachment to this area, she and her husband have not only brought a coffee and an

Dekk and Nancy Monteyro Serve Customer Michael Wyly

ice cream shop to town, they have brought jobs employing from six to fourteen people depending on the season.

Serving a varied and delicious menu, they also provide a warm and caring gathering place where they make people feel welcome. They post daily specials on their Facebook page and they also provide take-out home-cooked meals.

POPonOVERs is located in downtown on Main Street in what was formerly Lagorios where school children in the 1950's would buy penny candy. Over the years it has been site to a beauty parlor and floral shop as well as a take-out restaurant and now a cafe and bakery.

Blue Sky Produce

Lynn Thurston with Jane Woodruff

Lynn Thurston was looking for a strategic location for her cooler. As a wholesaler and distributor of wild blueberries, she had previously been renting space in Addison, Maine to house the berries from Down East. For ten years, she had scrambled to find coolers to rent for the season. Not finding the right-sized place to purchase, she decided to build.

She chose a site in Pittsfield's Industrial Park because of its central location and the community's positive attitude. The cooler found its home there in a new building she had constructed in 2016. Berries are pre-cooled there and orders made up to sell to retail chains in New England and farm stands. She has cooler space available for other producers to rent also. Lynn continues to expand the market and distribution for wild blueberries. She received a grant from the Maine Dept of Agriculture to do in-store demos for fresh berries in NY and NJ this year. Like she said, "They don't know what wild blueberries are down there!"

Stony Knolls Farm

&

Drooling Goat Bar-B-Que

Ken Spaulding

Lots of folks have been pleasantly surprised to see Drooling Goat BBQ setting up on Somerset Ave at Hathorn Park on Thursdays since July 2017. It might come as more of a surprise to note that we (Ken & janice Spaulding) are not new to serving the people in the Pittsfield area.

We have been selling "roadside" in Pittsfield for over 10 years. We were privileged to be members of the Pittsfield Farmers' Market, setting up every Monday and Thursday, since 2007 selling our farm-raised goat cheeses, soaps, home-baked breads along with pickles, jellies, and jams.

A few years ago, a decision was made to look into transitioning from livestock to a less demanding enterprise. Having traveled to Texas on numerous occasions to purchase goats, Ken got his first taste of Texas-style slow-smoked BBQed meats. This proved to be the niche market we could handle. We contracted with a local welder to build our smoker/cooker and in May of 2014 started perfecting our recipes. And as they say the "rest is history". We have expanded to three days a week selling "roadside" Thursdays in Pittsfield, Friday in Newport, and Saturday in Dexter.

Pittsfield Farmers' Market

Tom Roberts

A farmers' market organized in early 1997 by Tom Roberts of Snakeroot Organic Farm, with the support of the Town allowing the market to use the parking area at the Central and Somerset Ave corner of Hathorn Park. The founding members include area farmers, gardeners, cooks, and artisans, offering locally produced fruits, vegetables, herbs, home baked pies, garden seedlings and plants. It is hoped that additional local producers will join in to increase the offerings available to residents who wish to support fresh, local food, and home-made products. Open May Day until Halloween each year.

Outland Farm Brewery

Heather & Michael Holland

Outland Farm Brewery is a small, artisanal, farmhouse brewery housed on a beautiful 72-acre farm in Pittsfield, Maine.

The brewery, owned by Heather and Michael Holland, has an emphasis on providing new and interesting beers made with locally sourced ingredients. In addition, the brewery functions as a vehicle for agricultural education, allowing customers to experience the direct link between the field and the glass first hand.

The brewery is housed inside the 2,400 square foot converted barn located in the center of the property, nestled between the two apple orchards, community garden, and expansive hay fields. Ample space is dedicated to a warm and inviting taproom where customers can sample and enjoy all the brewery's offerings. An outdoor grassed recreation area is provided for outdoor enjoyment during the spring, summer, and fall. The taproom is available for private events, meetings, and parties throughout the year.

Renys in Pittsfield

Mary Kate Reny

The Pittsfield Reny story began almost fifty years ago, when R.H. Reny opened his department store at 131 Main Street, in the building known as the Charles Vickery Building/Block. Designed in 1908, the building is 110 years old this year. The original blueprints of the building were found in a wall when Renys renovated the store in 2007.

When the Pittsfield Renys store opened in 1969, it became the seventh Renys store location; the Renys' chain of stores has since grown to 17 locations throughout Maine. R.H. had opened a store in Dexter and Madison, Maine in 1958 and 1960, respectively, making Pittsfield a natural next location when planning the distribution of goods via truck from the company's Damariscotta "warehouse."

The first manager of the store was Dick House of South Bristol. Tom Burr was the store manager from 1997 to 2010. Tom still works for us and is currently a regional supervisor. Our current manager in Pittsfield in Josh Bickford. Renys hopes to continue its "Maine Adventure" for many years to come and as some of our customers say, "If Renys doesn't have it, I don't need it."

Local Store Manager Tom Burr on Left with Renys Management on the Occasion of Re-opening the Basement after Its Renovation in 2007

Robert H. Reny, Sr. opened his first store in Damariscotta, Maine in 1949. Today Reny's employs 525 employees and has 17 store locations in Maine. Renys is one of the oldest family-owned businesses that still exist in the State of Maine.

U.S. Senator Olympia J. Snowe and former Governor John R. McKernan, Jr. issued a statement on the passing of Bob Reny in 2009, remarking that Reny had been "a dear friend to us since our days in the state legislature. Bob was a true entrepreneur and visionary business owner whose pioneering spirit turned a unique business idea into a staple of communities throughout Maine."

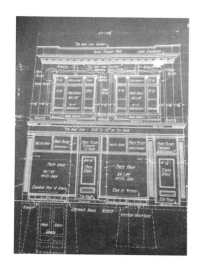

The Tack Stop

Stephen Rickens

The Tack Stop began in 1997 with Carolyn's unbreakable habit of buying barrel racing equipment. Her husband Steve suggested she open a barrel racing supply store in the hopes that it would curb her appetite for buying new equipment.

Carolyn took the challenge! She started selling used equipment on her front porch and soon her business exploded.

Carolyn and Steve are very active members of the barrel racing community. Carolyn competes in barrel racing and pole bending. Her horse Mona's Little Guy was a Top 10 at the 2002 All American Quarter Horse Congress in Senior Pole Bending. Carolyn continues to compete in AQHA, NBHA, NPBA, and local jack pots.

At The Tack Stop we try to keep in touch with what the barrel racers and pole benders are looking for, both in products and service. We may not have competed in the NFR, (yet, we're still dreaming!) but we also want to have the best equipment for our barrel horses. We strive to find the latest and most dependable equipment that barrel racers want! We have the opportunity to carry hundreds of products, however we have a motto, "If we won't use it on our horses, we won't sell it". We are not here to sell quantity, but QUALITY! We think of our customers as "clients". We strive to have the best customer service out there. We try to share our knowledge, but we also gain vast amounts of knowledge from our "clients".

The Tack Stop is located at 1519 Main Street in Pittsfield. Situated in a small rustic building surrounded by open fields and horses grazing nearby. When you enter the building you are immediately hit with the deep leather scent of saddles and equipment. Followed by blingy halters and show equipment! 2 rooms filled with training equipment, bits, reins, horse boots and gear for the barrel racer to choose from. Not only do we have our store, but we have a website that we sell to customers all over the world!

Pittsfield Redemption Center

Kurt Dodge with Jane Woodruff

On April 1, 2016, Lori and Kurt Dodge opened their business, the Pittsfield Redemption Center, on South Main Street. Kurt had previously been employed in Clinton doing similar work and waited for an opportunity to start his own business. He explains that only one state license per town is issued unless the service is attached to a grocery store such as the one at Bud's.

Anyone entering their building can't help but note the large number of tall cartons holding returnables

and realize the diversity of bottles and cans that Kurt and his staff must sort. While customers may at times be disgruntled that some cans or bottles aren't returnable, the staff must be vigilant to ensure that the items have the symbol designating a ME deposit. Heavy fines can be levied against the Dodges if this practice isn't followed.

The Redemption Center is open daily except Sunday and works with community groups in taking massive amounts of containers from their bottle drives. The Dodges also have a weekly drawing where a customer can win a $25 gift certificate from a local business.

PERSONAL SERVICES

Stan Trembly

Stan Tremblay has not only seen the changes on Main Street, he has been part of them. Stan has been on the east side and the west. He has been in five different locations in over the fifty years that he has been barbering in Pittsfield.

After three years working with Frank Jacques, Stan bought the business in 1968 that he has been running ever since. With no plans to retire, it is his "hope that it's another twenty years" that he will be barbering on Main Street.

Eden Day Spa

Jillyann Butler

Eden Day Spa - once known as Amici Nail Spa - opened its new location at 145 Main Street in Pittsfield on December 7, 2016 by Jillyann Butler. The new building was purchased in May of 2016 and renovations were done by Jillyann's husband, Jacob Butler, and family. It truly was a labor of love. At Eden Day Spa, we offer nail services by Jillyann Butler including manicures, pedicures, and acrylics; while Molly Ferguson offers hair services for men, women, and children including cuts, color, and facial waxing. We have hosted 2 open houses, one shortly after our December opening, and one to celebrate our one-year anniversary in December of 2017. This event allowed us to open our doors for the community to take a peek into our new space and see what we were all about. We have enjoyed a very good first year meeting new people and making new clients and look forward to the year ahead. This spring we are adding a new nail tech to our team to help keep up with our growing clientele and hope to be adding a massage therapist/esthetician to expand our services in the near future. We are so grateful for how the people of Pittsfield have welcomed us into their community and look forward to the coming season.

Copper Salon

Debra Higgins

Copper is a hair salon owned by Debra Higgins and started in 2014. Originally located on Main Street, it is now on Sebasticook Street in the building considered "The Old Credit Union".

Copper offers hair services from cuts, colors, highlights and many other color techniques that include freehand painting and bright fashion shades. Copper has three talented hair stylists: Debra Higgins, Alexandra Faria and Eve Condon who take time to further their education and love their jobs making people feel and look their best. Stylists at Copper focus on healthy, beautiful hair and work hard to educate their clients on how to maintain it with low maintenance, easy styling and lovely natural products. As we celebrate our fourth year in business, we are grateful to our families, community, and clients from afar for the support and encouragement.

Loretta's
Loretta Martin

Pittsfield welcomed me as I opened my first salon 40 years ago!

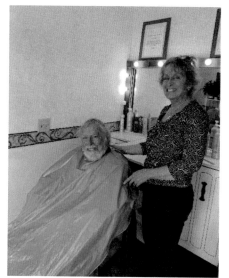

After working a short while in Bangor, as a hairstylist, I was encouraged and supported by friends and family to "be on my own". The location and size of Pittsfield seemed to be just right, and finding an available spot on Main St. was perfect! It felt great and proved to be successful for over 9 years.

My following shop location was North Lancey Street. For more than 6 years it was a nice "step up", joining other businesses, making new friends and enjoying a larger, brighter place, with extra parking.

The summer of '94 I was introduced to 152 Hartland Ave. and the possibilities of being a home owner, along with space for my shop, LORETTA'S. Another Dream Come True! I can hardly believe 24 years at this address will soon total 40 years enjoying Pittsfield and all it has to offer, hoping that I have been able to give back to this wonderful community I am proud to call HOME.

TNT SALON & SPA

Tuyet Clark with Jane Woodruff

Her husband Ken calls her "Dynamite" because of the initials of her Vietnamese name: TNT which stands for Tuyet Ngoc Tu. This is the name she has chosen for her salon where she performs facials, hair and nail care as well as eyelash extensions. She traveled to California with her husband to take a week-long course in lash extensions and become certified from Daniel Phu Dinh, inventor of Longori Lashes, who at the encouragement of Priscilla Presley has received a patent for his product.

Besides operating her own shop, Tuyet works at DK Nail Salon in Waterville. She also does the "paperwork" for her husband's business as she took classes in Vietnam for accounting and computer work which she loves. Before she became so busy at home, she had volunteered in the Human Resources Department of Sebasticook Valley Hospital where she did this type of work. Like her husband, she basically works seven days a week and any "vacation" they take is work-related.

Detail & Color Tattoo

Joe Staples

Detail & Color Tattoo was established in March 24th, 2000. Located at 137 Crawford Road, in Pittsfield, our business spent fifteen years in Skowhegan and now has been in Pittsfield for two and a half years. Pictures of my work can be seen on Facebook at: Detailandcolortattoo/facebook. We have a clean and friendly atmosphere and an easy to find location just one mile from the Interstate 95 exits. With twenty-one years of experience, we are still going strong after many other studios have come and gone. Check us out next time you are thinking about getting a tattoo and you will be glad you did. Get your next tattoo at Detail & Color Tattoo.

Cindy's Heart Felt Day Care

Cindy Emery with Jane Woodruff

For nearly three decades Cindy Emery has been running a day care program out of her home. Licensed to care for up to twelve children, she looks after youngsters from 2 to 12 years of age. Cindy also is a licensed HomeStart provider, meaning that the children in her care have access to special services and consultants. This program from Kennebec Valley Community Action Program combines Early Head Start and Family Child Care. She was one of only three providers in the state designated to field-test the HomeStart program when it first began.

Cindy began working in this field when as a stay-at-home mom doing bookkeeping work for her husband's Exxon business, she wanted to have other children in her home for her daughter to socialize with. This evolved into her now full-time occupation.

Darlene's Daycare

Darlene Steeves

Darlene's is a family childcare home licensed through the state of Maine. My business originally started in 1998 unlicensed with the birth of my second son and taking care of just two children plus my own. I became licensed originally in the year 2000 and ran a very successful childcare until the year 2007. Later, working in the school system for seven years as a special ed tech, I helped children with special needs. I went back into childcare in order to care for my grandchildren in 2014.

The daycare is currently licensed and at full capacity with eight children, two of which are my grandchildren. I am also a Home start childcare provider, offering Headstart educational activities in my home. HomeStart is a federally funded program based out of KVCAP in Waterville. HomeStart provides me with lots of support: such as funding for better activities and equipment, and a weekly visit from a HomeStart education consultant to help me to be able to provide these services for the families that I serve. I enjoy my job, love working with the children and families that I care for and being able to work from home.

Artful Alterations

Rebecca Thompson

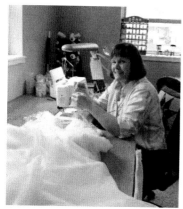

Artful Alterations, owned and operated by Becky Thompson, is located in the old Grammar School building on North Lancey Street. With a degree in Home Economics education and previous years of teaching experience, Becky is putting over 30 years of sewing experience, into her work, specializing in altering wedding, prom and other formal gowns. During slower times, she mends and repairs casual clothing. In 2018, at 6 years old, Artful Alterations grew from a one-woman operation to a workforce of three, which is very exciting.

As a former teacher, Becky feels at home in the old school building and her clients love the cheerful character it offers. As one of a few professional seamstresses in Maine, to specialize in wedding gown alterations, Becky is happy with the response to her work

and referrals leading her to be booked up months in advance. With clients being drawn from all over the state, lunch is often enjoyed in local eateries on Main Street, followed by a recommended walk in the park. Frequently a trip to Renys is on the agenda for clients to round out their visit to Pittsfield. Becky's children were raised in Pittsfield and Detroit and the UU Church, now Meetinghouse. "Pittsfield is a gem, and it's fun to share it with visitors and offer a service so welcomed by brides and their families!"

Dianna's Laundromat

Richard Bellows with Jane Woodruff

Dick Bellows and his wife, Dianna, opened the laundromat adjacent to Richie's Pizza on South Main Street in 2003. Originally, the structure was built in 1996 and for years, housed a variety of businesses such as equipment rental, a cleaning service, and a roofing business.

When Sessa Menendez' bowling alley and laundromat burned nearby, the Bellows' waited for 6 months to see if these would be rebuilt. When that didn't occur, they decided to open a laundromat which is available the same hours as Richie's.

Health Services

Chiropractors

Paul K. West, D.C. & Jeremy P. West, D.C.

The chiropractic office of Dr. Paul K. West was established on Somerset Avenue in Pittsfield, on April 1, 1986. Dr. West, being a graduate of MCI high school in Pittsfield, decided to return, after graduating from chiropractic college in St. Louis, Missouri. He began his family-centered practice as a home office at 221 Somerset Avenue. He and his wife Patty lived in an apartment, over the office until 1990. With their third child on the way, they purchased a farm on Route 100, in Pittsfield, where they reside today.

The first anniversary of his practice opening was marked by the flood of '87. Before the water got too high, around 5 AM, Dave Moody came to the office, to help remove the furnace motor, from the basement. Paul and Patty were evacuated by Lyford Beverage in his boat. Patty was eight months pregnant, getting into and out of the boat was a little tricky! That day was marked not only by the flood, but also neighbor helping neighbor.

Over the years, his practice grew and served Pittsfield and surrounding towns with chiropractic care. In 2014 Dr. Paul West was pleased to announce, the addition of his son, Dr. Jeremy West to his practice. Jeremy attended the same chiropractic college as his dad. Together they provide comprehensive chiropractic care at their Somerset Avenue office.

Dr. Paul and Dr. Jeremy are members of the Maine Chiropractic Association and the American

Chiropractic Association. Dr. Paul is past president of the local Kiwanis club; he also has been a youth baseball coach and a high school assistant baseball coach. The Drs. West office, is pleased to be part of the fabric of this community, providing contemporary care in a nostalgic, home office setting.

Eye Care of Maine

Eye Care of Maine has been caring for patients in central Maine since the early 1920's. In the early 80's, Dr. Fred Lagomarsino performed cataract surgeries at the Sebasticook Valley Hospital and clinic patients were seen out of a house on Hartland Ave. About a decade later in 1993, Pittsfield native Peter Kohler, MD started working for the practice. By the year 2000, Dr. Michael Parks had joined the practice at their current location, 123 Somerset Plaza, and continues to work for them to this day. Eye Care of Maine takes pride in continuing to serve the Pittsfield community with the highest quality of care and service for their patients.

A New You Massage Inc.

Terri Jean Grant

A New You Massage Inc. was opened originally in 2015, located in the Copper Salon. In March 2017, A New You Massage Inc. relocated to 113 North Lancey Street. Terri Jean (Grant) Wilkinson is a licensed massage therapist specializing in trigger point release. Her technique as a massage therapist is designed to incorporate therapeutic massage in order to achieve a higher state of relaxation and stress reduction. The business donates one-hour massages to numerous fundraisers as well as giving discounted chair massages to local school educators and small businesses. Terri and her siblings grew up, attended schools and participated in local sports, creating lifelong relationships in Pittsfield. A New You Massage Inc. is lucky to be welcomed with open arms by the community of Pittsfield.

Personal Counseling Practices

Sarah Williams

- Sarah Williams, LCSW
- Tina Meadow, LCSW
- Chris Kerr, LCSW
- Leslie Marchus, LCPC-CC

We are a four-person group of counselors serving our local community. We meet with individuals, couples, and families to assist them in creating positive change. We accept all ages of clients and a wide range of health insurance plans. We are trained and board certified to treat clinical depression, anxiety, Post Traumatic Stress Disorder, Personality Disorders, grief, and personal stress, as well as many other issues. To access our services we prefer a referral from your primary care provider but individuals may call directly as well. Our offices are located in 113 North Lancey Street downtown.

Group Fitness Classes & Personal Training

Shawna Melanson

Shawna Melanson is a Certified Personal Trainer and earned her B.S. in Exercise Science. In 2011, she opened her own Group Fitness Classes and Personal Training business attracting clients from the

Pittsfield & Newport area. Shawna offers fitness training for small groups, large groups, and individuals. The most popular class is the Outdoor Bootcamp program in which she brings participants to various parks in town, utilizing the lay of the land, their own bodyweight, and various pieces of fitness equipment such as sand bags, slosh sticks, fire hose, weights, bands, and more, to challenge the fitness levels of her participants. Shawna travels to clients' homes and offices, as well as offering classes at the local recreation centers in the Central Maine area. Shawna teaches fitness to those of all ages and abilities; with classes offering stretching, strength training, cardio endurance training, athlete conditioning, and senior strength & flexibility programs.

Shorey-Nichols Funeral Home & Cremation Services

Glenn & Rachel Nichols with Jane Woodruff

Glenn and Rachel Nichols aptly stated, "It's a calling." This husband and wife team are available to grieving families 24/7 and are never more than a forty-five minute drive from Pittsfield. They have dedicated their lives to serving Pittsfield area residents with their kind and compassionate care in providing end-of-life services for eighty to hundred families per year.

Both received pastoral training in a 3-year program as well as later earning their associates degrees with its two thousand hour apprenticeship to become licensed funeral directors. Along with their daughter Mikaela, who works in the administrative aspects of the business, the Nichols function as team. Working part-time as licensed funeral attendants are Michael Havey, Ronald Tasker, Jeff Vanadestine and Christopher Rines.

Honoring Donald Shorey who moved the funeral home to its present location on Hartland Avenue in November 1961, the Nichols added their name to his. They carried forward the tradition of an independent and local funeral home when they purchased it from a corporate funeral business in 2007. They have felt embraced with open arms by the community that they serve.

ANIMAL SERVICES

Right on the Mark Dog Training, LLC
Stephani Morancie

Right on the Mark Dog Training, LLC (ROTM) was started in 2012 by Stephani Morancie. ROTM offers positive reinforcement-based group dog training classes and in-home private lessons in the Pittsfield area and the Belfast area. Group classes usually consist of no more than 5 students per class and run for one hour a week for four weeks. Dogs from age 8 weeks to senior are welcome in class (Yes! Old dogs CAN learn new tricks).

ROTM is a proud member of the Pet Professional Guild, which promotes force and fear free training for all animals. Force and fear free training means that no shock, no pain, no choke, no fear, no physical force, no compulsion-based methods are employed to train or care for a pet.

The Dog House
Danielle Aziz

My name is Danielle Aziz and I have been grooming since 2004. I bought The Dog House from the former owner in 2006. I am at a convenient location in town. I treat each dog as if they were my own. I work alone and offer one on one grooming services by appointment.

Canine Insights, LLC

Breanna Norris KPA-CTP (certified dog trainer)

Canine Insights, LLC was established in July 2016 by Breanna Norris, a Pittsfield native.

Canine Insights is a professional dog training business that offers group and private lessons in the Pittsfield and Waterville areas. Breanna specializes in puppies, fun with dogs, shy and fearful dogs and

assisting families to help make their dog easier to live with.

Canine Insights works with schools and organizations to discuss dog bite prevention, safety, kids & dogs, and dog body language. Breanna has worked with several other domestic and some non-domesticated species including horses, rats, cats, and rabbits, but dogs are typically her focus.

Canine Insights offers modern training that is free of pain, force or frustration. Canine Insights training focuses on assisting people to have a better relationship with their dog and a lifetime of enjoyment together. Canine Insights is a proud member of the Shock Free Coalition.

Breanna has studied under Terry Ryan through the Karen Pryor Academy and holds several certificates in training as well as doing many hours of continuing education. She has been an active professional member in the Pet Professional Guild since 2013. She sits on the Advocacy Committee and Shelter & Rescue Committee for the guild. She is also on the board of Humane Society Waterville Area, the shelter that the town of Pittsfield contracts with. Breanna assists the shelter with dog enrichment and cat and dog behavior and occasionally works with other shelters, rescues, and veterinarians on special cases. website: canineinsightsllc .com

Somerset Veterinary Clinic

Tim Powers, D.V.M. with Jane Woodruff

Horses are what drew Dr. Tim Powers to Pittsfield in 1973 while working for Kennebec Veterinary Services. Tim spent one day a week treating horses at the Cianchette Stables owned by Ival, Alton, and Ken and located on South Main Street. At that time, twenty Standardbreds were stabled there and were raced throughout Maine and sometimes as far away as New York. Tim became known statewide as an equine specialist not only working for the Cianchette stables but covering horses at harness racing and training tracks throughout the state.

In 1987 just after the flood, the brothers sold their stables to Tim and he moved to town. Tim described the people in the area as "being very nice to me" and at their prompting in 1990-91, he added treating small animals to his practice. Today he still covers treating horses at tracks and training centers spending a day a week at Windsor where twenty horses are housed during the winter and over 100 seen in the full season. As Tim describes his work, a large cat emits a "meow" reminiscent of the cat's call in the Meow Mix commercial for which this cat is named. One time while on his tractor, Tim saw a black spot in his field discovering what initially he had taken to be a muskrat was in fact this cat who was hungry and freezing. Similarly, he saved his dog Dozer from being euthanized by its owners when its hip dysplasia was discovered. Standing nearby is Bob, his horse of 27 years. While Tim describes his practice as an "old school vet service", it is clear that his love of animals - large and small - is seen in the ones that surround him.

FUEL & AUTO

Dead River Company

Dead River Company has been family-owned, by the same Maine family for 109 years. An impressive stretch of history that saw the company evolve from a forest products enterprise on the banks of the Dead River in northern Maine to the largest home heating provider north of Boston, with 52 offices across Maine, New Hampshire Vermont, and western Massachusetts. Including one in Pittsfield, Maine.

As in every community it serves, Dead River Company enjoys being a part of the special events and day-to-day activities in Pittsfield. When people entrust the heating and safety of their homes to Dead River Company, they make sure to pay that forward by fully embracing the opportunity to become involved in what's important to Pittsfield.

Pittsfield is a place where neighbors pay attention to one another and offer help when it's needed. Because food and fuel insecurity are primary focuses of Dead River Company, it has donated to local food banks, and fuel assistance programs, as well as contributed fuel to various fundraisers in town. Because its other strong priority is education, Dead River Company has supported local schools by advertising in school programs and yearbooks. And because Dead River Company thinks building community bonds is important; it's also supported town-wide celebrations such as Pittsfield's signature event, the Central Maine Egg Festival. This year, it will be a part of the bicentennial golf tournament, too.

Dead River Company understands that these types of events and celebrations, where neighbors help neighbors and people volunteer to make a town the kind of place they want to live and raise a family are what create the fabric of a community. This bicentennial book is a perfect example of volunteers, working to give something to the town. Each of the family-friendly events happening throughout the year is the work of volunteers. The people of Pittsfield are what make it consistently ranked as one of the choicest places to live in Maine.

Dead River Company may share only recent history with Pittsfield, but at 109 years old, it shares the values of pride in founding, succession, evolution, and transformation as well as the community values of integrity, caring, and excellence.

Frost's Mobil Station

Forest Frost with Jane Woodruff

For years, the winged red horse was the symbol flying on the gas station known as Frost's Mobil Station. While the station now pumps APEX gas, owner Forest Frost is quick to point out that he carries the Mobil line of products, just not the gas. Apparently, there are few Mobil gas stations in Maine anymore.

Forest has been working out of this station since its original opening in December 1957 when it was built by J.R. Cianchette to service his construction company vehicles as well as the general public. Over the years, his brothers Roland and Dino have worked with him servicing vehicles and pumping gas. As Forest says, "Between them, his brothers have given him nearly fifty years." In June of 2001 Forest purchased the station from "Aunt Stell", J.R. Cianchette's widow.

Currently, he works 6 days a week over 10 hours a day and has one part-time employee. One of his loyal customers who has been coming to him to service her car for fifty to sixty years worried that Forest might consider retiring. She asked, "Who will I trust my car to?" She need not worry. Forest has no plans to retire.

Ron's

Ron Porter with Jane Woodruff

Since 2000, Ron Porter has owned and operated the business known as Ron's. Located in the heart of downtown on the corner of Easy and Main Streets, Ron provides comprehensive automotive repair services. As he says, "He does everything from bumper to bumper." Ron has been doing mechanical work since he was a teenager and had worked for the prior owner of the station before buying the business. At that time, it also provided gasoline, hence the name. For the past eight or nine years, he no longer has been pumping gas leaving him free to do service work on vehicles.

Many may not know that Ron's stands on a historic site. This land originally was occupied by George

Brown who in 1800 built the first frame house in Pittsfield. This house later became an inn known as the Lancey Homestead in the 1820s before its last innkeeper Isaac Lancey built the hotel just down the street a block. The house once again served as a residence before becoming the parsonage for the First Universalist Church until its demise. It was sold to an oil company who had it demolished and the current building became a service station in the 1950s. And that it remains to this day serving its many customers well with its warm and friendly service.

Folsom's Used Cars
Greg Folsom

Folsom's Used Cars was started on Cross St. in 1952 by Neil and Lorraine Folsom as a part time car sales business. In 1954 they moved to Hartland Avenue. where it is today, owned by second generation Greg and Braunda Folsom. It is and always was a "Mom and Pop" business. Over the years, we've seen many makes and models of cars, both good and bad. We're looking forward to being a part of Pittsfield for many more years. Happy 200th Birthday.

Varney Chevrolet

Sonny Spratt with Jane Woodruff

From cows to cars. Some townspeople may remember the farm with the gambrel barn and silo where J.R. Cianchette grazed Herefords. An image of this scene was captured in a large-scale photograph that, for years, hung in the First National Bank of Pittsfield. This farm was transformed into an auto dealership by J.K. Wright where trucks and cars replaced the cattle on the street-side of Somerset Avenue. The barn was turned into a showroom, the silo into a waiting room for customers.

Varney Chevrolet purchased this dealership in February of 2005. A scant two months later the barn caught fire taking with it five vehicles including a shop truck and wrecker. The apparent source was electrical. The large new structure they have today houses its showcase as well as the service department.

Varney Chevrolet is a customer-oriented dealership that draws clients from central Maine from Augusta to Bangor and as far away as Aroostook County. While part of a larger dealer group, they have the feel of a small hometown dealership. As Sonny says, "No matter what's going on, we will have transportation (for our customers)."

Ken's Classics

Ken Clark with Jane Woodruff

California, New Zealand, Missouri, North Carolina, Michigan, Texas ... all cars from away, cars in various stages of restoration find their way to Ken Clark and his re-converted chicken barn on Route 100. When asked which of the autos are his favorite, his response: "They are all my favorites."

Ken specializes in the restoration of the Cord, the first front wheel drive car that was manufactured by the Auburn Automobile Company of Indiana from June of 1929 to December 1931. In 1994, Ken joined the Auburn Duesenberg Club (ACD) and three years later, he has been restoring an auto from club members every year since. He is not limited to the restoration of this automobile only as evidenced by the Ford Model T truck or the 1923 Graham Brothers Truck that are parked in his shop.

Ken initially wanted to be a farmer but working with George Flood "cured" him of that. Fixing cars was easy for him as he helped his uncle in Unity. In the fall of 1979, when "Chuck" Cianchette lost his mechanic for his antique cars, "Babe" Tozier of Unity suggested contacting Ken who was working as a truck driver for H.E. Sargent at the time.

By the following spring, Ken started this work and has been doing it ever since. By December of 1982, he had moved to his current home in Pittsfield while still working for "Chuck" and three years later he started his own business where customers began bringing vehicles to him.

The restorations that he performs require a multitude of skills from mechanic work to woodworking to metalwork to upholstery. Cars that have been outdoors for 50 years may require his manufacturing parts - be they metal or wood. With over 25.000 parts per car, he needs to be a magician. Each restoration is an act of artistry and love and as Ken says, "I have been 'retired' for 40 years because I love my job. It has been quite a ride." Working 7 days a week, as one might expect he has no plans of ever retiring.

Scrub-A-Dub

Brady Snowman with Jane Woodruff

Pittsfield's car wash has been available to residents since 1987 when local realtor Jim Moorehead had it built. It is located on the lot adjacent to the house that was once part of J.R. Cianchette's cattle farm on Somerset Avenue. A prominent decorative Scrub-A-Dub sign indicates the entrance to its site and it is conveniently located next to Varney's Chevrolet.

Ownership has changed hands over the years. It is currently operated by Brady Snowman who took ownership in 2016. Originally it had 4 self-serve bays, but in the early 1990s, one of the bays was converted to automatic - a "touchless" one - meaning that no brushes are used, only high-pressure sprays. Adjacent to the bays is a vacuum system available for cleaning car interiors.

A & D Towing

David Lyons with Jane Woodruff

As a sixteen-year old, David Lyons learned some of his trade from his father who ran a junk yard in Hartland. In 1971, he and his wife Arlene moved to Pittsfield where he started a business called Pittsfield Car Crushers. Basically, Dave would use his loader to crush cars then load them onto a trailer to truck them to Portland or Waterville for recycling. Over time his business evolved into towing vehicles as well as trading and selling cars and trucks which he had repaired. Dave has hauled vehicles from Kittery to the County. As the focus of his business changed, so did its name going to Lyons Towing and then most recently to A & D Towing. Wisely he placed his wife's initial first.

213

HOME BUSINESSES

163 Design Company

by Mark Schumpert

Driving along back roads across the state of Maine, dreaming up ideas together; that's what we've done for a long time. In 2012 we made the leap from dreaming to creating and haven't looked back.

We are a family business; husband and wife, daughter and son-in-law and even grandsons who love to pitch ideas and help package. We live in the same town, on the same street, and enjoy celebrating life together.

There is always a new idea around every corner; our shop is constantly evolving. Our name comes straight from Proverbs 16:3..."Commit to the Lord whatever you do, and He will establish your plans." We've experienced that to be true, time and time again. While this business supports our families, we are also passionate about giving back. So please know that your purchases feed and clothe not only us, but whenever God plants a giving opportunity in our hearts, we follow His lead!

Smiling Otis Studio

Russ Cox

Author & Illustrator

Russ Cox was born and raised in the hills of Tennessee. After studying art,

Smiling Otis

especially graphic design and illustration, he met his wife in Pennsylvania. Through a series of fortunate events, he and his wife found themselves settling in the town of Pittsfield. They were looking for a small town with charm and scenic beauty. After driving through many areas of Maine, they found their future home in Pittsfield. They tell folks that Pittsfield picked them. From the first moment they drove

through the town, it was love at first sight. The charming downtown, the many parks and bodies of water in the town limits, and the people. The towns folk greeted the two out-of-towners with open arms, and have treated them as family ever since.

Since moving to the area, Russ has built a career in publishing. He has illustrated over 20 books for children, and has written, as well as illustrated, his own book, *Faraway Friends*. When he is not at his drawing table, he enjoys playing the banjo, hiking and traveling throughout Maine, and running amok in the snow. He can often be found at the town library, sketching, writing, and reading books in the children's book section. He is the one too large for the kiddie chairs.

The House Next Door Bed and Breakfast

Milton Webber

The House Next Door Bed and Breakfast was established in 2011. The name is quite simple and was created in part, because of its close proximity to MCI. Because of the school's burgeoning international student body, and parents who were bringing their sons and daughters to the campus, the B&B was the logical choice to become home away from home to them.

The B&B started out in space that originally was my grandfather's medical office and waiting room, and now has finally found its new space, inhabiting the entire second floor. Overnight stays come with a home-cooked breakfast in the morning. The B&B is within walking distance to all of Pittsfield's numerous parks, shops, and restaurants.

Identities @ 303 Main

Milton Webber

Identities @ 303 Main was established in 2017. It was created as gallery space to showcase artwork designed by Milt Webber and is in shared space with The House Next Door Bed and Breakfast.

Original work is and has been created by Milton Webber i.e. Identities by M.A. Webber. A 1975 graduate of MECA (formerly the Portland School of Art), Milt for many years worked in advertising agencies throughout New England. He finally came "home" saying "What can I create for you?"

Ollie Loops
Amanda Todaro

It all started for me in March 2013 when a few of my photography friends were in search of a prop

designer for all their adorable newborn photo shoots. Loving the idea of learning a new craft, I went to the store and picked up some yarn, the basic crochet hooks, and a 'How to Crochet Book'. Well, that book was written in a WHOLE new language to me! I got frustrated very quickly and almost wanted to quit right then and there…but I couldn't, I was determined to learn!

I ended up searching online and founds some great blogs, tutorials, and videos. I sat in my computer chair and just followed along. My first work is embarrassing as I'm sure any first timer's was. It was supposed to be a square- Yet, I don't even think there is a name for the shape I created. It was just a warped mess. BUT, I have it hanging over my computer desk to remind me of how far I've come since then. By the end of October, I felt comfortable enough in my craft to start taking orders and seeing what I could create. Now, almost 5 years I'm still at it!

I've been able to create pieces for new babies that they can carry with them through their lives. I've made decor pieces, that many of my customers have set out for display. I've even been able to piece together a precious heirloom for a family, and now every Christmas they get to enjoy the tree skirt their Grandma had started, but sadly, passed before finishing.

For now, I still just receive orders by Facebook or Email. One day I'm hoping to open a small online store. You can reach me at Facebook .com/OllieLoops or by Email – ollieloopscrochet @ gmail .com

Steve Martin, Inc.

Steve Martin

Steve Martin started his construction business in Pittsfield in 1980. He worked during the winter months delivering oil for Pittsfield Coal & Oil and in the spring would do his contracting work. He did this for about 5 years until the business grew enough that he could do it year round. He built six homes in Forest Park and many in the surrounding area. In the past forty years, he has done improvement to many homes in Pittsfield. One of the most memorable projects was remodeling MCI's Alumni Hall classrooms where several handwritten names of the original carpenters were discovered during the construction. It has been rewarding for this company to see the many improvements they have made in the town of Pittsfield and the community.

Tom Chadwick, Inc.

Sharon Chadwick

Tom and Sharon Chadwick moved to Pittsfield on Valentine's Day in 1966 to be closer to Sharon's family in Clinton. Tom had acquired a job at MCI in the maintenance department after learning of an opening from his sister Marion Mosher whose husband David was an instructor there. While still working at MCI as Head of Buildings and Grounds, Tom went to night school and got his Master Electrician's license in 1973. Soon after that, he started his own small electrical business called Tom's Electric.

In 1990, Tom incorporated his business changing the name to Tom Chadwick, Inc. A large portion of the community supported Tom and his business. By this time he had acquired faithful, returning industrial, commercial, and residential customers. Later the industrial businesses closed or moved out of town just leaving his commercial and residential work.

Over the years Sharon has done all of Tom's bookkeeping compilations in addition to her health-related employment in town. In 2002, Sharon opened their home to become a Bed & Breakfast which was in operation for twelve years.

Now both Tom and Sharon are happily working part-time, keeping involved, and busy with no plans to retire.

Dan Higgins - Residential Carpentry

Daniel Higgins

I got my start working for Jock Lasselle in the late 1980s doing foundations and framing. In 1999, I went on to work for myself doing small residential carpentry projects. I've had good fortune to work with people like Steve Rollins and Dale Duplisea. They've shared a lot of knowledge and skills of the trade with me over the years.

J & D Builders

Billie-Jo Reed

J & D Builders is honored to be a part of Pittsfield's Bicentennial, for the business is celebrating its 40th Anniversary this year. Jock Lasselle began his General Contractor business 40 years ago in this small town of Pittsfield. J & D Builders completes residential and commercial properties from the ground up.

J & D Builders has completed many projects and jobs to help this community over the years with some being the following:

Built the Little League sign for the sponsorships

Built the Snack building at Warsaw

Built tower for the visiting football team at MCI

Built an addition onto the Husky Hut

Built dug-outs for MCI baseball at Manson Park

Put in the slabs for the Warsaw at both girls softball and boys baseball fields

Put in the foundation for the goal posts

Put in the concrete for the Pittsfield Town pool

Dave's Gas Service

Dave Quint

My business, Dave's Gas Service, was started in 2009. I started this business to provide service for individuals and companies that need natural gas and propane equipment installed and serviced.

Dave's Gas Service was originally purchased by my parents, Marty and Mary in 1959. They bought the business and property on North Main Street where my parents started a successful propane business and raised seven children.

I decided to name my business after the original enterprise in an effort to come "full circle" and remember the roots from which our family has grown and been blessed. I am very fortunate to have had the opportunity to grow up, work, and raise a family here in Pittsfield. To everyone, live, laugh and enjoy life. Dave & Pat

JMR's Roofing & Painting

Jason Ramsdell

JMR's is a locally-owned painting and carpentry business located in Pittsfield. Our expertise is in all aspects of complete home remodeling, both interior and exterior. We pride ourselves on customer service, top-notch quality work, and affordable services. We have lived in Pittsfield for fifteen years and have worked all over the state. It's a great central location to be based out of. We look forward to working lots of years to come. The JMR's team thanks Pittsfield for including us in the bicentennial.

Harriman Electric

Don Harriman

Don Harriman has been in the electrical/electronic trades since 1966. While attending the University of Maine, he worked as an electrician in the greater Bangor/Brewer area. Don has worked in the town of Pittsfield for thirty-eight years along with his son Chris who joined him after completing college. They both hold Master Licenses and are fully insured. The duo has been in the majority of the homes in the town to repair electrical problems and to install new electrical systems. They also do residential and commercial work in Somerset County and adjacent counties.

They have done pro bono work in conjunction with the Town and KVCAP. Central Maine Power Company would bring a hazardous situation to the Town's or KVCAP's attention and then call Don. One unusual story is that of an elderly resident. As Don tells it, "Her service had burned out. She could not believe that we would be so kind to as to help her at no cost. She was so very happy and thanked me profusely. The power company re-energized the service around 11 AM. Sadly, she passed away around noon time of a heart attack. About 1 PM after being told of what had happened to her, I stopped at the foot of Grove Hill to the site of pick-up trucks being loaded up with her personal effects. I was greeted with 'Do we owe you money?' I told them 'no' and added that I was sorry for their loss."

The company motto is "There is no right way to do a wrong thing." All work will be done to the current national electrical code standards (we don't do shortcuts). Don also renovated the Riverside School at the foot of Grove Hill to include five two- bedroom apartments and a karate school. They have since sold the Riverside School property.

Young's Lawn Car & Plowing

Chris Young

Young's Lawn Care & Plowing owned by Chris Young started in 2009. Since I was young, my father was always trying to persuade me to start a lawn care service. After working at SAS Shoe for nearly 20 years, I followed my father's advice. I decided to start Young's Lawn Care & Plowing so I can provide quality work at reasonable rates. I believe people should be treated the same way that I would expect to be treated. I take pride in reliability and quality services.

I provide lawn care & plowing services. Services include; mowing, weed whacking, spring & fall cleanups, leaf removal, hedge trimming, mulch, bush-hogging, tractor services, compost, plowing. In the summer and during school vacations my son David has been working with me. I enjoy working side by side with my son and teaching him along the way.

It seems fitting to end this business section with a tribute to Pittsfield by someone drawn here by his wife and her connections to it and who has come to love this town.

Pittsfield Plumbing
Rick White

I started my career as an apprentice plumber in a family owned plumbing and heating company in Manchester, Connecticut, and moved on to a job as a plumbing foreman for a company that was hired to plumb a remodel in UCONN Health Center, a 7 acre healthcare facility in Farmington CT. While the pay was great, the bumper to bumper commute to and from work every day was long and stressful, and being a foreman was not as rewarding for me as the plumbing itself. My wife and I longed for a more peaceful existence in a small town, and since she was born in Maine and much of her family lived in Maine, we decided that's where we wanted to be.

My wife had family in Pittsfield and she'd often visited the town as a child. Many of her ancestors attended MCI and the town always held a special place in her heart. After visiting the town myself on many occasions it didn't take much to convince me to make the move, which we did in 1988.

We thought we knew what to expect. We thought we would be giving up some major conveniences in exchange for our small-town dream. What we found was quite the opposite. Most things were actually more convenient in general. For example, I could pay my taxes and register my car in the same building where I renewed my driver's license. I could WALK there from my house and there'd be no long lines. In Connecticut, I'd need a day off from work if I tried to do all three at once. I used to sit in a line at the drive thru window of the bank for 15 minutes or more just to make a deposit, and it was longer if I went inside. And red lights ... I've waited less time for a train to go by in Pittsfield than I did at some of those red lights. You could buy pizza and BEER at gas stations up here... another convenience that was unheard of in CT at that time. To this day you can't buy a bottle of wine in a supermarket. I am not sure about the beer.

But the biggest treasure we found when moving to Pittsfield was in its people. We quickly realized that people knew who we were long before we knew any of them. I was Virginia's daughter's husband. My wife was Gordon and Marion's granddaughter. We moved up in January. In the spring I went to the

town office to get a fishing license and the clerk filled in all of the information on the form for me, except for height and weight and the color of my eyes.

Not long after moving up to Maine, I entered into a partnership and we opened SEBCO, a successful plumbing and heating business located in Bangor Maine. We were a multi-million dollar company and our success story was written up in a national trade magazine. We hired 14 employees to tackle the plumbing and heating and I found myself in the office, working long hours doing exactly the kind of work I did not enjoy doing, and commuting 45 minutes to do it. I needed to get back into plumbing.

After years at SEBCO, I decided to sell out and open a plumbing business in my own home town of Pittsfield in 1993. It was scary at first, staring at a phone on the desk with a separate business line, and waiting for it to ring, but the people of Pittsfield were supportive and ring it DID. Word of mouth advertising, and an ad in the Rolling Thunder was all it took, and before I knew it, I had all the work I could handle.

Today, most of my work is right here in town. I also open and close many camps in the area when the seasons change. I have opened camps for people from out of state that have been my customers for over 30 years and I've never even met them in person. I went to someone's house recently and they had a teenage girl sitting at their table, and I realized she's that little baby I remember, all grown up now. Time does fly.

I work alone, and I have been very fortunate to stay busy. I can't tell you how many times I'd dial a wrong number, and the person on the other end of the line would say "By the way Rick, while I've got you on the line, I've got a job I'd like you to look at." I meet people at Buds, and sometimes we'll set up an appointment, right then and there. I did this not long ago, and I showed up at the guys house at the specified time, and he wasn't expecting me. When I saw him I realized why. I had the wrong guy. I apologized and explained that I made an appointment with a guy that looked just like him, and he said "OH... that's so and so. He lives on such and such a road!" and he was RIGHT! Only in a small town!

There are so many funny stories I could tell and my wife says I should write a book. I wouldn't need to use last names. You all know who you are. As a plumber I could tell stories that could gross you out as I am sure you can well imagine. But the one that takes the cake is when I was at Ralph Gary's place. I was up on a ladder reaching over my head pulling on some insulation, with my head way back and my mouth open .... and a mouse landed in my mouth! I quickly spit it out and it darted across the floor and Ralph said "What was THAT!". I said "A mouse." He said "what was he doing in your MOUTH!!!"

I love my job, and I enjoy the wonderful people I have met.

CONTRACT SERVICES

Argo Contact Centers

Patrician DeFosse

In 2003, Jason Levesque, a former U.S. Army infantry man and drill sergeant, founded Argo Marketing Group, Inc. His aim was to fulfill the growing need for third-party call center management; Jason built Argo into a full-service customer engagement center.

In 2012, Argo announced plans of a major expansion of its operations to the Pittsfield Area. Argo acquired the former GCS call center in the Somerset Plaza. The goal was for the addition to present up to 50 new jobs. These goals were achieved and much more. Twenty-two of the 25 employees working at the new Argo contact center in Pittsfield were former workers at GCS. The support flooded in, not only from the new employees, but also from the community of Pittsfield. Founder, Jason Levesque said, "The Pittsfield contact center and its strong workforce has been crucial to our success and will continue to be for many years to come."

In 2013, Jason saw the opportunity of expansion to the Lewiston-Auburn area with financial support, the renovations of the old McCrory's Department Store began. By 2014 the renovation was complete with space for up to 250 new jobs, a café and retail storefronts.

Argo believes deeply in the importance of connecting the business and employees to the community to help others help themselves by providing financial support for numerous organizations that include local schools, a theater, a toys for kids program, the Wounded Warriors Project, Make-a-Wish Maine, and more. Argo participates in the Welcome Table every month at the Universalist Church of Pittsfield. There is a Thanksgiving Food Drive in the Pittsfield center every year and during Christmastime Argo "adopts a family". The Pittsfield Team set up and ran an internal Texas Fundraiser for Hurricane Relief, raising $600 total and for every dollar the employees raised, Jason matched. All funds were donated to the Salvation Army.

In 2017, Argo Marketing Group re-branded and now does business as Argo Contact Centers. The re-brand is a more accurate representation of Argo and reflects the services Argo provides its clients. Today. the goal of Argo Contact Centers is, as it always has been and will continue to be, the success of our employees.

Matrika Press

Marie Manning

Matrika Press is an independent publishing house dedicated to publishing works in alignment with Unitarian Universalist Values and liberal religious principles. Matrika Press publishes stories and works that would otherwise remain untold, including anthologies, memoirs, art, poetry, prayer and ritual manuscripts, and other books to bring transformation to the world.

Matrika Press also resurrects out-of-print manuscripts to ensure our historical works remain accessible. Its founder is Pittsfield resident and former Town Councilor, Rev. "Twinkle" Marie Manning. She says the name "Matrika" pays homage to the 50 letters of the Sanskrit alphabet called "the mothers." As the story goes, the Goddess Kali Ma used the letters to form words, and from the words formed all things. Similar to the account in the Christian Bible and Jewish Torah, "in the beginning was the Word…" Many cultures and spiritual faiths around the world have similar beliefs in the creative power of sound. Matrika's is founded in this belief: *Words are powerful.* More than that: *Their vibration are creative forces; they bring all things into being.*

Matrika Press titles are automatically made available to more than tens of thousands of retailers, libraries, schools, and other distribution and fulfillment partners, including Amazon, Barnes & Noble, Chapters/Indigo (Canada), and other well-known book retailers and wholesalers across North America. Also: in the United Kingdom, Europe, Australia and New Zealand and other Global partners. Matrika has published authors from Maine and throughout the United States, to Canada and even overseas. Its fiscal sponsor is UU Women and Religion, a 501c3 organization.

FARMS

Balfour Farm
Arianna Medeiros

Heather and Doug Donahue started off their adventure with a few farm animals as a hobby. Eighteen years later, they have expanded their hobby into a small business. They now produce organic aged cheese, fresh cheese, yogurt and other cultured dairy items, fresh eggs and woodland pork. They are located at **461 Webb Road** in Pittsfield. Their products can be purchased at retail locations and farmers' markets. For more information or questions visit the website at balfourfarmdairy .com or call the farm at (207)213-3159.

Heather and Doug with Joy the Normande

Bellows Farms
Jane Woodruff

Driving along the Snakeroot Road, one passes by cattle on what was once Jim Richmonds' farm. Grazing in the fields are not the dairy cows once seen but Herefords. In 2011, Richard Bellows Sr. and his son Richard Jr. purchased the farm to raise and sell grass-fed beef. FDA-inspected, slaughtered and packaged by Maple Lane Farms of Charleston, Bellows Beef is sold exclusively at Richie's Pizza as is their all-natural pork.

Fletcher Farm

Walter Fletcher with Jane Woodruff

For nearly 40 years, Walter and Edna Fletcher have been milking cows at their farm on the Snakeroot Road. Their son, Austin Fletcher, became a partner in 2009. If you ever wondered about where their milk is shipped, look no further than to one of their barns for a clue. The distinctive black and red plaid barn where the cows are milked is a clear indicator of their being a member of the Cabot Creamery Cooperative. Walter is on its board of directors.

Cows to milk. Walter and Edna began shipping milk in May of 1980. They started with just 20 cows and now - nearly 230 of them - take up much of the day as they are cleaned and hooked up to milking cups attached to a mechanical milking system. Taking about 3 1/2 to 4 hours per shift, the cows are milked at 3 and 10:30 AM and 5:30 PM. As if this weren't enough work, there are young stock - well over 300 - to feed and care for, not to mention other farm tasks of plowing, planting, harvesting, machine maintenance to name just a few.

The Fletchers are a family-owned business, but also employ others to work at their farm. As Walter says, "We have had a lot of kids come through," meaning that they have hired high school students over the years to work milking their cows with them. It is evident that he loves his work as he clearly states, "I am doing what I always wanted to do."

Alex Rizza - Mushroomologist

Barbara Denaro

Alex Rizza, Mushroomologist, moved here in 2003 from Boston where he began to forage for prized mushrooms such as 'Oyster' and 'Hen of the Wood'. Alex shares his fondness and findings of wild mushrooms and has sold to local natural food stores. He also creates recipes for those who appreciate their flavor and natural healing abilities.

Born near Roma Italy, his knowledge of mushrooms began at age 5 with his curiosity to find edible varieties and learn about their nutrients and how they stimulate the immune system. Alex is licensed by The Town of Pittsfield.

Waggin' Tail Farm
Arianna Medeiros

Dante Bachman Helping Out at the Farm

This small family owned farm started out with a couple of goats to clear the yard. Then they got more goats and made a garden to be more self-sustainable. They wanted to be able to provide healthy and nutritional products for their family and customers. Soon it evolved into planning a barn and acquiring more farm animals. They took classes to be able to properly care for the animals. Now they have a fully functioning farm and provide fresh fruits and vegetables, various different breeds of chicken, fresh pork, and maple syrup. Their farm is located at 58 Hussey Rd, Pittsfield, ME. You can contact them through their phone (207-469-8119) or email WagginTailFarmME @ gmail.com They also have a website for more information at waggintailfarmme .com

Mark Mancini Gives Loving Care

Corson Farms
Allison Jamison

Located at 198 Webb Road in Pittsfield, Corson Farms produces and sells maple products of all kinds. In addition to selling their products, they host a Sugar Shack Open House during Maine Maple Syrup weekend. You can find more information at their website: corsonfarms .com

Windy Corner Farm
Matthew Hatch

Windy Corner Farm is a small, family operated farm located at 473 Higgins Road that offers many things alpaca. Contact Matthew and Stacey Hatch at 487-8028 or 355-5577 for raw alpaca fiber, fiber batts, roving, and alpaca yarn, or to arrange a farm visit.

M&M Farm
Allison Jamison

Pittsfield's own U-cut Christmas tree farm is located at 188 Canaan Road. Open seasonally every holiday season, they offer Christmas trees, wreaths and kissing balls ready-made or custom-ordered. For more information find them on facebook at M & M Farm or call Mo Pollard at (207) 951-7215.

Snakeroot Organic Farm
Tom Roberts

Snakeroot Organic Farm started in 1995 when Tom Roberts and Lois Labbe moved from Dixmont, where they had been farming together for five years. We moved onto a run out hayfield in an opening in the woods, and immediately began to improve the soil with cover crops and compost. Today we grow a wide variety of mixed vegetables, fruit, and culinary herbs on 5 acres of gardens. We sell almost all of our garden produce at four farmers markets - Pittsfield, Unity, Waterville, and Orono - each of which we helped start. Occasionally, folks also come by the farm to shop.

We have a heated 2,600 sq. ft. greenhouse and 4,820 sq. ft. in five unheated greenhouses where we grow seedlings for planting and for sale at market. During the winter months the greenhouses are planted with spinach, beet greens, radishes, lettuce, spicy greens, turnips, and carrots for harvest starting in April before the field crops are ready. Then we transplant tomato and cucumbers in the greenhouse for early harvest of those crops also.

In 2000, we began tapping maple trees in our sugarbush, and currently set a little over 400 taps to make our own maple syrup. In 2017, we added Jess Moquin, Sam Gerry, and their son Malachite to the farm. They brought with them a love of poultry and a flock of 100 ducks, geese, turkeys and chickens, thus diversifying our offerings even further.

Freshening Farm

Don Neville, Jr.

We have 5 equine: 2 horses, 1 adopted abused mini pony, & two mini donkeys. No cows or pigs anymore. We have a nice size flock of chickens & ducks, only 2 Chinchillas, and a Great Dane named Tinkerbell (haha). We sell chicken and duck eggs and will hatch some out if there's enough interest. We do sell some hay and bunnies. We no longer make canoe & kayak paddles, due to Don Sr.'s health issues. We are just a small family farm, plus can farm sit for others as needed. We do pet sit so you get the chance to go on vacation and not worry so much about your pet family member. We, Donny and Sandy, are both PSS (personal support specialist, State Certified Home Care Nurses). We luv our little farm and take in needy critters to rehab and they either stay here or we find them a forever home.

Bag End Suri Alpacas of Maine, LLC
Arianna Medeiros

Bag End Suri is a family run farm that breeds award winning alpacas. Jill is one of the owners and began her journey with farming when she was offered a job by a local breeder. She was taught about alpacas and how to care for them for two years. She loved the alpacas at first sight and working with them. So, she carried her knowledge into a family business. They now sell Alpacas, Herdsires, fiber and fiber products, Alpaca themed jewelry, and Nigerian Dwarf dairy goats. Their store hours are on their website at bagendsuris.com. Their phone number is 207-660-5276.

Blueberry Court Farms

Cody Southard

Blueberry Court Farms is a family-run farm on Route 100 near Burnham. It was established in 2012 by Todd Southard, growing both fruit and vegetables on a 12-acre lot. The farm includes over 300 high-bush blueberry shrubs that are open for u-pick. Raspberries, apples, pears, plums, and peaches will be offered for u-pick once they mature. Vegetables offered include potatoes, carrots, tomatoes, beans, peppers, squash, pumpkins, and corn. In the springtime, a small old  fashion maple syrup house called Pappy's Sugar Shack opens selling maple syrup. The family is always trying out new ideas to help further the growth of the family farm.

Somerset Farms

Brenda & Tom Cote

Somerset Farms, located on the Barney Cianchette Road south of Pittsfield on Route 100, was established in 1979. The family of Robert and Gloria Cote then owned a flock of eight hundred sheep, which were sold in 1983. From 1983 to 1987, the farm produced crops for other local farms.

In 1987, Robert's son Thomas purchased a small herd of dairy cows. We have continued to grow the dairy herd and are currently milking four hundred dairy cows along with raising approximately four hundred more replacement heifers. The farm harvests crops of corn and hay off of one thousand acres of land, both owned and rented. The farm currently employs six full time employees and we purchase supplies from many local merchants.

Somerset Farms was selected as the 2007 New England Green Pastures Dairy Farm award winner for the State of Maine. The New England Green pastures award is given every year to an outstanding dairy farm for each of the New England states. The award is presented annually at the Big E Fair in West Springfield, Massachusetts.

Outland Farm
Arianna Medeiros

Heather and Mike Holland offer fresh non-certified organic tree fruits (apples, peaches, pears, plums, and nectarines). They also produce fresh chicken and pork meat and have a community garden at no cost to their members. They have hiking trails on their property that are open to the public and can host private events such as wedding and farm-to-table dinners. There is a 10-barrel brewery opening in the main barn of the farm this coming year. Other future plans include a hop yard, small grains, educational workshops, new farmer support, and community outreach. Heather studied agriculture in high school and college. She carried her knowledge into farming as a passion of hers. They sell primary retail directly from the farm at 404 Phillips Corner in Pittsfield ME. Their products can also be found at the local Pittsfield farmers' market, area buyers' club, and local specialty markets. They offer wholesale for local breweries and wineries. For further information, you can go to their website: Outlandfarm .com or contact Heather through her email at Heather at outlandfarm .com or their phone number is 207-509-3031.

West Farm
Patty and Paul West

The West Farm is located at 696 Main Street in Pittsfield. The farm has been there since the mid-1800s.

Paul and Patty West currently own the farm and run it as a certified organic farm providing certified organic vegetables, hay, baleage, and pasture for sale.

Paul and Patty purchased the farm in 1989 from Lance and Judy Richmond. The Richmonds purchased it from Lawrence Coffin of Pittsfield whose father owned and operated the farm processing and selling meats.

During the 1990s and early 2000s Paul and Patty ran the farm as a certified organic dairy farm. Today certified organic vegetables are sold at the farm store on the farm.

MILLS AWAITING NEW OWNERS

Edwards Company
Norman Clarke

Robert Edwards worked in a laboratory with Thomas Edison and it was there he realized electricity was going to become the trend of the future. He started out making buzzers/ignitors for gas lamps but soon changed over to making just the buzzers. He opened a factory in a basement in New York City in 1872. This began one of the best manufacturers of buzzers, bells, signaling equipment and communication devices in the country. Soon outgrowing the New York plant, he moved operations to Norwalk Connecticut in 1937.

A major expansion move was needed and Pittsfield was selected. The Pittsfield Kiwanis members and several local businessmen formed the Pittsfield Development Corporation. These people were instrumental in bringing Edwards to town. It was to be erected next to the closed Pioneer Woolen Mill. One of the driving decisions of Edwards management was the willing labor force and the area in general. Many more details can be found in Sanger Cook's book *Pittsfield on the Sebasticook*. In 1956, the new plant was open and in production. Contractor K & H Foster, of Wilton, was chosen to build the plant. Local help was secured in building the facility. Edwards succeeded in becoming a major manufacturer of bells, small and large buzzers, fire alerting equipment and many more products. After a period of growth, Owen Sound Ontario, Canada and Burbank, California locations were added to the operation. Production soon tripled and due to the Maine work ethic, the Norwalk plant was closed and all manufacturing was moved to Pittsfield. The three main facilities were kept and Edwards soon had sales and service operations all over the country and Canada.

The plant added smoke detectors, alarm systems and modern products to its line and expansion and upgrading was soon added to Pittsfield. Facilities were opened in many foreign countries, some of which are still in operation. After a while, Edwards was bought by General Signal and that relationship lasted until General Signal sold off all of its nationwide manufacturing facilities. The once famous and prosperous Edwards was soon purchased by a few companies until it finally closed the doors in Pittsfield in 2015.

Some highlights from Edwards past:

The N.Y. Stock Exchange bell that opens and closes each session was made in Norwalk and has been refurbished in Pittsfield on occasion. Locals Forest Frost, Mike McGowan and Greg Libby helped lay the steel and worked on construction of the new building in 1956. Edwards made and delivered a massive fire alarm system for the Jedda, Saudi Arabia Airport. A hospital on wheels was set up at Edwards when Dow Air Force Base was in operation. The plant stored a 36-bed emergency hospital in the basement of the plant then, too. The small red "pull in case of fire" devices you see in so many TV shows and movies were made right here, in Pittsfield. During the flood of 1987, Edwards was the only facility in Pittsfield to remain running as employees sandbagged day and night to divert the water from entering the plant. An all-time shipping record was also set that week, in spite of the flood. Local area businesses donated food and many people from town and neighboring towns pitched in to help. The Edwards employees took pride in all of the fine products they helped make and sent all over the world.

Waverly Mill

Jane Woodruff

For over 125 years the Waverly Mill has stood near the Waverly Dam of the Sebasticook River. Once again, it awaits new occupants. Over the years, this three-story brick structure has been the site of a woolen mill and several shoe manufacturers. The opening for its first tenant, a woolen mill, was heralded with a two-day celebration beginning with a concert at Union Hall the first night. This was followed the next evening with a ball at the mill culminating with a midnight dinner serving 600 people.

In the late 1920s and early1930s, the work at the mill became sporadic to the point of being shut down for two years until it finally was put up for auction in 1934. It lay vacant, as it still does today, with people asking as did Clyde Martin his April 1941 letter to *The Advertiser* asking, "Why don't we do something about the Waverly Mill?' Later that year, a group of Kiwanians met after one of their meetings and at the suggestion of J.R. Cianchette, they determined that they would work to open the mill. That they did - they found a tenant: Pinchos Medwed, a shoe manufacturer. He would later sell the mill in 1950 to Northeast Shoe Company which by 1965 had become Pittsfield's largest employer with over 450 employees.

But again, hard times hit and Northeast Shoe closed its doors in 1983. One year later, it was re-opened as San Antonio Shoe or SAS as it came to be called locally. A former Northeast employee, Terry Armstrong, along with his partner Lew Hayden had started SAS in 1976 and expanded its operations to Pittsfield. Making walking shoes along with their standard penny loafers brought people and jobs back to this factory. In 2004, SAS made national news when its employees were given a holiday bonus of $1000 for every year that they had worked for the company. Unfortunately, times changed and with it the tastes in footwear. By 2008, the shoes being made at the Waverly factory were no longer deemed valued and it was closed with 160 jobs lost. Once again, it became vacant and still awaits a new owner.

Pittsfield Woolen Yarns, Inc.

Gregory Wright

Pittsfield Woolen Yarns started in 1945 by Perley Wright in a building on Park Street where the town office sits today. Perley bought wool from the Foss Farm in Athens and manufactured socks for L.L. Bean. In 1946, he and Earl Hodgkins, who owned two small mills on Sebasticook Street, bought a warehouse on Central Street and moved manufacturing to that location.

Perley soon bought out Hodgkins' share and formed a corporation with his children, Virginia, Clifford, Carl, and Neil. In the early 50s, he hired Ralph Cianchette to put an addition on the east end of the building. (One of the first jobs of the company that would become Cianbro, according to Greg.) Through the 50s and 60s, Pittsfield Woolen Yarns manufactured woven cloth for Prince Luxury Fabrics made from cashmere, camel hair and other high-end fibers. Then when that company was sold, the company worked for many of the other textile companies in Maine and New Hampshire.

In 1973, weaving was discontinued and the company continued to do commission spinning of weaving yarn. In 1969, the company founder, Perley Wright passed away leaving the business to be run by Clifford and Neil. Clifford's son, Greg, also came on board in 1968.

In the early 80s, Carl's son, Randy came on board and in 1984, the company was passed to the next generation with Greg and Randy in charge.

In 1992, a larger addition was added, doubling the yarn making capacity. This was short-lived as by the late 90s, foreign competition caused mill after mill to close. By 2003, there were no longer any customers and PWY closed.

Appendix

Pond Fire

Photograph by Mark Schumpert

(Portions of this summarized history are borrowed from the <u>1969 Sesquicentennial Souvenir Book</u> and also from Sanger Cook's <u>Pittsfield On the Sebasticook</u>. This history was updated by Brenda Seekins with the help of former Town Manager Dwight Dogherty who reviewed it for errors or omissions.)

It was 1794, when Moses Martin, Pittsfield's first white settler, tramped through the woods from Norridgewock to the Sebasticook River. He was traveling in virgin land of Plymouth Gore, the easternmost frontier of the charter grant made by [English King] James I to the Plymouth Company in 1606. As the first white settler, Martin came to be respected by his Indian neighbors, members of the Abnaki nation, most likely the Norridgewocks.

It is unlikely that Martin could ever imagine that he would be the founder of a settlement that would endure to its 175th anniversary in 1994.

Many will ask if Martin was here, at the joining of the east and west branches of the Sebasticook River in 1794, why are we only celebrating 175 years?

It was 25 years after his arrival, in 1819, that the tiny settlement of Warsaw was first incorporated as a town, and still five years after that before the name Pittsfield was adopted. The name was selected in honor of William Pitts, Esquire, of Belgrade, who was a large landowner in town. The earliest settlers were mostly farmers who paid their taxes in corn and wheat.

In its early years, the small village had little resemblance to the thriving community it would become. Downtown Pittsfield as we know it consisted of little more than an inn, a gristmill, sawmill, blacksmith shops, a carriage shop and two to three stores. The inn was the first Lancey House opened by Colonel William Lancey about 1820 at the north end of Main Street. Indeed, the neighboring communities of Palmyra and Detroit were said to have greater promise. In fact, in those early years, there was not one, but two Pittsfields, an East and a West Pittsfield, but the coming of the railroad was to change that.

The Penobscot and Kennebec Railroad Company was incorporated April 7, 1845 with plans to construct a line from Gardiner to north of Waterville towards Bangor. The railroad was to be constructed before Dec. 31, 1860 or lose its charter. By 1845, the line was complete from Waterville to Pittsfield with the exception of a bridge over the Kennebec. In early July, 1855, the train was running between Waterville and Pittsfield, but that was the end of the line. Stages ran regularly between Pittsfield and Bangor. It was July 30, 1855, when the first scheduled run between Waterville and Bangor passed through Pittsfield. The railroad brought a new round of prosperity and established the village center forever, in what was once East Pittsfield.

In 1860, the population of Pittsfield was 1,495.

A little more than five years after the railroad opened, trains departed Pittsfield with fresh recruits to defend the Union and ultimately reunite the United States in the "War Between the States."

In the years following the Civil War, a variety of men rose to prominence as businessmen and left a mark on the community. Going Hathorn is among the most notable. He was a manufacturer and constructed the first woolen mill in 1869 at the site of today's Edwards Company/G.S. Building Systems. The mill was subsequently sold to Robert Dobson and ultimately became the Pioneer Mill of American Woolens in 1914. American Woolen also purchased the Waverly Mill and a Newport Woolen

Mill at the same time. The company closed in 1934, but the Pioneer Mill continued to operate until after World War II.

Hathorn constructed a large estate where Hathorn Park sits today. His home sat on the site of today's Parkview Apartments. His stables were lost to other locations in town and eventually removed to make way for progress and renewal.

In 1867, downtown Pittsfield had some similarity to today — the east side of Main Street had few buildings. These included the first Lancey House at the north end of the street, a few homes and apparently one store. Within 20 years, significant construction filled the east side with businesses including the large Lancey House Hotel that stood as a Pittsfield landmark until 1965. In fact, the *Pittsfield Advertiser* reported a total of 71 buildings in 1867 Pittsfield, compared to 260 by 1887.

One of the significant additions of that double decade was the construction of Maine Central Institute. The school was actually incorporated in 1866, but construction did not begin until 1867. Apparently at the urging of Going Hathorn, the Institute building, now Founders Hall, was constructed in its entirety rather than in sections as originally planned. The total cost was $40,000 for the building, equipment and landscaping. The contractor was paid $29,000 for his portion of the work upon its completion in 1869.

In the 1880's, Main Street was evidence of a thriving community. While businesses continued to fill Main Street, east and west, side streets were developing with businesses as well. It is also in the last half of the 19th century that Pittsfield manufacturing began, in addition to the growing woolen industry, the town boasted a harness shop, a manufacturer of ladies underwear, and a brick yard. A public water system was established in 1895 with six and a half miles of pipe and 62 hydrants. Electricity followed in 1900 with the Pittsfield Light and Power Company. A sewer system was established and the town hall, Union Hall on Park Street, constructed.

It was also in the last decade of the 1800's that Col. Walter Morrill, Pittsfield's Civil War hero, moved from Dexter to Pittsfield and opened a livery stable. His move is credited with the rejuvenation of Union Trotting Park, the site of today's airport, and the establishment of Pittsfield as a horse racing center. In the same time period, the Waverly Mill opened in

1892. The Sebasticook and Moosehead Railroad opened and offered passenger and freight service to Hartland, Great Moose Pond and Castle Harmony. In 1893, the Tuesday Club began regular meetings as a social and civic women's club.

From 1880 to 1900, Pittsfield's population grew from 1,909 to 2,891.

With the coming of a new century, progress apparently slowed according to historians. It was not so much a lack of growth, but the loss of leadership that had led the previous development. The Pittsfield Public Libary, a Carnegie Library design, was dedicated in 1904. Other developments included the extension of sidewalks and sewers, the establishment of Burnham dam and the Sebasticook Power Company, the founding on the new St. Agnes Parish and the renovation of Pittsfield National Bank. Two fires brought destruction to Main Street. One fire severely damaged the Lancey House, leaving the town without a hotel for nearly five years. Another destroyed several businesses on the west side of Main Street.

Between 1900 and 1920 population dropped to 2,146. By 1930, growth had returned with a population of 3,075.

One of the most influential developments of the period, after the turn of the century, according to Sanger Cook, was not the physical changes of the town, but the demand for labor and the people it ultimately brought to town. The influx of Italian Immigrants was a significant addition to the community, one that is cited as bringing new spirit and enthusiasm. One history cites the efforts of a young Dominic M. Susi who brought many of his countrymen to Pittsfield. The construction of the Burnham dam created a need for barracks that came to be known as "Little Italy."

World War I was the next significant event in Pittsfield's history. With the return of the war veterans, social clubs, entertainment and athletics were developed. The Bijou Theater began to show the popular films of the time. MCI began to establish itself as a leader in athletics, in particular its baseball team which apparently beat all four Maine colleges in one season.

By the centennial year of 1919, Pittsfield had established itself as an important hub of commerce in central Maine.

In 1922, the era of automobile travel came to Pittsfield with the opening of a Ford dealership by Earle Friend.

The first community hospital was established in 1924, but it would be 1963 before a permanent health care facility would stand.

In 1928, the former boys dormitory, a wooden structure, burned at MCI, in its place Alumni Hall was erected. One year later, 1929, Pittsfield lost several businesses with the beginning of the depression. Even the Pittsfield National Bank was forced to close, only to reopen six months later never to close again.

The construction of the municipal airport was completed in this time period with government work project funds.

In 1935, Manson Park was donated to the town by J.W. Manson in memory of his mother, Mary Ann Lancey Manson. The donation was followed in later years with funds from Mr. Manson's will that also included plans for the development of the park. The will has often been the subject of controversy each time any group has proposed changes and additions in the park. A year later George M. Parks bequeathed funds for a new gymnasium at MCI. The Parks Gym served all indoor athletics at MCI until the construction of the Wright Gym in 1989.

From 1935 to 1940 is a time period recognized by Pittsfield historian Sanger Cook for the growth of its construction companies, mostly with Italian names, the second generation now. L.A. Dysart opened a 5 and 10 cent store on Main and shoe manufacturing established a toe hold in the community.

In 1936, Pittsfield did not escape the great flood. The red bridges to the island in the Sebasticook had to be blown out to relieve the danger of an ice jam. The water went over North Main Street flooding out the mill yard and threatening bridges and dams downriver all the way to the Kennebec. The road through the flats south of the village was reported impassable and there was three feet of water over the road leading into Burnham. The water height of that flood was not equaled again until 1987, when downtown Pittsfield was cut off from traffic because of the rising waters, and an entire residential district was flooded.

Also in the 1930's, the town manager form of government was adopted, but not without a rocky start. It seems the first manager, A.L. Thorndike, a graduate of Tufts College, lasted but a year before resigning. A local man, C.R. Ames, was appointed and was ultimately succeeded by Ray Badger, who had previously served as superintendent of the water works, before that position was assumed by the first town manager.

In 1940, the Kiwanis Club was organized and has served as a strong civic group for more than 50 years. It was also in this year that new interest in airport construction brought more government funds in to make improvements to Pittsfield's small airfield and left it with one of the best small airports in the state. As a result, the Navy took over the field in 1943 as a training ground for World War II cadets, many of whom filled dormitory space at MCI.

Pittsfield's close proximity to Bangor and Dow Air Force Base placed it in a danger zone. Volunteers were called upon to man an observation post, first in the tower of the Lancey House and later at the airport for the duration of the war. A total of 54 volunteers served the effort. In 1945, the end of the war was marked with enthusiasm in Pittsfield with an impromptu parade of fire trucks, cars and bicycles amid horns, sirens and whistles. The event culminated with a large bonfire.

By 1940, Pittsfield's population was 3,329.

In 1941, the Waverly Mill had stood vacant for a number of years. A meeting of the Kiwanis Club that year was to provide the basis of a continuing tradition in Pittsfield—interested and committed businessmen willing to fund and support industrial growth. The mill was repaired and sold to a shoe manufacturer. In 1950, the mill was sold again to Northeast Shoe, the company that ultimately built the new facility now occupied by San Antonio Shoe.

In 1950, population stood at 3,898.

In the early 1950's, Pittsfield businessmen were again called on through the Kiwanis Club to create The Pittsfield Development Associates, an apparent predecessor to today's Pittsfield Development Corporation. This time their goal was to find an occupant for the abandoned Pioneer Mill, closed by American Woolen Company in 1953. A long legal battle apparently followed as the corporation established itself, sought ownership of the mill and found a potential tenant. It was 1956 before construction was underway for a new building to join the old mill and house the Edwards Company.

In 1952, a new elementary school was built at Manson Park, followed by the construction of the Vickery School in 1958. In July 1953, the Kiwanis Club spearheaded another construction project for Pittsfield with the creation of a municipal swimming pool at Manson Park.

In 1960, population had grown again, now totaling 4,010. Soon after, a young women's club, Athenaeum Club, initiated the fundraising for Sebasticook Valley Hospital. The facility opened on Grove Hill in 1963.

Three significant changes came from the 1960's that mark a change in focus and lifestyle for the next decades. In 1964, Interstate 95 opened a section connecting Fairfield with Newport and bypassing Pittsfield's Main Street. This, coupled with the loss of railroad passenger service in the same decade, spelled decline for Main Street businesses and the famed Lancey House. In 1965, the Lancey House suffered its final blow with an October fire that eventually saw it torn down and committed to memory.

Waterville Savings Bank opened a branch bank on the site shortly after, and today houses Peoples Heritage Bank.

In 1966, Sanger M. Cook published the history *Pittsfield - On the Sebasticook.* In his preface, he noted that Pittsfield is no ordinary town, but one with "youthful aggressive spirit that was at once idealistic, yet practical. In things spiritual, cultural and industrial, it sought the best, but with characteristic Yankee caution."

In 1969, Pittsfield stopped to reflect on 150 years of history with the celebration of its Sesquicentennial, From June 14 through June 21, each day had a full schedule of activities with two parades providing appropriate bookends to the celebration.

By 1970, population stood at 4,274.

Another new decade, a declining business district and available government funds brought another renewal. Early in the decade, environmental concerns brought about the town's sewer treatment project and eliminated the long-time practice of using the river for sewage disposal.

The community also marked the new decade with a new form of government, a process that streamlined decision-making and enabled Pittsfield to progress and take advantage of numerous opportunities for growth. In 1971, the first town council was elected and functioning. Paul Susi, Jr. already a seasoned selectmen, was elected as first mayor and chairman of the board.

Celebration was again on the minds of townspeople in 1973, when the Central Maine Egg Festival was born. The now-annual celebration was intended to honor the community's long-standing egg industry, but also to create an identity for Pittsfield. Coinciding with the traditional Kiwanis Karnival, the festival has become a mainstay on the agriculture circuit in the state, as well as national and international recognition for Pittsfield, Maine.

In 1976, a Community Development Block Grant removed abandoned and dilapidated buildings on the north side of Park Street. Mill Pond [Park], also known as Stein Park, was created in their place. An Economic Development Administration project in 1977 removed the deteriorated portion of Union Hall and created today's municipal building and fire station. An Urban Development Action Grant, a plan to leverage public funds and improvements with the commitment of private development and improvement tackled the east side of Main Street before the end of the decade. Pittsfield's Sunnyside Up project removed deteriorated and abandoned buildings and saw in their place the construction of Cianbro Corporation's headquarters. About the same time, a shopping center was developing next to the new Craig Hardware on outer Somerset Avenue. A new grocery store, a department store, a laundromat and flower shop were part of the package. The new structure eventually took Bud's 'n Save and LaVerdieres from their downtown locations. The decade of the 1970's was also the time period when government funds were secured for the development of the Pittsfield Industrial Park, and new businesses joined the ranks of Pittsfield employers.

By 1980, population stood at 4,125, a decline of about 150 people over the decade. In 1990, the trend reversed slightly and population totaled 4,190.

In 1989, Cianbro Corporation celebrated a 40-year anniversary. It was 1949, when brothers Carl, Ival (Bud), Ken, and Alton (Chuck) incorporated as Cianchette Brothers. It was 1970 before the name "Cianbro" was adopted. Construction work for the Cianchette brothers was a natural progression as they followed in the footsteps of their father, Ralph, an Italian immigrant. Today, the company has grown to national prominence with offices, and projects, up and down the east coast.

The developments of the 1980's and early 1990's remain with us today with few exceptions. Among the most notable is the continuing growth of the Edwards Company, now G.S. Building Systems. The company has expanded its facility on the river repeatedly and in 1994 negotiated a lease with the town to occupy the former Bud's Shop'n'Save property on Hunnewell Avenue. The town's purchase of the building was made possible by economic development funds from the state and federal governments and tax increment financing on the local level. The unique project saved the loss of 125 jobs, and the expected downsizing of the company at the Pittsfield site. The addition of lab and testing facilities, as well as expansion and addition of a new state-of-the-art product line in the larger plant, is expected to insure jobs for Pittsfield for a long time to come.

Entering the 1990's, Pittsfield is a recognized leader in the central Maine area. The town initiated and continues to operate one of the best voluntary municipal recycling programs in the state. Its success has allowed repeated expansion of the program with state grant funds. Success in economic development and the utilization of state and federal grant money has brought in additional grant awards. Funding has been funneled into the town's own loan programs to enhance future business development and housing rehabilitation programs.

It is an obvious impossible mission to tell this town's varied history in a few short pages. This effort is just that — a simple attempt to convey to today's Pittsfield residents what has gone before and made what we are today. For some people these are memories and accomplishments. For others it is simple getting acquainted with the history of their new home.

Since the Septaquintaquinquecentennial

Changes have been many since Brenda Seekins summarized the town's history in her piece *Pittsfield 1794-1994* on the occasion of Pittsfield's Septaquintaquinquecentennial or its 175th birthday of its incorporation. Perhaps the best way to view these alterations to the town is simply to list the gains and losses.

Gains or Expansions	Losses
Argo Contact Center	Country Creations
Walpole Woodworkers	C. Jones Inc.
Dollar Store	Heidi Ann Floral Shop
Sonoco	TD Bank
Blue Sky Produce	Skowhegan Savings Bank
Nitro Trailers	Corner Cupboard
SVFCU	San Antonio Shoe
SVH Addition	United Technologies Corp.
Medical Waste Facility	Woodworth Construction
Cianbro Solar Farm	The Chalice
Insource Renewables	Nancy's
AE Robinson	Catholic School
Dysarts	Birch Grove Nursing Home
SVH Rehabilitation Center	SV Nursing Home
Vittles	Tuesday Club
POPonOVER	Local News Coverage
Kwong Lee Restaurant	
A New You	
Eden Day Spa	
Copper Salon	

Balfour Farm

Waggin' Tail Farm

Outland Farm

Bag End Suri Alpaca Farm

Corson Farms

Snakeroot Organic Farm

Pittsfield Farmers' Market

Pittsfield Redemption Center

Fendler Park

Veterans' Park

Warsaw sport field development

Pennywise

MCI sports fields

Cianchette Science Building

Bossov Ballet

Pool replacement

Tennis courts replacement

The Beauty of Pittsfield in Winter

by Mark Schumpert

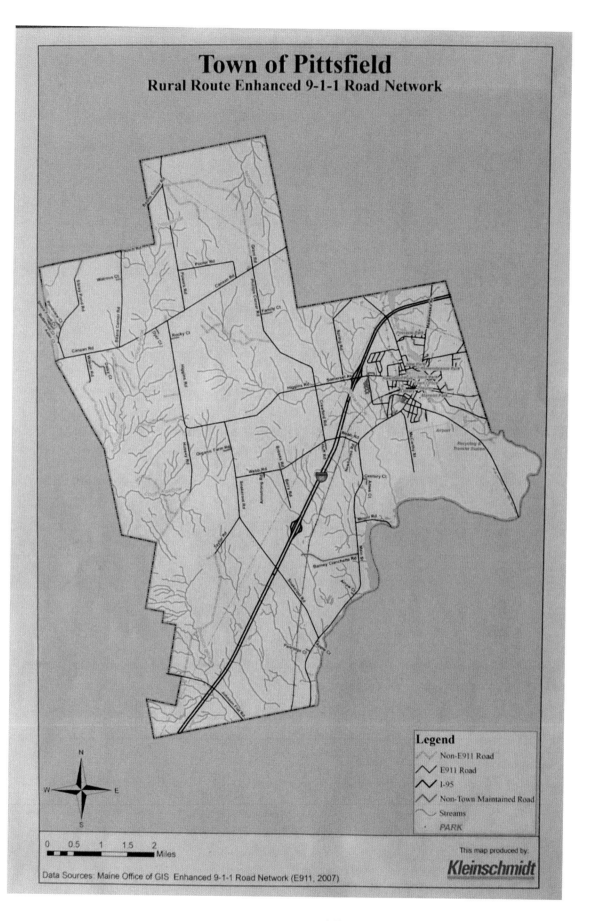

Town of Pittsfield
Rural Route Enhanced 9-1-1 Road Network

Legend
- Non-E911 Road
- E911 Road
- I-95
- Non-Town Maintained Road
- Streams
- *PARK*

0   0.5   1   1.5   2 Miles

This map produced by:
Kleinschmidt

Data Sources: Maine Office of GIS Enhanced 9-1-1 Road Network (E911, 2007)

Whence Came the Ballet

Michael Duncan Wyly

Founder, Bossov Ballet Theatre

Pittsfield, Maine, population 4200, boasts a ballet school and performing company that does the classics with professional aplomb. This under the strict discipline and extraordinary artistic sense of its Russian Artistic Director, Choreographer, and International Performer.

I started Bossov Ballet Theatre in 1996 mainly for my then 13-year-old daughter who had developed an interest in Ballet taking lessons in the Washington, D.C. area before I retired from the Marine Corps. I had met Maestro Andrei Bossov and seen him teach and perform, but now he had returned to his native St. Petersburg. There was something about him that was extraordinarily authentic. It manifested itself in his on-stage talent and his dedication to the art.

How could I get him to fly to the United States and consider full-time employment? I obtained the visa needed to employ him temporarily and began the process for a "Green Card" for permanent resident status. To speed the process, I went to the State House in Augusta and incorporated "Bossov Ballet Theatre" as a non-profit. In five years' time, we would have Andrei's full U.S. Citizenship. It was January 1996, when I greeted him at Boston Logan Airport, just-in from Russia.

At this same time, I was discovering Maine Central Institute (M.C.I.), in Pittsfield. My older daughter had matriculated there as a high school freshman in the fall of 1995. My original intent was to set up a ballet studio in Waterville following Andrei's employment by Colby College in their dance program, which, we succeeded in obtaining. But the more I learned about M.C.I. and its role as a boarding high school, the more the idea grew in my head: establish a ballet school as part of the M.C.I. curriculum! Then build from there. The college girls at Colby had already formed habits that did not conform to the Russian standards Andrei demanded. And, already enrolled as Colby College students, dance had become a pastime; not a life's goal for a profession.

We started to make Pittsfield our home in the summer of 1997 with just a 5-week Summer Program on the M.C.I. campus, dancers coming from "away" and living in the dorms. Andrei culminated that first summer's training with a near professional level performance of "Cinderella", the Russian version, with music by Sergei Prokofiev. The ballet was laced with humor as well as romance and was well-attended in its opening in Waterville.

As years passed, more and more out-of-state Summer dancers inquired whether they might go to high school in Maine and continue to study under Andrei year-round. The answer was obvious: incorporate ballet in the M.C.I. curriculum and then bring them in as year-round boarding students.

The better I became acquainted with Andrei, the more I watched, the more I read, and the more excited and involved I became. We were on to something special. I said to Andrei: "Let's make this as close as we can to *your* school experience. Of course, we were "a far cry" then from Andrei's school in St. Petersburg, the famed Vaganova Academy, established in 1738 in pre-Soviet days as the "Imperial Ballet School of Russia". But we were on to something special all the same. We added examinations and a course on Ballet History. We stressed the intensive work ethic required for daily classes, including Saturdays. In addition to getting to know Andrei, my interest was driven by my study and reading. Russian émigré and danseur Mikhail Baryshnikov (who in his early days took class along with Andrei) in his personal reminiscence said it best:

"When I entered the ballet school ballet didn't become less mysterious to me, it became more so. Here was a community of people dedicated to this art. They were servants of something – messengers. They all had their own places in the company, each place very important and needed. They had a duty, and not to everyday life. The whole thing seemed to me like a ritual, haunting. "I thought ' what a beautiful way to live! ' " *

And, as I read the words of Maestro Baryshnikov, who had left his country to come to ours, it occurred to me: what a beautiful experience for our young Americans to have growing up – those of whom are so moved!

In this way, Bossov Ballet Theatre was born. Right here in Pittsfield. The company's first full-length Christmas *Nutcracker* (when we finally could afford such an extravaganza – December 2000) was performed at the Waterville Opera House. It filled the house and became an annual event. Other full-length performances included *Giselle, Coppelia, Carmen, The Sleeping Beauty, Don Quixote, Scheherazade, Le Corsaire*, and Andrei's original *The Red Shoes*. While the Waterville Opera House remained a regular venue for performing, other theaters included the Ogunquit Playhouse, University of Maine's Collins Center in Orono, U. Maine Machias, and The Nashua Playhouse in New Hampshire."The dancers from Pittsfield" had made a name. And it continues to grow.

Soon it became standard that families would send a daughter or son to Pittsfield for the summer program, and then, if qualified and invited, would join the year-round program as a full-time M.C.I. student. Some came from as far as Germany, Israel, and Australia.

As our school matured and gained its reputation, graduates entered the professional ballet world, competitive though professional ballet is. Graduation was and is a crossroads for each: which road to take? Professional ballet? Or college? Or, ballet first and college later? Their diploma gives them credentials for either fork in the road. The profession is one that must be entered while young and that is limited by the endurance of physical stamina.

As we moved into the 21st century, growth continued. I hired Natalya Getman who now serves as Bossov Ballet Theatre's Artistic Director, post-Andrei's retirement in 2013. Finding Natalya and selecting her, I often think, was the smartest thing I ever did. She has maintained the standard!

With Natalya as with Andrei, my motivation to continue growing the company was especially driven by deeply ingrained emotions carried over from the thirty-five years I spent in uniform, finally retiring as a U.S. Marine colonel. Andrei, Natalya, both of them born and bred in the old Soviet Union, the empire I fully expected all my adult life to one day have to fight on a bloody battlefield; here we were now, fast friends, sharing values of excellence, discipline, dedication, and tradition. All with a common appreciation of beauty. How much we had in common! Tchaikovsky, *The Nutcracker*. Our common love of freedom, their appreciation of our Declaration and Constitution; our appreciation of a deep and glorious culture steeped in literature, poetry, and music. There would be no war between us. Every day we discovered more that we had in common. The Bossov Ballet had become my life's calling. And, for our up and coming youth, there was – and is - that special sense of purpose. As the great Baryshnikov observed: "What a beautiful way to live!

---

*Mikhail Baryshnikov quoted in Greskovic, Robert. *Ballet 101; A Complete Guide to Learning and Loving the Ballet*. New York: Hyperion, 1998; Introduction by Baryshnikov pp. xiii and xiv.

Pittsfield Voting Districts

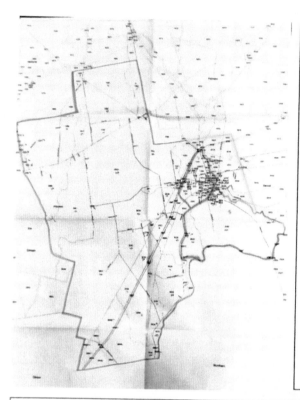

District 1 (yellow): Chandler, Cottage, Curtis, Davis, Deer Run, Detroit, Dobson, Dogtown, Easy, Fairview, First, Fourth, Glen Eagle Court, Harriet, Hartland 375 -379, 381-589, Hunnewell, Leighton, Leonard, Lincoln, Livingston, Madawaska, Mill, N. Lancey, N. Main 115-604, N. Orchard, SAS, Second, Third, Washington, Waverly

District 2 (Orange): Ames, Century, Chester, Cianchette, Crosby, Cross, Estelle, Franklin, Harrison, Institute, Lancey, Libby, Library, Main even 148-912 and odd 149-427, Manson, McCarthy, Meadow, Mount even 2-146, Nichols, Peltoma, Pittsfield, Powell, Stinson 101-230, Summer, Sunset, Weymouth

District 3 (Magenta): A, Arbor, b, Bates, Birchwood, Bow, Business, C, Cardinal, Central, Connor, D, Dorothy, E, Elm, F, G, George, Greeley, H, Hamilton, Hartland 101-374 and 376-378, Hathorn, Hemlock, Highland, Industrial Park, June, Main odd 101-147 and odd 429-467, Maple, Middle, Morrill, N. Main 101-114, Noble, Raymond, Rice, Ruth, Ryan ,School, Sebasticook, Somerset 101-506, South, Staples, Stinson 231-430, Union, West, Westbranch

District 4 (Blue): Apple, Armstrong, Arrow, Aster, Barney Cianchette, Beans Corner Road, Berry, Blueberry, Brooks, Bush Clan, Buttercup, Canaan, Crawford, Daisy, Dyer, Family, Grant, Hartland 380-590, Higgins, Hood Brook, Huff, Hussey, Johnson Flat, Mae, Main odd 469-1679 and even 914-1680, Mount odd 1-145, Newhouse, Notch, Organic Farm, Partridge, Phillips Corner, Pondview, Pooler, Powers, Reynolds, Rocky, Shore Front, Sibley Pond, Snakeroot, Somerset 507-724, Spring, Taylor, Watrous, Webb, Wilson

NOTES

Chapter 1 Along Her Banks

The writings and photography about the Town Farm Property or Peltoma Woods was a project of the 8th Grade Class of Warsaw Middle School calling themselves the "Pioneers of Peltoma". Their work is showcased in a kiosk that they built to the entrance to this area near the Snowmobile Club. They acknowledged that students of the "Take a Hike" 2013 expeditionary learning program had laid the groundwork for the stewardship of this land.

The quote about Moses Martin's outdoor skills is from his obituary written by brother Drew noted in Sanger Cook's book about Pittsfield.

Chapter 2 Pittsfield Then & Pittsfield Now

While the book focuses particularly on showcasing the town as it is now, it is in the context of its history. Traditions and landmarks help reflect the changes from then to now.

Chapter 3 Her Families & Their Recollections

Though many families could have been represented, these 14 are the ones that took the time to share their stories. Special thanks to William Cunningham for reaching out to notify townspeople of this project, for collecting their stories and putting this chapter together.

Chapter 4 Her Organizations

Over the years, there have been a number of organizations that unfortunately folded. Three were chosen to represent that group for either their uniqueness or for their lasting impact on the community.

Chapter 5 Her Culture

Whether they were born, lived or were schooled in Pittsfield, these folks were included as creative people listed in this chapter. MCI graduates are identified by their class year after their name. Pittsfield is rich in having so many creative people associated with her and is reflected in the sheer number of people listed. It is regretted that more in-depth information couldn't be given.

The students in the group photo of Bossov Ballet Theatre practice are Abigail DeSchiffart, Sophie Flyn, Olivia Durkee, Sarah Trimarchi, Hanna Holtsclaw, Julia Bluhm, Celia Merritt, Hannah Folan.

Chapter 6 Her Schools

With the exception of MCI, there have been no new school buildings built in Pittsfield in the last 50 years with Warsaw Middle School being the youngest having been built in 1965.

Chapter 7 Her Parks & Recreation

According to Sanger Cook, a lot was purchased on the Hathorn Estate for a burying ground, later changed to an area near the Universalist Church, and changed once again to its current location on Peltoma for the town's cemetery.

Chapter 8 Vital Services

Current Cash Expenses Chargeable to Fiscal Year 1881.

Paid and Incurred.

Stove..	$9 00
Insurance on town farm buildings	12 50
Signs for bridges.............................	3 50
Cemetery fence near L. F. Rolfe's	243 86
Attorney fees and legal expense.................	60 57
Constable's fees.............................	13 14
Fire of March 16, 1881	76 25

From the *Town Report*, it notes expenditures for the Fire of 1881 that would seem to indicate the existence of a fire department. This was the earliest indicator found.

The code that most townspeople

had posted in their homes to alert

them as to the location of a fire.

The town whistle would blow

according to the particular code

with school children often anxiously

awaiting to hear 6 blasts ......

indicating "No School."

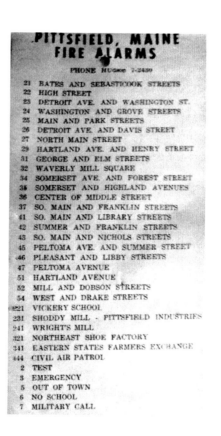

PITTSFIELD, MAINE
FIRE ALARMS

PHONE HUgson 7-2480

21	BATES AND SEBASTICOOK STREETS
22	HIGH STREET
23	DETROIT AVE. AND WASHINGTON ST.
24	WASHINGTON AND GROVE STREETS
25	MAIN AND PARK STREETS
26	DETROIT AVE. AND DAVIS STREET
27	NORTH MAIN STREET
29	HARTLAND AVE. AND HENRY STREET
31	GEORGE AND ELM STREETS
32	WAVERLY MILL SQUARE
34	SOMERSET AVE. AND FOREST STREET
35	SOMERSET AND HIGHLAND AVENUES
36	CENTER OF MIDDLE STREET
37	SO. MAIN AND FRANKLIN STREETS
41	SO. MAIN AND LIBRARY STREETS
42	SUMMER AND FRANKLIN STREETS
43	SO. MAIN AND NICHOLS STREETS
45	PELTOMA AVE. AND SUMMER STREET
46	PLEASANT AND LIBBY STREETS
47	PELTOMA AVENUE
51	HARTLAND AVENUE
52	MILL AND DOBSON STREETS
54	WEST AND DRAKE STREETS
221	VICKERY SCHOOL
231	SHODDY MILL - PITTSFIELD INDUSTRIES
241	WRIGHT'S MILL
321	NORTHEAST SHOE FACTORY
341	EASTERN STATES FARMERS EXCHANGE
444	CIVIL AIR PATROL
2	TEST
3	EMERGENCY
5	OUT OF TOWN
6	NO SCHOOL
7	MILITARY CALL

Chapter 9 Her Infrastructure

With the change to the Council form of government, the town was divided into 4 geographical districts such that there is one person elected from each of the districts and 3 elected from at large.

Chapter 10 Her Businesses

Vital Services: Pittsfield's Municipal Airport: Owner of Union Trotting Park, Colonel Walter Morrill received the Medal of Honor for his actions at Rapahannock Station, Virginia on November 7, 1863. He was in many skirmishes and key battles, the most famous being Gettysburg where Colonel Joshua Chamberlain led a bayonet charge down Little Round Top against the enemy while Morrill and is Co. B skirmishers mounted a surprise attack to the enemy's rear. His life is recounted in Robert L. Haskell's historical novel *Yankee Warrior.*

Appendix

Pittsfield 1794-1994 is reprinted from *Milestones and Memories* by Brenda Seekins written on the occasion of Pittsfield's 175th birthday.

Pittsfield has four voting districts. The lines are redrawn from time to time to reflect changes in the number of citizens in the areas in to trying to keep the districts equal in population.

In 2006, Pittsfield underwent many changes in street numbers and names with the installation of the 911 system. Some streets such as Llewellyn, Pleasant and Forest were completely eliminated as they were subsumed into other streets such as Bates, Library and Central, respectively.

References

Books

Chatto, Clarence I. Chatto & Turner, Claire E., *The East Somerset Register 1911-12,* Auburn, Maine: Chatto & Turner, 1912.

Cook, Sanger, *Pittsfield on the Sebasticook,* Bangor, Maine: Furbush-Roberts Printing Co., Inc., 1966.

Mitchell & Daggett, *The Pittsfield Register 1904,* Kents Hill, Maine: H.E. Mitchell Publishing Co., 1904.

Seekins, Brenda, *Images of America - Sebasticook Valley,* Maine: Arcadia Publishing, 2004.

Miscellaneous Articles & Publications

Numerous articles by local reporters - Ann McGowan, Sharon Mack, Brenda Seekins - found through Marvel! Maine's Virtual Library using ProQuest Newspapers to access US Newsstream offering access to local and regional newspapers from 1980 to present.

The Alumnus Magazine, online: mci-school .org/page .cfm?p=409

Seekins, Brenda, *Milestones & Memories,* Pittsfield, Maine: Valley Graphics.

Websites

http:// maineanencyclopedia .com/

http:// pittsfield .org/

http:// pittsfieldhistoricalsociety .org/

http:// libraries.maine .edu/mainedatabases/

https:// wikipedia .org

Contributors

They wrote. They photographed. They shared their stories.

So many thanks to you all for making this book possible.

A   Alan Grover   Alex Rizza   Alfred Bachrach   Allison Jameson

    Amanda Todaro   Ann McGowan   April Smith Stock   Arianna Medeiros

B   Barbara Denaro   Barbara Pomeroy   Beverly Breau   Beverly Rollins

    Bernard Williams   Beth Smith   Bethany Knowles   Billie-Jo Reed

    Bob Ballard   Bobbie Goulette   Brady Snowman   Brad Fisher

    Bre Graffam   Breanna Norris   Brenda Cote   Brenda Seekins

C   Caleb Curtis   Carole Vigue   Carolyn H. Taylor   Cindy Emery

    Chad Caron   Chris Anthony   Chris Young   Clermont Spencer

    Cody Southard   Connie Thies   Cyndra Knowles

D   Dan Boreham   Daniel Higgins   Danielle Aziz   Darlene Steeves

    Dave Barden   Dave Lyons   Dave Quint   Dean Homstead

    Deidre Heaton   Don Chute   Don Hallenbeck   Don Harriman

    Donald Neville Jr.   Don Woodruff   Donna Laux   Debra Higgins

    Douglas Fernald   Douglas Quint

E   Elizabeth Audet   Emma Gallimore   Erin Plummer

F   Floyd Humphrey   Frank Woodworth   Forest Frost

G   Gayle Middleton   Gary Fitts   Gary Jordan, Sr.   Glenn Nichols

    Greg Folsom   Gregory Wright

H   Heather Donahue   Heather Holland   Holly Zadra

J   James Cianchette   James Dunphy   James Hammond   Jane Woodruff

    Jason Ramsdell   Jeremy West   Jillyann Butler   John Campbell

Joseph Staples   Josh Miville   Jill McElderry-Maxwell

K Kathy Phelan   Ken Clark   Ken Spaulding   Kellie Brooks

Kerma Cordice   Kim Post   Kurt Dodge

L Laura Woodcock   Laurie Clement   Lee Southard   Leigh Hallett

Loretta Martin   Lyn Smith   Lynn Thurston   Lynn Cianchette

M Mark Mancini   Mark Schumpert   Marie Manning   Marge Downing

Mary Kate Reny   Matthew Bagley   Matthew Hatch   Megan Hart

Melinda Nyman   Melissa Flewelling   Michael Dugas   Michael Fendler

Michael Lange   Michael Lynch   Michael Raven   Michael Wyly

Milton Webber

N Nancy Monteyro   Natalya Getman   Norman Clarke

P Pam Dorman   Patty West   Paul Bertrand   Paul West

Patricia DeFosse   Patty West   Penny Oliphant   Peter Snow

R Rachel Nichols   Rae Hersey   Rebecca Johnson   Rebecca Thompson

Rena Hodgins   Richard Bellows   Richard Bryant   Rick McCarthy

Rick White   Robin Chase   Robert Ballad   Robert Duplisea

Robert Matthews   Ron Porter   Ross Fitts   Russ Collier

Russ Cox

S Sandra Friend   Sarah Williams   Scott Noble   Scott Varney

Sharon Chadwick   Shawna Melanson   Sonny Spratt   Stan Trembly

Stephani Morancie   Stephanie Valente   Stephen Kennedy   Stephen Martin

Stephen Quint   Stephen Rickens   Steve Peterson   Steve Vance

Sue Liebowitcz   Sue Nile   Susan Quint Cassidy   Suzy Morton

T Ted Bragg   Terri Jean Grant   Terri deNatale   Thomas Gates

Timothy Hoyt   Tim Powers   Tim Roussin   Tom Chadwick

Tom Cote   Tom Gordon   Tom Roberts   Trudy Ferland

Tuyet Clark

V Vaughan Woodruff

W Walter Fletcher   Warsaw 8th Grade Class   Wesley Burton   William Cunningham

Y   Yvonne Blake

Map, Illustration & Photo Credits

Cover

Mill Pond Photograph: Mark Schumpert

Design: Barbara Denaro

Contents

Pittsfield Skyline: Vaughan Woodruff

Pittsfield Logo: Barbara Denaro

Chapter 1 Along Her Banks

Chapter Header: Evergreen: Barbara Denaro

Town Farm Property or Peltoma Woods Project: 8th Grade Class of Warsaw Middle School

Peltoma Bridge Postcard: Courtesy of Brenda Seekins

Chapter 2 Pittsfield Then & Pittsfield Now

Chapter Header: Postcard of Main Street: Courtesy of Laura Woodcock

Chapter Header: Photograph of Main Street: Mark Schumpert

Valley Times Building: Courtesy of Laura Woodcock

Lancey House Post Card & Recipe: Courtesy of Laura Woodcock

Brownies Crossing Bridge: Courtesy of Pittsfield Historical Society

Dr. John C. Manson: Courtesy of Maine State Archives

Scout Cardboard Sled: Megan Hart

Kiwanis Fish Pond: Courtesy of Pittsfield Historical Society

Watering Trough - Hartland Avenue: Courtesy of Pittsfield Garden Club

Map of Downtown Pittsfield: Courtesy of Kleinschmidt

Chapter 3 Her Families & Their Recollections

Chapter Header: "Bessie & Lou": Penny Oliphant

Higgins Home   - 1800s: Courtesy of Daniel Higgins

Forest Frederick: Courtesy of Kellie Brooks

Cunningham Home: Courtesy of William Cunningham

Chapter 4 Her Organizations

Chapter Header: "The Start": Penny Oliphant

Baptist Church: Mark Schumpert

Catholic Church - Then: Courtesy of Rena Hodgins Now: Mark Schumpert

Nazarene Church - Easter Service: Courtesy of Nazarene Church

Congregational Church: Courtesy of Congregational Church

Kiwanis Club - Pinnacle Ski Slope: Courtesy of MCI; Bike Rodeo - Courtesy of Kiwanis

Cub Scouts: Megan L. Hart

Boy Scouts: Courtesy of Robert Matthews

Girl Scouts - Then: Courtesy of the Pittsfield Historical Society

Girl Scouts - Now: Kellie Brooks

Pittsfield Historical Society Depot: Mark Schumpert

SVH Auxiliary: Elizabeth Rougny

Eastern Star: Courtesy of Eastern Star

ARTS Club: Beverly Rollins

Senior Citizens: Cyndra Knowles

Welcome Table: Trudy Ferland

Community Garden: Courtesy of Community Garden

Driftbusters Snowmobile Club: Mark Schumpert

Chapter 5 Her Culture

Chapter Header: Public Library: Terri deNatale & Milton Webber

Pittsfield Public Library: Interior Courtesy of Library, Exterior Mark Schumpert

Pittsfield Community Theatre: Courtesy of MSAD #53

Deb Susi with Lexie LaMarre: Courtesy of MCI

Natalya Getman: Hayim Heron, Courtesy of Bossov Ballet Theatre

Mykayla Weinstein and Arjan Orr: Hayim Heron, Courtesy of Bossov Ballet Theatre

The Pittsfield Band: Courtesy of Pittsfield Historical Society

Summer & Christmas Concerts: Mark Schumpert

Aerial of Pittsfield: Courtesy of People's United Bank

Black Bananas: Vera Bryant

Stephen Peterson: Mark Schumpert

Colby Thomas & Stephen Quint: Courtesy of Stephen Quint

Chapter 6 Her Schools

Chapter Header: One Room Schoolhouse: Courtesy of Pittsfield Historical Society

Chapter Header: Maine Central Institute Postcard: Courtesy of Laura Woodcock

Manson Park School: Mark Schumpert

Maine Central Institute: Oren Cheney, early MCI campus, Powers Hall, Caravan, Parks   Gym, Ella Night, Lunar New Year: Courtesy of Maine Central Institute

MCI Campus - Winter Carnival and In Fall Foliage: Mark Schumpert

Chapter 7 Her Parks & Recreation

Chapter Header: Hathorn Sunset: April Smith Stock

Chapter Header: Hathorn Park & Manson Park in Winter: Mark Schumpert

Legge's Diamond: Steve Kennedy

Manson & Fendler Parks: Mark Schumpert

Rail Trail Aerial: Courtesy of Pittsfield Historical Society

Community Pool: Courtesy of Richard McCarthy

  Batter: Suzy Morton

Skydiving: Courtesy of Vacationland Skydiving

Sibley Pond: Gary Fitts

Chapter 8 Vital Services

Chapter Header: Firefighters: Courtesy of Pittsfield Historical Society

Chapter Header: Current Gear: Jane Woodruff

Sebasticook Valley Hospital: Aerial, SVH & Care Staff: Courtesy of SVH

Hometown Health Center: Courtesy of Hometown Health

Chapter 9 Her Infrastructure

Chapter Header: Lagoons: Jane Woodruff

Town Government Post Card: Courtesy of Laura Woodcock

Chapter 10 Her Businesses

Chapter Header: Business Establishments: Courtesy of Pittsfield Historical Society

Manufacturers

  CM Almy Stitchers: Courtesy of CM Almy

  Nitro Trailers: Courtesy of Innovative Specialties

  Pittsfield Hancock Opening: Courtesy of Hancock Lumber

Engineering & Construction

  Cianbro Brothers, Penobscot Narrows Bridge, Headquarters & Institute: Courtesy

  of Cianbro

Scaffolding: Courtesy of NES/NIS/NSS

Scientist Taking Readings: Courtesy of Kleinschmidt Assocatiates

Insource Renewables with Amish: Courtesy of Insource Renewables

Hydroseeder & Sod Cutter: Courtesy of hydrograsscorp

AAA Buildng & Van: Courtesy of AAA Service

Legal, Financial, & Business

Michael Lynch: Courtesy of Northeast Planning Associates, Inc.

Food & Retail

Bud's Shop 'n Save Opening, Then & Now: Courtesy of Dean Homstead

Barbecue: Courtesy of Stony Knolls Farm

Beer: Courtesy of Outland Farm Brewery

Renys Celebration & Floor Plans: Courtesy of Renys

Carolyn Rickens Racing & The Tack Shop: Courtesy of Stephen Rickens

Personal Services

Stan Trembly: Courtesy of Stan Trembly

Health Services

Drs. Paul & Jeremy West: Courtesy of the Wests

Dr. Michael Parks: Courtesy of Eye Care of Maine

A New You Massage: Courtesy of Terri-Jean Grant

Glenn, Mikaela & Rachel Nichols: Courtesy of the Nichols

Animal Services

Breanna Norris: Monty Sloan, Courtesy of Canine Insights, LLC

Fuel & Auto

J.R. Cianchette Farm: Courtesy of Varney Chevrolet

Home Businesses

163 Design Company: Mark Schumpert

Russ Cox: Courtesy of Smiling Otis Studio

The Webber House: Courtesy of Milton Webber

MCI Bell Tower: Milton Webber

Ollie Loops: Amanda Todaro

Rick White: Courtesy of Pittsfield Plumbing

Contract Services

Pittsfield Argo Crew: Courtesy of Argo Contact Center

Farms

Doug & Heather Donahue: Courtesy of Balfour Farm

Alex Rizza: Courtesy of Alex Rizza

Dante Bachman & Mark Mancini: Courtesy of Waggin Tail Farm

Alpaca: Courtesy of Windy Corner Farm: Matthew Hatch

Christmas Trees: Courtesy of M & M Farm

Lois Labbe & Tom Roberts: Courtesy of Snakeroot Organic Farm

Freshening Farm Logo: Courtesy of Donald Neville, Jr.

Alpaca & Wool: Courtesy of Bag End Suri Alpacas of Maine

Blueberries: Courtesy of Blueberry Court Farms

Outland Farm Collage: Courtesy of Heather Holland

West Farm: Paul West

Mills

Waverly Mill Postcard: Courtesy of Laura Woodcock

SAS Property: Mark Schumpert

Appendix

Chapter Header: Pond Fire: Mark Schumpert

The Beauty of Pittsfield in Winter: Mark Schumpert

Pittsfield Voting Districts: Town of Pittsfield

Town of Pittsfield Rural Route Enhanced 9-1-1 Road Network: Courtesy of Kleinschmidt and the Town of Pittsfield

Notes: 1881 Fire Expenses & Fire Alarm Code: Courtesy of Pittsfield Historical Society

Photos not otherwise specified: Jane Woodruff

A Good Place to Call Home

47712321R00150

Made in the USA
Middletown, DE
09 June 2019